BEGINNING GLASSBLOWING

EDWARD T. SCHMID

Edward T. Schmid

August 2004

GLASS MOUNTAIN PRESS

BELLINGHAM, WASHINGTON

2

BEGINNING GLASSBLOWING © 1998

I.S.B.N. 0-9638728-2-6

AUTHOR: SCHMID, EDWARD T.

LIBRARY OF CONGRESS CATALOG CARD NUMBER 98-93002

SUGGESTED RETAIL PRICE $ 24.95

GLASS MOUNTAIN PRESS

BELLINGHAM, WASHINGTON

★ WHERE WE WRITE BOOKS THE OLD-FASHIONED WAY☞ BY HAND!

CONTACT ME AT:
GLASS MOUNTAIN PRESS
927 YEW STREET
BELLINGHAM, WASHINGTON
98226
U.S.A.

THIS ADDRESS IS GUARANTEED FOR AT LEAST ONE YEAR — AS OF SEPTEMBER 1998

PRINTED ON RECYCLED PAPER

Table of Contents

Forward

MOLTEN GLASS IS AN AMAZING MATERIAL TO WORK WITH. AS ART MEDIA GO, IT IS A VERY UNIQUE SUBSTANCE. GLASSES MANY INHERENT QUALITIES OFFER LIMITLESS POSSIBILITIES FOR EXPLORATION AND EXPRESSION. HOT GLASS BEHAVES LIKE A LIQUID, PRODUCES IT'S OWN LIGHT AND IS PROBABLY HOTTER THAN ANYTHING YOU'VE EVER ENCOUNTERED. WHEN COOLED PROPERLY, GLASS IS MORE SOLID (AND PERMANENT) THAN THE ROCK OF GIBRALTOR.

TAMING THIS WILD MATERIAL REQUIRES A WHOLE HOST OF EQUIPMENT AND SKILLS. FIRST-OFF, IT REQUIRES A SUBSTANTIAL AMOUNT OF ENERGY AND EXPENSE IN ORDER TO TURN SAND INTO HOT GLASS. HOT SHOPS (GLASS STUDIOS WHERE THEY MELT GLASS) ARE FORTUNATELY POPPING-UP ALL OVER THE WORLD. THE STUDIO GLASS MOVEMENT IS RESPONSIBLE IN A LARGE WAY FOR MAKING IT POSSIBLE TO BLOW GLASS IN VIRTUALLY EVERY MAJOR CITY IN THE UNITED STATES. NEVERTHELESS, YOU SHOULD CONSIDER IT A PRIVILEGE AND HONOR TO WORK WITH MOLTEN GLASS.

IN THE 2000-PLUS YEARS OF BLOWING GLASS, SURPRISING LITTLE HAS BEEN WRITTEN ABOUT THE PROCESS. MOST METHODS AND SECRETS ABOUT THE "ART" WERE PASSED DOWN THROUGH THE FAMILIES OF GLASSMAKERS – NEVER TO BE REVEALED TO "OUTSIDERS". WHEN THE STUDIO GLASS MOVEMENT BEGAN SOME 30 YEARS AGO ~ MANY OF THOSE TECHNIQUES KEPT SECRET INSIDE OF THE FACTORIES STARTED TO COME TO LIGHT.

BACK IN '89 WHEN I STARTED TEACHING BEGINNING GLASSBLOWING (WHILE IN GRAD' SCHOOL) ALL WE HAD WAS "WALT'S GUIDE FOR GLASSBLOWERS" – A SMALL 'HOW-TO' HANDOUT (HEAVILY XEROXED) WRITTEN YEARS EARLIER BY WALTER LIEBERMAN. I FOUND IT A HELPFUL AID IN GETTING THE STUDENTS TO REMEMBER THE NAMES OF TOOLS AND SOME TECHNIQUES, BUT MORE INFORMATION WAS NEEDED.

IN 1993 I WROTE AND SELF-PUBLISHED ED'S BIG HANDBOOK OF GLASSBLOWING TO FILL-IN SOME OF THE GAPS. BEGINNING GLASSBLOWING IS THE NEW & IMPROVED VERSION OF THAT BOOK. IT IS EASIER TO READ, MORE INFORMATIVE, AND SPORTS AN INDEX ~ MAKING IT A BREEZE TO FIND WHAT YOU NEED AT-A-GLANCE.

IN MOST SECTIONS I'VE ADDED SUGGESTIONS FOR PRACTICING YOUR SKILLS. THESE EXERCISES FOCUS MORE ON TECHNIQUE-BUILDING RATHER THAN OBJECT-MAKING, THE IDEA BEING "YOU NEED TO LEARN HOW TO WALK BEFORE YOU CAN RUN".

THIS BOOK IS INTENDED TO SUPPLEMENT THE INFORMATION "THROWN AT YOU" IN YOUR BEGINNING GLASSBLOWING CLASSES. SOME THINGS MAY BE DIFFERENT IN HERE THAN WHAT YOUR INSTRUCTOR SAYS – BUT SUCH IS THE NATURE OF THIS EVER-EXPANDING (GLASS) UNIVERSE. MY ADVICE IS: TO ARM YOURSELF WITH AS MUCH KNOWLEDGE AS YOU CAN, TO TRAIN YOUR HANDS AND MIND WITH THE SKILLS AS BEST YOU CAN ~ IN ORDER TO ULTIMATELY GAIN A HANDLE ON THIS ELUSIVE MATERIAL. AND THEN GO TRY IT OUT FOR YOURSELF!

I HOPE YOU ENJOY THE PAGES THAT FOLLOW. THE INFORMATION CONTAINED WITHIN WILL CONTINUE TO BE VALUABLE FOR YEARS TO COME, AND IF YOU FIND IT USEFUL – please – PASS IT ON! REMEMBER – WE'RE ALL IN THIS TOGETHER, AND THE GLASSMAKING COMMUNITY CONTINUES TO BE ONE OF THE MOST SHARING GROUPS OF PEOPLE THAT I'VE EVER COME IN CONTACT WITH. SEEK THEM OUT FOR ADDITIONAL INFORMATION AND GUIDANCE.

GOOD LUCK WITH THE LAVA and REMEMBER: HOT GOOD – COLD BAD.

Edward T. Schmid

APRIL 14TH 1998

Introduction

You're about to embark upon a one-way voyage of information and practical experience. All of which will undoubtedly make you a more diverse and interesting person.

This knowledge will never leave you (although some steps and methods will often "take vacation" at inopportune times). Try to learn from every attempt you make.

Feel free to share your knowledge or enhance it by communicating with others.

Communication is one of the easiest ways of learning. It allows a dialogue or forum with which the whole process becomes easier and more fun.

hello hot glass... my name is...

There are an infinite number of objects that this "super-cooled liquid" may be transformed into, and I can't stress this enough: your **sketchbook** will be your most valuable **tool** in your workspace. **Draw, DRAW, DRAW!** You'll find by sketching already existing objects (called "studies"), your ability to visualize qualities of the medium will become more acute.

A simple sketch or drawing serves to create a base for your own innovations and adaptations. It exists as a concrete manifestation of your brain and creative desires. A sketchbook may be a journal of your ideas for the present time, and some day be a useful resource for generating new concepts from old ones.

Even the crudest line drawing can aid in communicating what it is that you want to create with others, or by yourself. Drawing allows you the ability to execute dozens of objects per hour and not get cut, burned, or consume vast quantities of natural resources. plus **IT'S GOOD FOR YOU!**

"I can't draw" — is the lamest and unfortunately the most common excuse I hear from students. "Do you practice?" — is my response. Drawing, like glassblowing, is an acquired skill. In order to get better at it, you must make an effort. Study and practice. Sound like going to school? ya sure, ya betcha!

6 ? ? Q. "CAN I BLOW GLASS?. I MEAN, I'M NOT REALLY AN **ARTIST**... BUT I'M INTERESTED IN WHAT I SEE..." "**WHAT DOES IT TAKE?**"

A. VIRTUALLY ANYONE CAN BLOW GLASS. **1ST**, IT TAKES A DESIRE AND A WANT TO WORK WITH HOT, MOLTEN MATERIAL. BUT, JUST BECAUSE YOU CAN BLOW GLASS, DOES NOT MEAN YOU'RE AN "ARTIST". NOR SHOULD YOU LABLE YOURSELF SUCH.

    SECOND, GLASSBLOWING IS SOMEWHAT PHYSICALLY DEMANDING. "IF YOU CAN'T STAND THE HEAT, STAY OUT OF THE ~~KITCHEN~~ HOT SHOP!" IT IS NOT FOR EVERYONE. THE HEAT ALONE CAN BE TOO INTENSE FOR SOME (A "TURN-ON" FOR OTHERS.) **YOU WILL GET ~~CUT~~. YOU WILL BE BURNED. I GUARANTEE IT!** YOU WILL BE AMAZED AND FRUSTRATED BY YOUR HANDS ABILITY NOT TO PERFORM THE FUNCTIONS WHICH YOUR BRAIN DESIRES.

    THE NATURAL FORCES OF **GRAVITY** AND THERMAL DYNAMICS WHICH WE ALL TAKE FOR GRANTED WILL COME BACK TO YOU IN A NEW AND CHALLENGING FASHION.

    THIRD, IT REQUIRES **SKILL** TO BLOW GLASS. THIS CAN TAKE SOME TIME TO DEVELOP. **LINO** DIDN'T JUST 'HAPPEN' TO BE A PHENOMENAL GLASSBLOWER, HE HAD TO WORK VERY HARD AT IT - YEARS AND YEARS OF TRAINING HIMSELF AND THE TEAMS OF PEOPLE HE WORKS WITH. SOME PEOPLE 'PICK IT UP' QUICKER THAN OTHERS. IT NEVERTHELESS TAKES PERSEVERANCE. IF YOU ABSOLUTELY CANNOT TOLERATE THE OLD ADAGE "IF AT FIRST YOU DON'T SUCCEED, TRY TRY AGAIN" GLASSBLOWING MAY NOT BE FOR YOU. THERE ARE MANY OBSTACLES AND HURDLES TO OVERCOME IN THE PROCESS OF BLOWING GLASS. LEARN HOW TO BLOW OFF STEAM, AND NOT BLOW YOUR COOL.

    FOURTH, IT COSTS MONEY. BUNCHES OF IT!...... ....ouch!

    FINALLY, GLASSBLOWING REQUIRES AN OPEN MIND. **FOCUS** YOUR ENERGY INTO MAKING EACH EXPERIENCE, REGARDLESS OF THE RESULTS INTO A

POSITIVE LEARNING SITUATION. UNDOUBTEDLY THROUGHOUT THE COURSE OF YOUR FORMATIVE YEARS YOU WILL HAVE SEVERAL DIFFERENT GLASS INSTRUCTORS, EACH WITH HER OR HIS OWN VIEWPOINT ON HOW TO BLOW GLASS. — SOMETIMES THEY'LL BE IN DIRECT CONTRADICTION TO WHAT SOMEONE SHOWED YOU PREVIOUSLY. W H O A ! SO IT GOES...

I'VE FOUND BEGINNING GLASSBLOWERS OFTEN HAVE THE FRESHEST OF IDEAS AND MOST INNOVATIVE DESIGNS, YET THEY BECOME DISCOURAGED WHEN THEIR SKILLS DON'T PERMIT THEM 100% REALIZATION.

I HAVE ALSO SEEN SOME BEAUTIFUL SCULPTURAL WORKS CREATED BY BEGINNERS WITH THE SIMPLEST OF FORMS, AND THE VISION TO SEE THEIR OBJECTS IN MORE THAN ONE LIGHT.

Explore THE WORLD OF HOT GLASS OPENLY, ASK QUESTIONS AND ABOVE ALL : K E E P   I T   F U N ! THERE ARE WAY TOO MANY PEOPLE ON THIS PLANET CONCERNED WITH BEING "SERIOUS" AND CONSEQUENTLY TOO UPTIGHT. RELAX ! KEEP YOUR EYES ON THE BUBBLE, REMEMBER: GRAVITY IS YOUR FRIEND, HOT GOOD - COLD BAD, AND HOT GLASS IS A LIQUID ↝ YOU MUST BE FLUID! BLOW YOUR BRAINS OUT. AND REMEMBER, NO MATTER HOW BAD THINGS GET, YOU CAN ALWAYS RECYCLE YOUR CLEAR GLASS — THUS ERASING YOUR MISTAKES AND GIVING YOURSELF A CHANCE TO DO IT ALL OVER AGAIN!

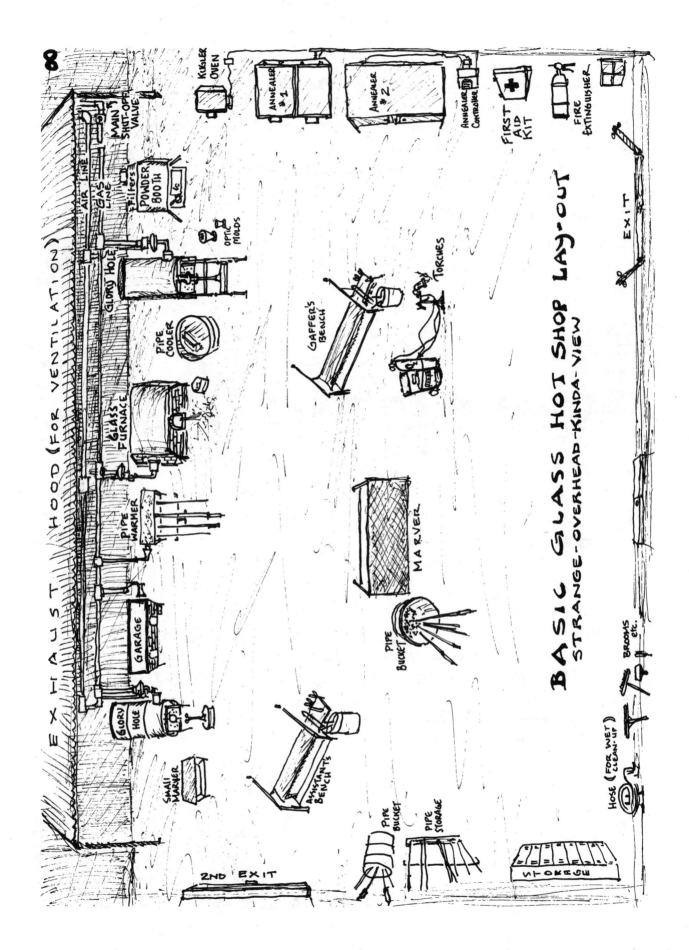

BASIC GLASS HOT SHOP LAY-OUT
-STRANGE-OVERHEAD-KINDA-VIEW-

Orientation

Many tools are needed in the generation of hot-formed glass objects. What follows is a brief discussion of the essentials which will rapidly become familiar to you.

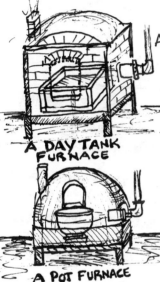

You are here

SKETCHBOOK: First and foremost,

your **#1** resource that should always be at hand. It can be the most valuable tool in your studio, and amongst the easiest to maintain. Don't leave home without it!

GLASS MELTING FURNACE: A heavily insulated chamber

whose temperatures exceed 2,000°F and which is kept hot constantly ~ 24 hours-a-day, 365 days a year, in order to melt the **BATCH** or **CULLET**. They may be heated electrically or more commonly with either propane or natural gas and forced air.

Furnace designs and sizes vary considerably. The largest ones, usually found in industry are **CONTINUOUS MELTING** - where you **CHARGE** in one side, and remove molten glass out the other (not shown). The next largest size are **DAY TANKS**. They are constructed with alumina-zircon liner bricks specifically designed to withstand the corrosive nature of melting glass. Ideally, these furnaces get charged and melted over-night, and used-up the following day. They usually exceed 400 lbs capacity, and because of their cost are often found in school situations, casting studios or in "production" facilities.

A **POT FURNACE** is one which has a **CRUCIBLE** - either "free standing" or "invested" (also know as a "POT") for melting glass. The sizes of the crucibles range from 5-to-500 lb capacities or more. Because of their smaller size and cost of operation, they are commonly found in private studios.

← ## GLORY HOLE: A gas & forced-air fired drum-

shaped chamber used for heating and reheating glass which is on a pipe or punty. It is kept running only while working. It enables the glassblower to keep their work hot and "plastic". A fairly recent invention; in the "good ol' days" you used to have to reheat pieces in the furnace - (a practice which still goes on in many glass facilities world wide.)

10

THE YOKE:

THESE UNITS MAY BE SET UP AS STATIONARY OR MOBILE (ROLLING) DEVICES. IT IS WHERE THE GLASS-WORKER RESTS THEIR PIPE DURING REHEATS AT THE GLORY HOLE. A PAIR OF BALL BEARINGS ARE INSET IN THE YOKE TO AID IN FRICTION-FREE PIPE ROTATION. FROM TIME TO TIME THE BEARINGS MAY REQUIRE A SMALL DOSE OF POWDERED GRAPHITE TO KEEP THEM LUBRICATED.

PIPE WARMER:

A SMALL, INSULATED OPEN-FACED BOX FIRED WITH SOME TYPE OF BURNER. IT IS WHERE PIPES AND PUNTIES ARE PREHEATED PRIOR TO USING THEM. (MOLTEN GLASS DOES NOT STICK VERY WELL TO COLD METAL.) THE PIPES ARE WARM (pre heated) WHEN THEY EXHIBIT AND ORANGE/RED GLOW ON THEIR TIP.

Hand Tools

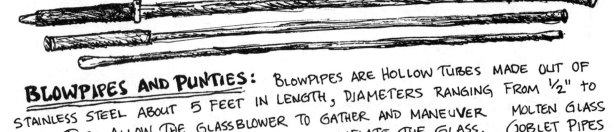

BLOWPIPES AND PUNTIES:

BLOWPIPES ARE HOLLOW TUBES MADE OUT OF STAINLESS STEEL ABOUT 5 FEET IN LENGTH, DIAMETERS RANGING FROM ½" TO 2". THEY ALLOW THE GLASSBLOWER TO GATHER AND MANEUVER MOLTEN GLASS AS WELL AS AN OPPORTUNITY TO BLOW AND INFLATE THE GLASS. GOBLET PIPES ARE USUALLY SHORTER, LIGHTER, AND MORE RESPONSIVE THAN THEIR HEAVY-WEIGHT COUNTERPARTS (USED FOR BLOWING LARGE AND HEAVY OBJECTS).

PUNTIES, ON THE OTHERHAND, ARE SOLID RODS DESIGNED TO TRANSFER GLASS-EITHER THE OBJECT BEING MADE OR FOR ADDING BITS, HANDLES, OR SOME FORM OF DECORATION. THEY, TOO, RANGE IN SIZES AND WEIGHT — FROM VERY LIGHT "BIT RODS" TO COUNTERWEIGHTED MONSTERS CAPABLE OF HANDLING **100lbs** OR MORE.

IF YOU TAKE GOOD CARE OF YOUR PIPES AND PUNTIES THEY SHOULD OFFER YOU YEARS OF DUTIFUL SERVICE. AVOID OVERHEATING THEM, OR HEATING THEM TOO DEEPLY IN THE GLORY HOLE. DO NOT QUENCH YOUR PIPES (OR PUNTIES) IN WATER WHEN YOU'RE DONE WITH THEM — IT PUTS UNNECESSARY STRESS ON THE WELD WHERE THE HEAD IS ATTACHED AND PREMATURELY FATIGUES THE METAL.

PIPES AND PUNTIES DO GET BENT FROM TIME-TO-TIME. IT IS USUALLY FROM SOMEONE GATHERING TOO MUCH GLASS ON THEM (MORE THAN THEY'RE DESIGNED TO HANDLE.). IF, WHEN YOU ROLL THE PIPE (OR PUNTY) DOWN THE BENCH, YOU NOTICE EXCESSIVE WOBBLE ON THE END, OR A BOW IN THE MIDDLE — DO NOT USE IT. IT WILL BE DIFFICULT TO BLOW THINGS SYMMETRICAL WITH IT. IT NEEDS TO BE

STRAIGHTENED BY THE MANUFACTURER (THEY'RE BEST SUITED TO DEAL WITH THE PROBLEM) OR BY AN EXPERIENCED SHOP TECHNICIAN.

ALSO, BEFORE YOU SET YOUR BLOWPIPES "UP" IN THE PIPEWARMER - YOU MUST MAKE SURE THEY'RE NOT CLOGGED. SIMPLY BLOW THROUGH THE END. IF YOU FEEL RESISTANCE YOU CAN BE PRETTY CERTAIN THERE'S SOME GLASS JAMMED UP IN THERE. TO CLEAN IT OUT YOU'LL HAVE TO HEAT THE TIP REALLY RED AND BLOW IT OUT → EITHER WITH A STRONG PUFF FROM YOUR LUNGS OR A BLAST OF COMPRESSED AIR (MAKE SURE THAT YOU'RE NOT AIMING THE PIPE AT ANYONE → I'VE SEEN THAT SCHMUTZ FLY PRETTY FAR AND WITH FRIGHTENING VELOCITY)! YOU CAN USE A PAIR OF TWEEZERS TO PULL OR REMOVE ANY EXCESS GLASS ON THE TIP AND PROCEED AS NORMAL WHEN CLEANED.

BLOCKS:

THESE WOODEN, CARVED, LADLE-LOOKING TOOLS ENABLE THE GLASSWORKER TO SHAPE FRESH HOT GATHERS INTO A USEABLE SYMMETRICAL FORM. USUALLY MADE FROM CHERRY WOOD (WHICH BURNS SLOWLY) THEY ARE KEPT WET CONSTANTLY TO PREVENT THEM FROM CRACKING AND TO REDUCE THE CHARRING EFFECT. THEY ARE AVAILABLE IN ALL SIZES - FROM MARBLES TO BASKET BALLS (OR LARGER) AND EVEN IN LEFT-HANDED VERSIONS!

WET NEWSPAPER:

A SIMPLE YET EXCELLENT TOOL FOR SHAPING HOT GLASS. IT'S A FLEXIBLE **BLOCK** OF SORTS AND COMPLETELY RECYCLEABLE. A LAYER OF STEAM BUILDS UP BETWEEN THE SURFACE OF THE WET PAPER AND HOT GLASS - WHICH ALLOWS THE GLASSBLOWER TO GUIDE, GLIDE AND SHAPE THE GLASS THE WAY THEY WANT WITHOUT GETTING BURNED. IT'S THE CLOSEST YOU CAN GET TO THE GLASS AND ACTUALLY HAVE A 'FEEL' FOR HOW IT'S MOVING. THE N.Y. TIMES AND WALL STREET JOURNAL SEEM TO FARE THE BEST - BUT YOU CAN USE WHATEVER'S AVAILABLE. AVOID THE COMICS AND HEAVILY COLORED SECTIONS—AS SOME DYES AND INKS ARE TOXIC TO BREATHE WHEN THEY'RE BURNED (IN OTHER WORDS, **DON'T INHALE THE SMOKE!**). MANY PEOPLE HAVE THEIR OWN METHOD OF FOLDING THEIR NEWSPAPER (ALMOST DOWN TO A SCIENCE), for example...

HOW TO MAKE A NEWSPAPER BLOCK:

TAKE 5 or 6 SHEETS OF NEWSPAPER. OPEN THEM UP ALL THE WAY. FOLD IT INTO THIRDS.

FOLD AGAIN INTO THIRDS

SOAK ca. 10 MINUTES

SOME GLASSBLOWERS WILL TUCK THE FLAP INTO THE FOLD TO MAKE A NICE COMPACT SHAPE. PLUS, SOME BLOWERS LIKE TO TRIM THE CORNERS TO ALLOW EXCESS WATER TO DRAIN EASIER.

ED'S BIG HAND METHOD: LAY OUT SOME SHEETS OF PAPER, (ALREADY FOLDED AS IT COMES) → FOLD IT OVER ONCE. YOU'RE DONE! LOTS OF EXTRA WRIST PROTECTION

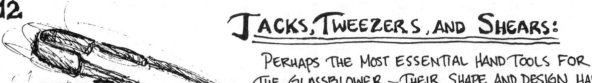

JACKS, TWEEZERS, AND SHEARS:

PERHAPS THE MOST ESSENTIAL HAND TOOLS FOR THE GLASSBLOWER — THEIR SHAPE AND DESIGN HAVE NOT CHANGED SIGNIFICANTLY IN THE PAST TWO MILLENIA OF GLASSBLOWING. THEY ALLOW YOU TO MANIPULATE THE MATERIAL WITHOUT GETTING BURNED.

JACKS ARE USED TO "NECK" THE BUBBLE, CUT LINES INTO THE WORK, OR AS A SCULPTING TOOL.

TWEEZERS MAY BE USED TO PICK THE HOT GLASS, TWIST IT, PINCH IT, POKE IT OR GUIDE OTHER TOOLS & \OR BITS IN THE PROCESS.

YOU MAY CUT OR TRIM HOT GLASS WITH THE VARIOUS SHEARS AVAILABLE. EACH PAIR HAS IT'S OWN UNIQUE DESIGN FOR FUNCTION. JUST REMEMBER THIS: **SHEARS ARE NOT HAMMERS!** i.e. TREAT THEM NICELY!

JACKS

TWEEZERS

STRAIGHT SHEARS

DIAMOND SHEARS

DUCKBILL SHEARS

THE MARVER: A LARGE SMOOTH STEEL SURFACE

ON WHICH HOT GLASS MAY BE ROLLED BACK AND FORTH TO SHAPE AND COOL THE SYMMETRICAL OBJECT BEING MADE.

ORIGINALLY MADE OF STONE, THE WORD MARVER COMES FROM AN OLD FRENCH TERM MEANING "MARBLE".

A MARVER

SAFETY GLASSES : MUST BE WORN AT ALL TIMES!

YOU ONLY HAVE ONE PAIR OF EYES! WHILE IN THE HOT SHOP
PROTECT THEM!

USE 'EM!

YOU NEED ADEQUATE ULTRA-VIOLET AND INFRARED PROTECTION WHILE WORKING FURNACE GLASS — MOSTLY DUE TO THE LIGHT PRODUCED FROM THE FURNACE AND GLORY HOLES. WELDERS GLASSES WITH A +2.3 RATING OR BETTER ARE ACCEPTABLE — ALTHOUGH THEY CAN LEAVE YOU A BIT 'IN THE DARK'. DIDYMIUM GLASSES — POPULAR WITH LAMPWORKERS ARE SOMEWHAT SATISFACTORY — BUT THEY DO NOT FILTER OUT QUITE 100% OF THE HARMFUL WAVELENGTHS YOU MAY ENCOUNTER. SOME NEWER MODELS OF LENSES SPECIFICALLY DESIGNED FOR FURNACE-STYLE GLASSBLOWING HAVE COME ON THE MARKET RECENTLY AND MAY BE WORTH THE INVESTMENT, IF YOU PLAN ON GLASSBLOWING WITH GREAT REGULARITY.

ANOTHER REASON TO WEAR SAFETY GLASSES IS THE PROTECTION THEY OFFER YOU FROM FLYING OBJECTS — ESPECIALLY THOSE PAIRS EQUIPPED WITH SIDE SHIELDS. FREQUENTLY, GLASS POPS OFF THE END OF COOLING PIPES, OR FROM ONES BEING PRE-HEATED. **GLASS BREAKS!** FLYING HAZARDS OCCUR. AN UNNECESSARY ACCIDENT MAY ONLY TAKE A SPLIT-SECOND AND NO AMOUNT OF "I SHOULD DA..." OR "IF ONLY I'D..."

WILL REVERSE POTENTIALLY PERMANENT DAMAGE. AND AGAIN, SAFETY GLASSES ONLY WORK IF THEY'RE ON YOUR FACE AND NOT JUST HANGING AROUND YOUR NECK.

THE BENCH: A METAL OR WOOD

CONSTRUCT USED FREQUENTLY DURING THE GLASSBLOWING PROCESS. THE METAL RAILS SUPPORT THE BLOWPIPE AS IT IS ROLLED BACK AND FORTH EVENLY DURING THE FORMING STAGES, THE SEAT SUPPORTS YOUR ASS AS YOU WORK THE GLASS, AND THE SIDE REST EXISTS FOR EASY ACCESS TO YOUR TOOLS.

NEVER, EVER REMOVE TOOLS (OR ANYTHING ELSE FOR THAT MATTER) FROM SOMEONE ELSE'S BENCH WITHOUT **ASKING FIRST!** YOU MAY UPSET A FELLOW GLASSBLOWER'S TIMING AND INVADE IN THEIR PRIVATE SPACE (GLASSBLOWERS CAN BE VERY PICKY ABOUT THEIR TOOLS!). PLEASE RESPECT EVERYONE'S OWN SPACE AND PROPERTY. IT IS PART OF WHAT SOME PEOPLE CALL "GLASSBLOWERS ETIQUETTE".

THE ANNEALER OR "BOX":

AN INSULATED OVEN, GAS OR MORE COMMONLY ELECTRIC-FIRED UNIT, WHERE THE GLASS OBJECT IS PLACED UPON COMPLETION OF THE HOT PROCESS. THE TEMPERATURE INSIDE IS "HELD" AROUND 900°F WHILE BLOWING AND LOADING IT. WHEN IT'S FULL, OR THE END OF THE DAY, IT IS PUT ON A TURN-DOWN CYCLE WHICH ANNEALS THE GLASS **i.e.** IT IS COOLED GRADUALLY TO RELIEVE THERMAL STRAIN/STRESS WITHIN THE GLASS. WITHOUT ANNEALING, GLASS WILL BREAK OR EVEN EXPLODE WHILE RAPID COOLING— A HIGHLY UNDESIREABLE SITUATION.

MOST OFTEN THE ANNEALERS ARE COMPUTER CONTROLLED AND OPERATED BY THE SHOP TECHNICIANS AND EXPERIENCED GLASSWORKERS — AND BEST LEFT THAT WAY IN THE BEGINNING.

FIRST AID KIT & FIRE EXTINGUISHER:

EVERY SHOP SHOULD HAVE THEM IN PLAIN SIGHT. KNOW WHERE THEY ARE~MEMORIZE IT - JUST IN CASE! BECOME INFORMED ON HOW-TO USE 'EM ~ JUST IN CASE!

CLOTHING FOR GLASSBLOWERS:

100% COTTON, OR OTHER NATURAL FIBER CLOTHES KEEP YOU COOL AND PROTECT YOU FROM THE HEAT. AVOID SHORT SLEEVES, SHORTS/CUT-OFFS AND OPEN-TOED SHOES OR SANDALS. SYNTHETIC FABRICS WILL MELT AND/OR BURN~ AND BE OVERALL UNCOMFORTABLE TO BLOW IN. YOU DON'T WANNA WEAR BLACK EITHER. NO, GLOVES AREN'T NECESSARY. AND IF YOU HAVE LONG HAIR- TIE IT BACK TO KEEP IT OUT OF THE WAY- ESPECIALLY WHEN LOADING INTO THE ANNEALER.

Getting Started

UPON WALKING INTO A HOT SHOP, YOU IMMEDIATELY BECOME AWARE OF A FEW THINGS. USUALLY THE ROAR OF THE FURNACE AND THE GLORY HOLES CAN BE HEARD AND THE GLOW & HEAT WHICH THEY PRODUCE ARE ATTRACTIVE, IF NOT A BIT INTIMIDATING. FOR EXPERIENCED GLASSBLOWERS IT'S LIKE THE MOTH-BEFORE-A-FLAME ANALOGY, YOU CAN'T HELP BUT BE ATTRACTED TO IT!

IT TAKES SOME TIME TO GET USED-TO WORKING AROUND TEMPERATURES IN EXCESS OF 2,000°F. IT MAY SEEM OBVIOUS... BUT DON'T STAND RIGHT IN FRONT OF THE GLORY HOLE OR FURNACE ⇒ IT'S HOT THERE! BELIEVE IT OR NOT, I'VE HAD SOME BEGINNING STUDENTS WHO FORGET THEIR COMMON SENSE AND B.B.Q. THEIR HANDS &/OR FACE BECAUSE THEY'RE CONCENTRATING SO HARD ON WHAT'S HAPPENING TO THE HOT GLASS ON THE END OF THE STICK (THAT THEY DON'T RE-ALIZE WHAT'S HAPPENING TO THEM!).

SO ... WITH THAT IN MIND – BE CAREFUL OF WHERE YOU STAND.

MAKE USE OF **HEAT SHIELDS** WHENEVER POSSIBLE. DO NOT EXPOSE YOURSELF TO UNNECESSARY HEAT ANY MORE THAN YOU HAVE TO. AND THAT GOES THE SAME WITH **GATHERING**. WHEN IT COMES TIME TO GATHER OUT OF THE FURNACE – ONLY OPEN THE DOOR AS MUCH AS YOU NEED TO GET THE PIPE IN AND OUT. IN FACT, CLOSE DOWN THE DOOR WHILE GATHERING TO KEEP YOUR HEAT EXPOSURE TO A MINIMUM.

EVERY FURNACE DOOR HAS IT'S OWN UNIQUE SYSTEM FOR OPENING. BE SURE YOU ARE FAMILIAR WITH HOW IT OPERATES BEFORE YOU START TAK-ING GATHERS. ALSO, CHECK OUT THE GLORY HOLE. SEE WHERE YOU CAN STAND (BEHIND THE HEAT SHIELD FOR EXAMPLE) WITHOUT EXPOSING YOUR-SELF TO TOO MUCH HEAT.

TAKE A MINUTE OR TWO TO SIT AT THE BENCH. SIT SNUG UP AGAINST THE RAIL ON THE RIGHT. THIS PUTS YOU CLOSEST TO YOUR TOOLS AND THE GLASS WHICH YOU WILL BE SHAPING. TRY ROLLING A PIPE OR PUNTY TO GET THE FEEL OF IT. ALWAYS ROLL THE PIPE WITH YOUR LEFT HAND. THIS ALLOWS YOUR RIGHT HAND TO DO THE SHAPING AND MANIPULATIONS.

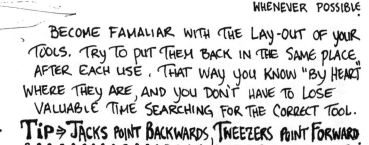

OVER-HEAD VIEW (GLORY HOLE)

HEAT SHIELD

STAND AWAY FROM THE H E A T! USE HEAT SHIELDS WHENEVER POSSIBLE

SITTING AT THE BENCH OVERHEAD VIEW

SIT SNUG AGAINST ↗ THE RAIL.

BECOME FAMILIAR WITH THE LAY-OUT OF YOUR TOOLS. TRY TO PUT THEM BACK IN THE SAME PLACE AFTER EACH USE. THAT WAY YOU KNOW "BY HEART" WHERE THEY ARE, AND YOU DON'T HAVE TO LOSE VALUABLE TIME SEARCHING FOR THE CORRECT TOOL.

TIP ⇒ JACKS POINT BACKWARDS, TWEEZERS POINT FORWARD

ANY "LEFTIES" OUT THERE? UH-OH!... YES, IT'S A CRUEL AND UNKIND RULE THAT THIS WORLD IS DOMINATED BY RIGHT-HANDED PEOPLE AND GLASSBLOWING STUDIOS ARE BY-AND-LARGE BUILT THAT WAY.

CAN YOU BLOW GLASS LEFTY? ya sure, ya betcha! BUT... IT AIN'T GONNA BE EASY..... 1st - LEFTY BENCHES ARE HARD TO COME BY. YOU CAN USE A RIGHTY BENCH AND HAVE A SMALL TABLE NEARBY (OR BOLT ONE ON) FOR THE TOOLS TO REST ON. CHECK WITH YOUR INSTRUCTOR OR SHOP TECHNICIAN FIRST.

YOU CAN ALSO TRY TO TRACK DOWN LEFT-HANDED BLOCKS. AND YOU CAN HOPEFULLY RELOCATE THE HEAT SHIELDS TO THE RIGHT SIDE OF THE GLORY HOLE. AND, HOW YOU GATHER IS UP TO YOU. OR YOU CAN DO LIKE I DO, (I'M A "LEFTY") - AND LEARN HOW TO BLOW "RIGHT HANDED" (ACTUALLY I'M AMBIDEXTROUS AND DO SOME-THINGS LEFTY ↝ like REHEATING & GATHERING - AND OTHER THINGS RIGHTY e.g. ALL THE ACTIVITIES AT THE BENCH).

MY THEORY IS THIS: GLASSBLOWING IS A STRANGE AND UNUSUAL ACTIVITY IN AND OF ITSELF. SINCE MOST SHOPS ARE ALREADY SET-UP RIGHT-HANDED, WHY NOT LEARN TO DO IT THAT WAY? BELEIVE IT OR NOT - TURNING THE PIPE WITH YOUR LEFT HAND SEEMS KINDA NATURAL FOR LEFTYS. THE MAIN DIFFICULTY THAT YOU WILL ENCOUNTER IS WHEN IT COMES TIME TO TRIM OR CUT HOT GLASS WITH THE SHEARS. I SUGGEST YOU TAKE TIME TO PRACTICE. YOU DON'T NEED HOT GLASS FOR THIS ↘

TAKE A COUPLE SHEETS OF PAPER. ROLL IT UP INTO A TUBE. GRAB A PAIR OF SCISSORS (THOSE WITH SHORT BLADES WORK BEST FOR THIS EXERCISE).

CUT "RIBBONS" OFF THE END OF THE TUBE WHILE SIMULTANEOUSLY TURNING / FEEDING THE TUBE WITH YOUR LEFT HAND (THIS SIMULATES THE PIPE-TURNING ACTION), WHILE TRIMMING OFF A HALF-INCH OR SO OF PAPER WITH YOUR RIGHT HAND. SURE IT FEELS AWKWARD! BUT IF YOU PRACTICE IT A FEW TIMES EACH DAY - FOR A WEEK OR TWO - IT SHOULD BECOME MORE 'NATURAL', AND WHEN IT COMES TIME TO TRIM HOT GLASS YOU WILL BE BETTER PREPARED TO DEAL WITH THE SITUATION.

TURN

LEFT HANDED? PRACTICE TRIMMING!...

>> WE NOW RETURN THIS STATION TO IT'S <<
  REGULARLY SCHEDULED PROGRAM ... ed.

"DANG! SCREWED-UP AGAIN! IF ONLY I HAD A LEFT-HANDED BLOW-PIPE..."

The Process

THE FIRST STEP TAKEN IN A HOT GLASS SHOP IS TO KNOW THAT EVERY-THING HAS THE POTENTIAL FOR BEING HOT AS HELL! USE THE SLOW-TO-TOUCH APPROACH WHEN PICKING UP TOOLS OR GLASS, REDUCING YOUR BURN FACTOR AS MUCH AS POSSIBLE. HAVING PICKED-UP A HOT PUNTY ROD ON THE WRONG END MY SECOND WEEK OF GLASSBLOWING SERVED AS A HARD LESSON FOR ME IN MAKING SURE THAT POTENTIALLY HOT OBJECTS ARE CLEARLY IDENTIFIED. USUALLY, YOU GET A SEVERE BURN ONCE. AFTER THAT, YOU BECOME PAINFULLY AWARE.

SHOULD YOU HAVE THE MISFORTUNE OF GETTING BURNED ⇒ DEAL WITH IT IMMEDIATELY! IMMERSE THE BURN IN COLD ICE WATER AS SOON AS POSSIBLE. THIS SUFFOCATES THE WOUND. AFTER INITIAL CONTACT, A BURN CONTINUES BURNING UP TO TWENTY MINUTES GIVEN THE OXYGEN TO DO SO. SEVERE BURNS MAY REQUIRE PROFESSIONAL ATTENTION. KEEP BURNS CLEAN AND DRY, DO NOT POP BLISTERS (IT'S YOUR BODY'S NATURAL BAND-AID) AND SEEK THE FIRST AID YOU NEED TO KEEP YOU HEALTHY AND BLOWING GLASS.

JUST FOR AMUSEMENT (AT THE SAME STROKE EDUCATIONAL), LET'S SUPPOSE YOU WERE TO CALL ON OF THOSE 1-900-HOT-BLOW NUMBERS TO LEARN WHAT IT TAKES TO GET STARTED WITH THIS MOST SEDUCTIVE OF MATERIALS. THE CONVERSATION MIGHT GO SOMETHING LIKE THIS: "Hi there, my name is I. Candy. How may I please you?" "uh...yeah, I want to know what's involved in the blowing process..."

"My pleasure...First, you grasp the rod gently in your hands, making sure that the head is hot and glowing red. Begin by rolling the rod in a relaxed motion, back and forth (you never get anywhere by being too tense or stressed). Make con-tinious rotations in one direction, open the door to the furnace and insert the tip inside. Angle the pipe, allow the head full penetration below the level of the glass. Continue the turning motion while driving deeper to gather up as much of the hot stuff as possible on the blowpipes head. Prepare to withdraw by coming out horizontally, gently, and keep the rod turning!"...

PRE-HEATED BLOWPIPE TURN
ENTER THE FURNACE. REST THE PIPE ON THE SILL, & BEGIN TURNING.

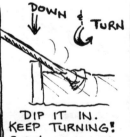

DOWN TURN
DIP IT IN. KEEP TURNING! 2 REVOLUTIONS minimum

DRIVE FORWARD & GATHER UP THE GLASS. LEVEL OUT.

ALLOW EXCESS GLASS TO TRAIL OFF. TURN IT TO MAKE A NICE EVEN GATHER.

EXIT THE FURNACE. KEEP IT TURNING!

Time Out!

LET'S CHILL FOR A MOMENT & DISCUSS

A FEW THINGS ABOUT THE PHYICS OF GLASSBLOWING

$E = mc^2$ i.e. SOMETHING ABOUT ENERGY MASS and LIGHT.

fig. A

fig. B

HOLDING THE PIPE CORRECTLY CAN EASE A GREAT DEAL OF UNNECESSARY TENSION DURING THE PROCESS OF PHENOMENAL GLASSMAKING. NOTE HOW fig. A (above) APPEARS GREATLY INTIMIDATED BY THE HOT MOLTEN MATERIAL. WITH BOTH HANDS TOGETHER, HE GRASPS THE PIPE AS FAR AWAY AS POSSIBLE FROM THE FEROCIOUS HEAT, THEREBY INCREASING THE PHYSICAL LABOR OF THE PROCESS BY A FACTOR OF FOUR.

FIGURE. B KNOWS THAT HOT GLASS IS AN ARTISTS FRIEND. SHE IS COMFORTABLE AND WELL-BALANCED, HER HANDS ARE SPREAD APART ~ EVENLY DISTRIBUTING THE WEIGHT OF GLASS AND MAKING FOR EASE OF PIPE ROTATION.

A PIPE COOLER
MANUALLY OPERATED...

SOMETIMES DURING THE GATHERING PROCESS, YOUR BLOWPIPE CAN GET QUITE HOT! IF YOUR STUDIO HAS ONE, CHILL THE PIPE WITH A PIPE COOLER. ESSENTIALLY YOU USE COOL WATER TO DISSIPATE THE EXCESSIVE HEAT. THAT WAY, YOU CAN GRIP THE PIPE CLOSER TO THE GLASS AND INCREASE YOUR CONTROL OVER HOW IT BEHAVES. THIS EFFECT BECOMES MORE EVIDENT AS YOU INCREASE THE WEIGHT AND SIZE OF YOUR GATHERS. ....CLIP & SAVE.

HEY KIDS! WHY NOT RECYCLE THAT OLD TURPENTINE / MINERAL SPIRITS CAN INTO A PIPE COOLER! JUST MASH THE BOTTOM IN TO FIT → THE PIPE, DRILL SOME HOLES FOR THE WATER TO DRIP OUT OF → AND OPEN THE TOP WITH A CAN OPENER . VOILÁ!

H_2O

18 AGAIN... THE BIG THREE FORCES WHICH EFFECT THE BEHAVIOR OF THE HOT GLASS ON YOUR BLOWPIPE ARE: **HEAT, GRAVITY, & YOU.**

GRAVITY IS THE ONE CONSTANT FACTOR WHICH YOU HAVE ABSOLUTELY NO CONTROL OVER, HOWEVER IF YOU RECOGNIZE AND UNDERSTAND IT'S INFLUENCE ON HOT GLASS ~ YOU WILL BE ABLE TO COMPENSATE FOR IT'S EFFECT. JUST REMEMBER THIS:

GRAVITY IS YOUR FRIEND!

"OH YEAH," GRAVITY...

BONK!

IN NEWTON'S ORCHARD...

HEAT IS ANOTHER FORCE YOU WILL BE CON- STANTLY WORKING WITH WHILE SHAPING HOT GLASS. THE MORE YOU WORK WITH HOT GLASS, THE MORE FAMILIAR YOU WILL BECOME IN RECOGNIZING WHAT HEAT CAN DO FOR YOU. **THE HOTTER GLASS GETS → THE EASIER IT IS TO MANIPULATE IT!**

MOST BEGINNING GLASSBLOWERS ARE FRIGHTENED TO GET THE GLASS HOT ENOUGH TO WHERE IT'S FULLY PLASTIC (A VERY UNSTABILIZED FEELING) — AND CONSEQUENTLY THEY STRUGGLE WITH GLASS THAT'S PRACTICALLY FROZEN — A VERY DIFFICULT WAY TO BLOW GLASS. REMEMBER AND <u>UNDERSTAND</u> WHEN WE SAY:

HOT GOOD! COLD BAD!

LASTLY, **YOU** ARE UNQUESTIONABLY THE MOST INFLUENCIAL FORCE GOVERN- ING THE OUTCOME OF OBJECTS ON THE BLOWPIPE AND PUNTY. YOU PROVIDE THE BREATHS THAT INFLATE YOUR BUBBLES WITH L I F E. YOU CONTROL THE TOOLS WHICH GUIDE THE BUBBLE INTO SHAPE. AND YOU PROVIDE THE AESTHETIC — THE IM- PULSE AND KNOW-HOW TO SEIZE THE MOMENT ~ FREEZE A PARTICULAR SHAPE AND KEEP IT IN THAT FORM FOR MILLENIUM TO COME (BY PUTTING YOUR PIECE INTO THE ANNEALER VS. PUTTING IT IN THE TRASH BUCKET / RECYCLING BIN).

PRACTICE. TRAIN YOURSELF. IT'S NOT TOO DISSIMILAR FROM HOW AN ATHLETE TRAINS FOR A PARTICULAR SPORT. THROUGH REPETITION AND EX- ERCISES YOU TEACH YOUR BODY AND MIND HOW TO RESPOND QUICKLY AND MORE EF- FICIENTLY. AND THEN THE HAPPY ACCIDENTS WILL OCCUR ~ THE CREATIVITY STARTS TO FLOW, AND THAT'S WHEN THE REAL FUN BEGINS.

KEEP THE PIPE TURNING AT ALL TIMES!

YES!

NO!

OTHERWISE THAT **GRAVITY** THING WILL PULL YOUR PHENOMENAL WORK OF ART BACK TO EARTH, and you don't want that to happen, see...?

GATHER IT UP!

AFTER SUCCESSFULLY GATHERING YOUR FIRST GLOB OF GLASS, YOU'LL IMMEDIATELY BECOME AWARE OF THE LIQUID NATURE OF MOLTEN GLASS. YOU ALSO BECOME AWARE OF GRAVITY'S EFFECT ON THIS LIQUID.

YOU MUST ROTATE THE BLOWPIPE EVENLY AND CONSTANTLY. IT ALLOWS YOU TO KEEP THE GATHER COMPACT, ON-CENTER, AND WHERE YOU WANT IT. YOU MUST ALSO KEEP YOUR EYES ON THE GLASS AT ALL TIMES! — IF YOU LOOK AWAY ~ THE GLASS SOMEHOW SENSES IT AND LIKELY WILL DO SOMETHING YOU DON'T WANT IT TO DO(LIKE PUDDLE ON THE FLOOR...).

KEEP IT HORIZONTAL...

IT STAYS PUT

IF YOU TURN THE PIPE AND KEEP IT PARALLEL WITH THE FLOOR - THAT IS, HORIZONTAL, THE GLASS WILL PRETTY MUCH REMAIN AT THE END OF THE BLOWPIPE.

IF YOU TILT THE HEAD OF THE BLOWPIPE DOWN, THE GLASS WILL WANT TO SAG OR FALL OFF THE END. CONVERSELY, IF YOU POINT THE HEAD OF THE BLOWPIPE UP - THE GLASS WILL FLOW BACK ON THE PIPE. WITH THESE SIMPLE ADJUSTMENTS IN THE ANGLE OF THE PIPE - YOU CAN DRAMATICALLY INFLUENCE THE SHAPE AND BEHAVIOR OF THE HOT GLASS — WITHOUT EVEN TOUCHING IT! WE SOMETIMES REFER TO IT AS "AIR MARVERING". MORE ON THAT LATER.

POINT IT DOWN...

IT FALLS OFF....

YOU WILL ALSO NOTICE THAT THE HOTTER THE GLASS IS ~ THE MORE RAPID THIS MOVEMENT BECOMES. AND AS DIFFICULT AS IT SEEMS, KNOW ALSO THAT YOU ARE IN COMPLETE CONTROL!

FOR PRACTICE: TAKE A MOMENT OUT OF YOUR BUSY DAY TO OBSERVE THE SIMPLE EFFECTS OF GRAVITY. SEE HOW MUCH YOU CAN SHAPE AND MOVE A FRESH GATHER OF GLASS SIMPLY BY TURNING THE PIPE AND ANGLING IT OFF THE HORIZONTAL AXIS.

REMEMBER: GRAVITY IS YOUR FRIEND! (and you don't wanna fight with your friends, see?)

POINT IT UP... AND IT FALLS BACK.

KEEP THE PIPE TURNING!

20   PRIOR TO BLOWING YOUR INITIAL "STARTER" BUBBLE, YOU'LL WANT TO SHAPE THE AMORPHOUS BLOB ON YOUR BLOWPIPE IN ORDER TO BEST UTILIZE ALL OF THE GLASS THERE. THE **MARVER** IS A CONVENIENT AND APPROPRIATE TOOL FOR DOING JUST THAT!

The Start:

Marvering

ESSENTIALLY YOU FIRST PUSH OR SQUEEZE THE GLASS OFF THE END OF THE PIPE (DON'T WORRY, IT WON'T FALL OFF - TRUST ME!). START WITH YOUR HANDS DOWN LOW, YOU ROTATE THE GLASS ON THE MARVER'S SURFACE - CLOSE TO THE EDGE. ROLL AND PULL THE PIPE TOWARDS YOU, TRY TO SQUEEZE THE GLASS OFF TO THE VERY TIP. BE GENTLE! DON'T FORCE IT! ALLOW THE WEIGHT OF THE PIPE COMBINED WITH THE ROLLING MOTIONS TO SHAPE THE GLASS, MORE OR LESS SYMMETRICAL.

Rotate the pod

Please HAL

TURN.   PUSH OUTWARDS.   OVERHEAD VIEW

SIDE VIEW

NEXT, YOU BRING YOUR HANDS LEVEL WITH THE MARVER AND ROTATE THE GLASS BACK AND FORTH TO CHILL THE SIDE WALLS AND EVEN-UP THE GATHER.

FINALLY, YOU BRING THE HANDLE END OF THE PIPE UP - SO AS TO ROUND THE END OF THE GLASS INTO A POINT OR CONESHAPE.

WHEN MARVERING - BE SURE TO KEEP YOUR HANDS SPREAD APART. THIS GIVES YOU GREATER LEVERAGE AND IMPROVED BALANCE.

EVEN IT OUT.

ALSO, I FIND IT EASIEST IF ONE HAND ACTS AS A GUIDE AND SUPPORT WHILE THE OTHER HAND DOES ALL OF THE TURNING. THEY THEN SWITCH ROLES WHEN ROTATING IN THE OPPOSITE DIRECTION.

TRY TO BE AS FLUID AS YOU CAN.

CHOPPY, UNEVEN MARVERING OR INCOMPLETE REVOLUTIONS MAY CAUSE YOUR GLASS TO BECOME UNEVEN AND OFF-CENTER.

POINT IT UP.

AT LAST, WHEN YOU OBTAIN A BULLET-SHAPE, HANG THE PIPE OVER THE BACK EDGE OF THE MARVER, AND B L O W! (SEE ALSO "BLOW N' CAP → PAGE 85).

& BLOW!

NOTE: IF YOU CAN ACHIEVE THE BULLET SHAPE QUICKLY, THE GLASS WILL BE EXHIBITING SOME MOVEMENT. THIS IS A <u>GOOD</u> INDICATION THAT THE GLASS IS STILL HOT AND SHOULD BE <u>EASY</u> TO BLOW. IF, ON THE OTHER HAND, YOU'VE CHILLED THE GLASS TOO MUCH, (BY EXCESSIVE MARVERING OR BY SIMPLY WORKING TOO SLOW) IT WILL BE NEXT-TO-IMPOSSIBLE TO GET IT TO BLOW OUT. IF THAT'S THE CASE, YOU'LL HAVE TO REHEAT THE GLASS IN THE GLORY HOLE AND TRY IT ALL OVER AGAIN.

A. THERE ARE THREE WAYS IN WHICH YOU CAN CHECK ON HOW YOUR BUBBLE'S PROGRESSING: ① HAVE SOMEONE ELSE WATCH IT WHILE YOU BLOW ~ AND THEY CAN LET YOU KNOW WHEN TO STOP ② USE A MIRROR PROPPED UP AGAINST THE FLOOR AND WATCH FOR YOURSELF ③ LOOK FOR A BULGE IN THE SIDES OF THE PARISON ~ A SURE SIGN THAT THERE IS SOME EXPANSION GOING ON DOWN THERE. LEAN OVER THE MARVER AND DOUBLE-CHECK IT FOR YOURSELF. IT'S IMPORTANT THAT YOU DON'T BLOW THE BUBBLE TOO THIN — OTHERWISE IT WILL BE VERY DIFFICULT TO GATHER OVER, AND MAINTAIN ITS SHAPE.

#1 THERE ARE A FEW RULES IN GLASSBLOWING WHICH HOLD TRUE. WE ALMOST ALWAYS WORK FROM THE PIPE ON OUT (EXPLAINED BELOW).

THE IMAGE DRAWN AT THE RIGHT EXHIBITS THE DESIRED SHAPE OF THE **PARISON / BUBBLE** AFTER THE FIRST GATHER, MARVER AND BLOW. WHEN WORKING WITH BUBBLES, OR BLOWING ANY KIND OF VESSEL, IT IS WISE TO SHAPE AND COOL FIRST CLOSEST TO THE PIPE (REGION "A"). THIS PROVIDES YOU WITH A STABLE BASE TO WORK OFF OF.

YOU MAY THEN DIRECT YOUR ATTENTION TO SHAPING AND COOLING REGION "B". SOMETIMES YOU MAY NEED TO MOVE BACK TO REGION "A" TO REINFORCE AND CHILL IT FOR INCREASED SUPPORT AND SYMMETRY.

FINALLY, BY SHAPING THE TIP (REGION "C") YOU ARRIVE AT THE IDEAL BULLET FORM. IT IS FROM THIS **Q-TIP** SHAPE THAT VIRTUALLY ANYTHING CAN BE MADE.

EVEN-WALL THICKNESS IS STRONGLY DESIRED. YOU'LL ALSO WANT ONLY ONE INCH OR SO OF GLASS ON THE PIPE AND THE REST OF IT OFF THE END WHERE YOU CAN MAKE USE OF IT. IF YOU ACCIDENTLY GATHER TOO DEEPLY IN THE FURNACE YOU'LL WIND UP WITH TOO MUCH GLASS ON THE PIPE. IT MAY BECOME A DISTRACTION OR NUISANCE LATER ON ~ SO YOUR BEST BET MAY BE TO TRASH THE WHOLE THING AND BEGIN AGAIN.

FOR PRACTICE: FORGET ABOUT MAKING ANY OBJECTS — JUST SPEND AN HOUR OR MORE AND PRACTICE MAKING **STARTER BUBBLES**. THE MORE YOU DO, THE BETTER YOU GET. IT WILL ALSO HELP YOU BY BECOMING FAMILIAR WITH THE FURNACE — WHERE THE LEVEL OF THE GLASS IS, AND HOW TO GATHER MORE COMFORTABLY WITHOUT GETTING FRIED. IT SHOULD TAKE LESS THAN A MINUTE TO GET YOUR BUBBLE SHAPED-UP AND BLOWN IN, WITHOUT THE NEED TO REHEAT IT.

"A GOOD "START" IS A GOOD START!"

—anobvious

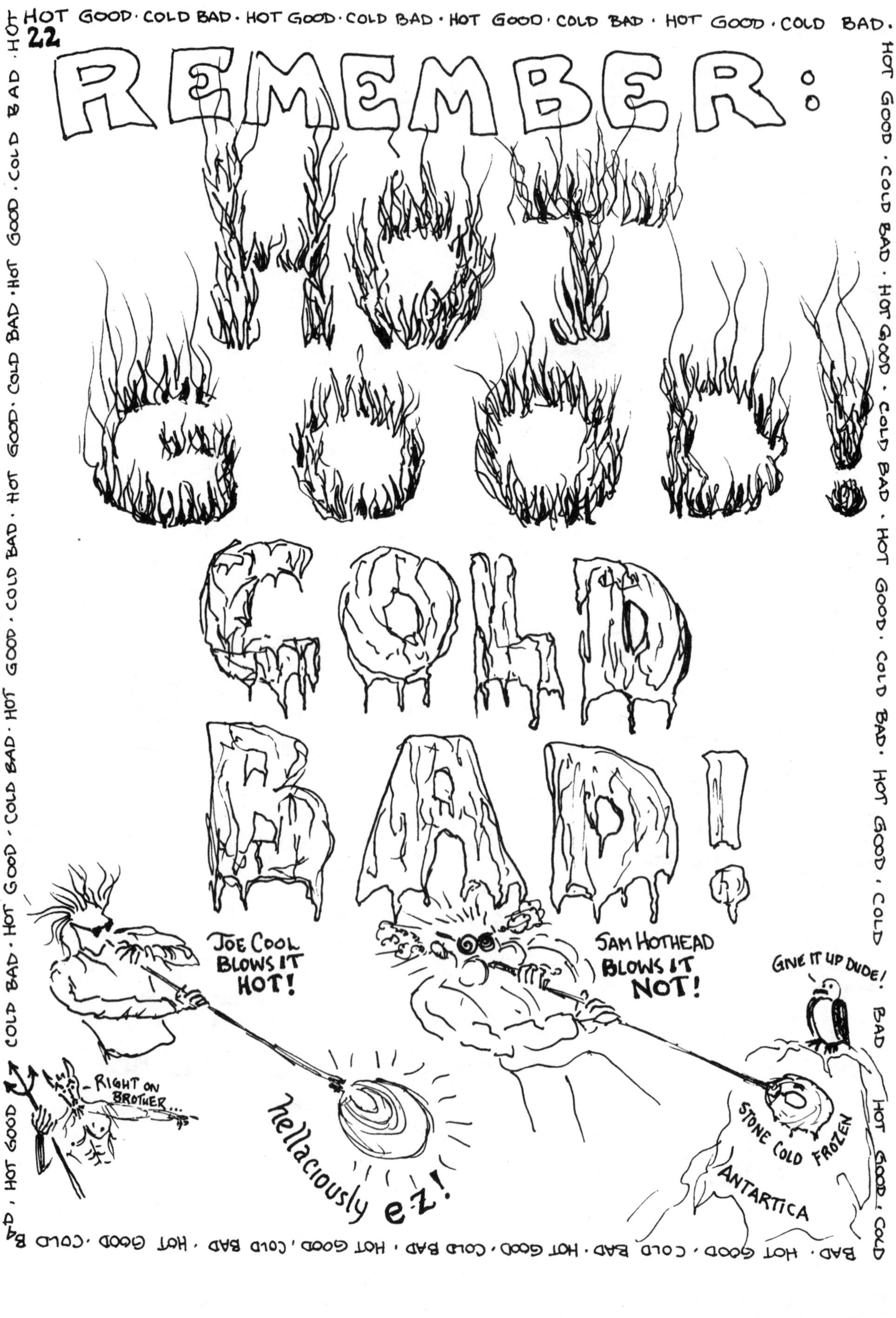

REMEMBER:

HOT GOOD! COLD BAD!

JOE COOL BLOWS IT HOT!

SAM HOTHEAD BLOWS IT NOT!

GIVE IT UP DUDE!

- RIGHT ON BROTHER...

hellaciously ez!

STONE COLD FROZEN

ANTARTICA

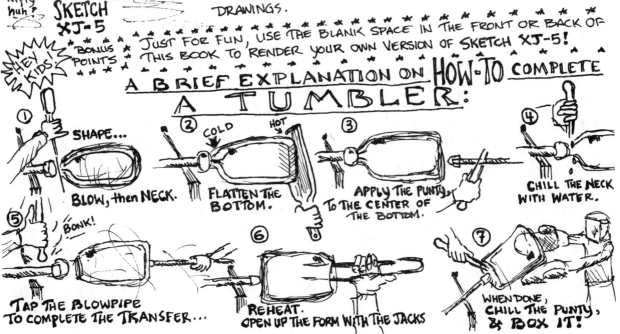

The Next Step

WHAT IS THE NEXT STEP? A GOOD QUESTION... FOLLOWED BY YET ANOTHER GOOD QUESTION: WHAT DO YOU WANNA MAKE? THIS VALID QUESTION SHOULD HAVE A RELATIVELY CONCRETE ANSWER *i.e.* <u>YOU SHOULD KNOW EVEN BEFORE YOU PICK UP A BLOWPIPE WHAT IT IS THAT YOU ARE TRYING TO MAKE!</u>

A SKETCH IS A BIG HELP 'CAUSE IT AIDS IN THE VISUALIZATION PROCESS AND ENABLES THOSE AROUND YOU TO KNOW YOUR INTENTIONS (SOMETIMES YOUR ASSISTANTS, TEACHERS, OR ANNOYING/INTIMIDATING ON-LOOKERS WANT TO BE "CLUED-IN").

DRAWINGS CAN SAVE HUGE AMOUNTS OF TIME AND VALUABLE RESOURCES, NOT-TO-MENTION AMBIGUOUS DIALOG SUCH AS: "IMAGINE IF YOU WILL... AN OBJECT LIKE NO OTHER ON EARTH..." OR "I'M MAKING A VASE-THING." SO, YOU SKETCH.

FOR THE SAKE OF ARGUMENT AND AMBIVALENCE, AND FOLLOWING THE PATH OF LEAST RESISTANCE, LET'S SAY WE'D LIKE TO MAKE A SIMPLE TUMBLER LIKE THE ONE DESCRIBED BY SKETCH XJ-5.

YOU WILL NOTE HOWEVER THAT THE OBJECT DEPICTED IN SKETCH XJ-5 IS MUCH DIFFERENT IN APPEARANCE THAN THE BUBBLE DESCRIBED ON PAGE 21. INDEED, IT REQUIRES A BIT OF WORK AND EXPLANATION TO MAKE IT COME ABOUT.

FOR EXAMPLE, XJ-5 SPORTS A FLAT BOTTOM TO SIT ON, STRAIGHT WALLS, AND AN OPEN TOP TO CONFORM TO THE TRADITIONAL VESSEL FORMAT. LET'S SEE HOW WE GO ABOUT ACHIEVING THIS FORM THROUGH SOME SIMPLE LINE DRAWINGS.

ELLIPTICAL CIRCLES SUGGEST 3-D VOLUME

SMALL SQUARE SIMULATES GLASSY SURFACE (cool trick, huh?)

Nifty huh?

SKETCH XJ-5

HEY KIDS! * BONUS * POINTS * JUST FOR FUN, USE THE BLANK SPACE IN THE FRONT OR BACK OF THIS BOOK TO RENDER YOUR OWN VERSION OF SKETCH XJ-5!

A BRIEF EXPLANATION ON HOW-TO COMPLETE A TUMBLER:

① SHAPE... BLOW, then NECK.

② COLD HOT FLATTEN THE BOTTOM.

③ APPLY THE PUNTY TO THE CENTER OF THE BOTTOM.

④ CHILL THE NECK WITH WATER.

⑤ BONK! TAP THE BLOWPIPE TO COMPLETE THE TRANSFER...

⑥ REHEAT. OPEN UP THE FORM WITH THE JACKS

⑦ WHEN DONE, CHILL THE PUNTY, & BOX IT!

COMPLETING YOUR VERY FIRST TUMBLER
THE WELL ENDOWED VERSION

UNLESS YOU WANT A TUMBLER THE SIZE AND THICKNESS OF A SHOT GLASS, YOU WILL NEED TO GATHER MORE GLASS IN ORDER TO INCREASE THE SIZE AND VOLUME YOU WANT. DESIRE. NEED. DREAM ABOUT....

Gathering More Glass

GATHERING YOUR SECOND, THIRD, FOURTH, AD INFINITUM LAYERS OF GLASS GOES JUST LIKE THE FIRST. WITH EACH SUCCESSIVE GATHER YOU SHOULD PLUNGE THE PIPE DEEP ENOUGH IN THE GLASS SO AS TO COVER THE PRE-EXISTING GATHER. MAKE AT LEAST TWO FULL ROTATIONS IN THE GLASS TO INSURE EVENESS.

YOU CAN DRAMATICALLY EFFECT THE A M O U N T OF GLASS YOU GATHER BY JUST CHANGING THE **METHOD** or **Style** BY WHICH YOU GATHER.

DIP IT IN. TURN.   MAKE FULL REV-OLUTIONS.   KEEP TURNING. WITHDRAW ON AN ANGLE.   EXIT THE FURNACE AFTER THE GLASS TRAILS OFF.

THE COAT METHOD ↵

WITH THE **COAT-STYLE** OF GATHERING, YOU END UP WITH THE LEAST AMOUNT OF GLASS PER GATHER. BUT BY ALLOWING THE GLASS AN OPPORTUNITY TO TRAIL OFF IN THE FURNACE - YOUR GATHER GETS A NICE EVEN SHAPE.

WITH THE **COLLECTIVE-STYLE** OF GATHERING (DRAWN BELOW) - YOU GAIN THE LARGEST AMOUNT OF GLASS PER GATHER. THEY DON'T NECESSARILY COME OUT AS CLEAN AS YOU LIKE, BUT THAT'S WHY BLOCKS WERE INVENTED.

DIP IT IN. TURN.   MAKE FULL REV-OLUTIONS. DRIVE FORWARD.   CONTINUE TO FEED MORE GLASS ON THE PIPE.   COME UP & OUT OF THE GLASS. TRY NOT TO TRAIL ANY EXCESS GLASS OFF.   EXIT THE FURNACE.

THE COLLECTIVE METHOD ↵

FOR PRACTICE : JUST TAKE GATHERS. PRACTICE TURNING AT VARIOUS SPEEDS. SEE WHAT IT DOES FOR YOU. [TAKE NOTES]. TRY CHANGING YOUR ENTRY ANGLE. SEE WHAT THAT DOES. THEN TRY CHANGING THE ANGLE AT WHICH YOU EXIT THE FUR-NACE. IF YOU GET THE HANG OF GATHERING - DIFFERENTLY - BUT WITH PRE-DICTABLE RESULTS ～ YOU'LL GO FAR! OF COURSE, THE TEMPERATURE OF THE GLASS IN THE FURNACE PLAYS AN IMPORTANT ROLE. IF IT'S REALLY HOT - YOU'LL ONLY BE ABLE TO GATHER A LITTLE AT A TIME. IF THE GLASS IS "COLD" - YOU'RE LIKELY TO GATHER LARGER AND HEAVIER.

BLOCKING

So... AFTER YOU TAKE THE NEXT GATHER, YOU'LL WANT TO SHAPE THAT AMORPHOUS BLOB INTO A USEABLE FORM. BLOCKING IS ANOTHER TECHNIQUE FOR DOING JUST THAT.

SIT AT THE BENCH, SNUG UP AGAINST THE RAIL. GRAB AN APPROPRIATE-SIZED BLOCK, (ONE SLIGHTLY LARGER THAN YOUR OUT-OF-CONTROL BLOB), FROM THE BLOCK BUCKET BEHIND YOU.

CONTINUE THE ROLLING MOTION WITH YOUR **LEFT** HAND, AND BLOCK THE MOLTEN MATERIAL WITH THE TOOL IN YOUR RIGHT. LET THE GLASS FALL INTO THE CAVITY OF THE BLOCK. BASICALLY YOU'RE PROVIDING A TROUGH OR MOLD THAT THE GLASS SPINS IN- WHICH SIMULTANEOUSLY SHAPES AND COOLS ITS SKIN.

SHAPE AND CHILL THE NECK AREA FIRST, STARTING SNUG AGAINST THE END OF THE PIPE. DON'T FORCE IT! VISUALIZE GUIDING AND COAXING THE BLOB INTO A SYMMETRICAL FORM. AFTER THE NECK, CONCENTRATE ON BLOCKING THE CENTER OF THE FORM, AND THEN FINISH THE VERY END. TRY TILTING THE PIPE. IT ALLOWS YOU TO SHAPE THE BOTTOM HALF OF THE PIECE. (SEE BELOW) TRY ALSO ANGLING THE BLOCK BACKWARD AND FORWARD, UP AND DOWN. THIS HELPS YOU COVER ALL THE AREAS.

IF YOU NOTICE EXCESSIVE SMOKE POURING OUT OF THE BLOCK, OR IF THE BLOCK STARTS STICKING TO THE HOT GLASS- YOU'LL HAVE TO RE-WET THE BLOCK IN THE BUCKET.

IN FACT, IT'S A GOOD IDEA TO "AIR MARVER" BETWEEN PASSES DOWN THE LENGTHS OF THE RAILS. IT GIVES YOU AN OPPORTUNITY TO REWET YOUR BLOCK IN ADDITION TO ASSESSING THE BEHAVIOR OF THE GLASS AND WHERE YOU NEED TO BLOCK NEXT.

BLOCKS HAVE PRETTY MUCH ONE PURPOSE: TO OBTAIN A NICE EVEN SHAPE SUITABLE FOR GATHERING OVER OR BLOWING OUT. THEY ARE ONLY A PRIMARY SHAPING TOOL. ONCE YOU GET A NICE SYMMETRICAL FORM, YOU CAN GO AHEAD AND USE THE MARVER, NEWSPAPER OR JACKS TO ACCURATELY SHAPE YOUR GLASS WITH.

...OR IF THE GLASS IS STILL HOT ENOUGH, YOU CAN TRY BLOWING OUT THE BUBBLE SOME MORE. USUALLY, THE GLASS WILL REQUIRE SOME ADDITIONAL REHEATING IN ORDER TO WORK IT **GOOD N' HOT**, AND SHAPE IT FURTHER...

ANGLE THE PIPE TO HELP BLOCK THE BOTTOM OF THE PIECE

Now, some tips on reheating your work. Since it consumes almost 50% (more or less) of the glassblowing process, you'll want to make the best use of your time BASKING IN FRONT of the Glory Hole.

HEY! First off — don't over-bake your-self! GET THE WORK HOT — NOT YOU!

Stand where it is most comfortable and where you can still maintain control of what's on the end of the "stick". Heat shields are very helpful. Well-constructed doors operated by a clued-in assistant can greatly reduce unnecessary heat-exposure to yourself — and heat loss by the Glory Hole.

NOTE: If you're "doing doors" (assisting the gaffer at the Glory Hole) pay attention to the gaffer's head NOT the work in the Glory Hole. Usually they'll tip their head, squint, or make some type of verbal command (such as "open please") to indicate that they're ready to come out of the Glory Hole. You MUST pay attention while participating in this capacity. You must respond with split-second reflexes. Also, **BE GENTLE WITH THE EQUIPMENT!** Doors are often cast insulation — which are vulnerable to breaking or cracking if they are slammed shut too hard. Take it easy! If they get stuck together — pry them apart SLOWLY, don't try to yank them apart. More-than-likely some hot glass has fused them together and may require cleaning when the Glory Hole is cold.

RULE: Reheat only those areas of the glass which you need to work. Keep in mind where it's hottest-both the work itself and those spots within the Glory Hole where the heat is concentrated the most.

Since a Glory Hole is simply a giant torch stuck inside of an insulated drum → you know that if you stick the glass in front of the burner (the torch), it will get hot FAST.

When the doors are closed, and the piece is "boxed in", there is considerable heat reflected inside of the doors. Thus — the closer you can get to the doors (without sticking to them!) — the hotter your piece will get.

Make sure you have enough room to get your piece in and out of the Glory Hole without tagging a door. **DOOR MARVERING IS NOT AN OPTION!** Have an assistant standing-by to give you access in and out of the

OVERHEAD VIEW
The Hottest Spots in the Glory Hole

BURNER

GLORY HOLE. ALSO, AVOID HEATING TOO DEEPLY IN THE GLORY HOLE. YOU RISK **27** GETTING YOUR PIPE (OR PUNTY) UNNECESSARILY [& UNHEALTHILY] HOT.

ONCE AGAIN I'LL REMIND YOU OF CERTAIN FORCES AT WORK, ESPECIALLY DURING THE REHEATING PROCESS. AS YOU TRANSFORM THAT SOLID BACK INTO A SEMI-LIQUID ~ THE CENTRIFUGAL FORCE CAUSES THE BUBBLE TO EXPAND IN THE MIDDLE AND CONTRACT SOMEWHAT IN OVERALL LENGTH.

THE EFFECTS OF HEATING AND PIPE ROTATION:

THE FASTER YOU ROTATE THE PIPE - PLUS THE LONGER YOU EXPOSE IT TO THE HEAT IN THE GLORY HOLE, THE MORE DRAMATIC THIS EFFECT BECOMES. IT IS NOT NECESSARY TO SPIN THE PIPE LIKE CRAZY. **RELAX!** TAKE IT EASY. YOU MAY REDUCE THE CENTRIFUGAL FORCE BY ROTATING THE WORK ONE HALF-TURN TO THE RIGHT FOLLOWED BY ONE HALF TURN TO THE LEFT— KEEPING THE WORK BALANCED AND "ON-CENTER" UNTIL YOU'RE READY FOR THE NEXT STEP.

THIS IS AN IMPORTANT METHOD OF REHEATING. IT ENABLES YOU TO JUDGE HOW HOT YOUR GLASS IS BY HOW MUCH THE GLASS SAGS WHEN YOU MOMENTARILY HALT THE PIPE ROTATION. IT WILL ALSO KEEP YOUR WRISTS FROM TIRING OUT BY BREAKING-UP THE REPETITIVE MOTION.

Q. "WHAT'S ALL THIS STUFF ABOUT KEEPING EVERYTHING **ON CENTER?** I JUS' WANNA BLOW GLASS..."

A. GLASSBLOWING REQUIRES THAT YOU **PAY ATTENTION AT ALL TIMES!** FOCUS ON THE BEHAVIOR OF THE GLASS ON THE END OF THE STICK, AND REALIZE THAT YOU'RE IN C O M P L E T E C O N T R O L (YOUR HANDS JUST MAY NOT KNOW IT YET.)!

IF THE BUBBLE SAGS DOWN

FLIP IT OVER

AND LET IT FALL

BACK ON CENTER & ...

IF YOU'RE BUBBLE SAGS OFF-CENTER - FLIP IT OVER SO THE HIGH SPOT IS ON TOP, STOP THE PIPE ROTATION FOR A SECOND OR SO AND ALLOW THE BUBBLE TO FALL ON CENTER - PARALLEL WITH THE PIPE. AS SOON AS IT'S EVEN - CONTINUE THE RO-TATION. IF YOU DON'T GET YOUR BUBBLE ON-CENTER YOU'LL END-UP STRUGGLING WITH A WONKY, OUT-OF-KILTER BLOB THAT WILL FEEL VERY AWKWARD TO DEAL WITH. **GET IT RIGHT** - ON... **KEEP IT THAT WAY!**

Shaping & Blowing

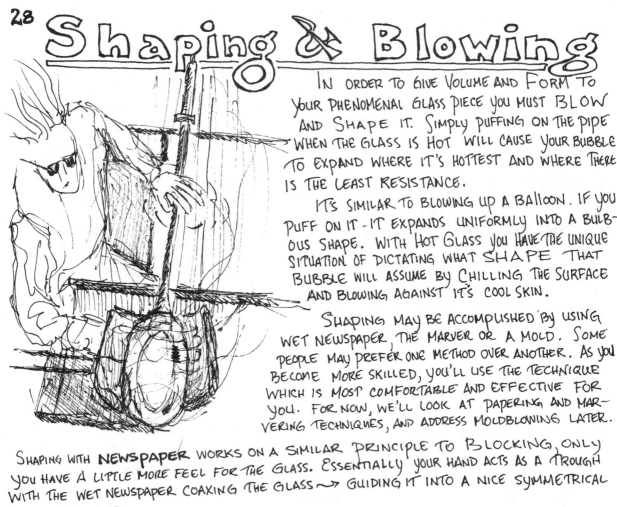

IN ORDER TO GIVE VOLUME AND FORM TO YOUR PHENOMENAL GLASS PIECE YOU MUST BLOW AND SHAPE IT. SIMPLY PUFFING ON THE PIPE WHEN THE GLASS IS HOT WILL CAUSE YOUR BUBBLE TO EXPAND WHERE IT'S HOTTEST AND WHERE THERE IS THE LEAST RESISTANCE.

IT'S SIMILAR TO BLOWING UP A BALLOON. IF YOU PUFF ON IT - IT EXPANDS UNIFORMLY INTO A BULBOUS SHAPE. WITH HOT GLASS YOU HAVE THE UNIQUE SITUATION OF DICTATING WHAT SHAPE THAT BUBBLE WILL ASSUME BY CHILLING THE SURFACE AND BLOWING AGAINST IT'S COOL SKIN.

SHAPING MAY BE ACCOMPLISHED BY USING WET NEWSPAPER, THE MARVER OR A MOLD. SOME PEOPLE MAY PREFER ONE METHOD OVER ANOTHER. AS YOU BECOME MORE SKILLED, YOU'LL USE THE TECHNIQUE WHICH IS MOST COMFORTABLE AND EFFECTIVE FOR YOU. FOR NOW, WE'LL LOOK AT PAPERING AND MARVERING TECHNIQUES, AND ADDRESS MOLDBLOWING LATER.

SHAPING WITH **NEWSPAPER** WORKS ON A SIMILAR PRINCIPLE TO BLOCKING, ONLY YOU HAVE A LITTLE MORE FEEL FOR THE GLASS. ESSENTIALLY YOUR HAND ACTS AS A TROUGH WITH THE WET NEWSPAPER COAXING THE GLASS → GUIDING IT INTO A NICE SYMMETRICAL "Q-TIP" SHAPE.

THE PAPERING PROCESS BEGINS BY "SETTING-UP" THE NECK AREA, CHILLING IT FOR STABILITY, AND THEN ADDRESSING THE WAIST AND LOWER SECTIONS. (SEE BELOW). THIS ENABLES YOU TO MAINTAIN SYMMETRY AND KEEP YOUR BUBBLE ON-CENTER. MAKE CONTINIOUS REVOLUTIONS OF THE PIPE, BACK N' FORTH ~ UP N' DOWN THE RAILS OF THE BENCH TO INSURE YOU UNIFORMLY SHAPE THE BUBBLE. AGAIN, DON'T FORCE IT! ALLOW THE WEIGHT OF THE GLASS - COMBINED WITH THE PIPE ROTATION, AND THE MOIST CRADLE OF THE WET NEWSPAPER, TO SHAPE THE GLASS.

TURN, TURN, TURN!

PAPER HERE 1st. THEN WORK YOUR WAY OUT

HOLD IT!

IF YOU NOTICE TON'S OF SMOKE POURING OFF YOUR NEWSPAPER,...

WET IT DOWN!

NOT ONLY IS THAT STUFF BAD TO BREATHE, THERE'S A GOOD CHANCE THAT THE ASH FROM THE BURNING NEWSPAPER IS ADHERRING ITSELF TO THE SURFACE OF YOUR GLASS FOREVER!

TRY TO KEEP 'WATERING' YOUR NEWSPAPER EVERY OTHER PASS DOWN THE RAILS UNTIL IT BUILDS UP A NICE LAYER OF CARBON (THAT BLACK STUFF). FRESH NEWSPAPER BLOCKS ESPECIALLY NEED A BREAK-IN PERIOD. ONCE SEASONED, THE PAPER SHOULDN'T SMOKE TOO MUCH, OR REQUIRE ALOT OF WATER ↝ JUST A SPRITZ OR TWO SHOULD KEEP IT IN GOOD SHAPE. AVOID TOO MUCH WATER - PUDDLES etc. IT CAN QUENCH YOUR GLASS - NOT WHAT YOU WANNA HAVE HAPPEN.

COUGH COUGH!

DON'T SMOKE!

NOW FOR THE EXCITING PART: AFTER AN INITIAL SHAPE-UP WITH THE PAPER, KICK BACK IN THE BENCH, SLIDE THE PIPE DOWN THE RAIL, AND GIVE A CONTINIOUS BLOW ON THE PIPE WHILE WATCHING YOUR BUBBLE EXPAND.

TAKE IT IN STEPS!

IF THE GLASS IS HOT ENOUGH (STILL), IT SHOULD INFLATE EASILY. WATCH IT! IT CAN BLOW-OUT TOO THIN AT ANY MOMENT ↝ A SITUATION YOU WANT TO AVOID AT ALL COSTS. ON THE OTHER HAND, IF YOU COOLED IT DOWN TOO MUCH (FROM EXCESSIVE PAPER-ING), YOUR EYES MAY BE BUGGING-OUT OF YOUR HEAD AND YOUR LUNGS MAY FEEL LIKE THEY'RE GONNA BURST BECAUSE OF THE RESISTANCE.

WATCH THAT EXPANSION!

HOT GOOD. COLD BAD.

REHEAT THE GLASS AND BLOW IT WHEN IT'S HOT. AGAIN, TAKE IT IN STEPS! A LITTLE AT A TIME. BLOW N' SHAPE. BLOW N' SHAPE. ALL THE WHILE KEEPING YOUR EYE ON THE BUBBLE. YOU WANT TO END-UP WITH AN EVEN BUBBLE, WITH CONSISTENT WALL-THICKNESS THROUGHOUT. IT'S BETTER AT FIRST TO KEEP YOUR PIECES ON THE

BLOWING SOLO AT THE BENCH

THICK-SIDE (NOT TOO THIN), THEY'RE EASIER TO HANDLE - LESS LIKELY TO CRINKLE OR COLLAPSE ON YOU, AND OFFER A HIGHER SUCCESS-RATE OF MAKING IT INTO THE BOX. YOU WILL, WITH PRACTICE, EVENTUALLY DEVELOP THE SKILLS TO BLOW THINNER, MORE DELICATE WORK IN THE FUTURE. BUT FOR NOW → BETTER-SAFE-THAN-SORRY!

AS STATED EARLIER, YOU CAN SHAPE AND BLOW AT THE MARVER AS WELL. LET'S CHECK THAT OUT. →

Marvering

The marver is a simple looking tool. It can be one of the easiest ones to use in shaping hot glass → if you understand how it works.

One way to explain this concept is to visualize a balloon filled with a "liquid sand mixture". At rest, it just sits there with one big flat spot.

If we tilt the board the balloon is resting on, it starts to roll. The skin of the balloon keeps the sand mixture contained. The rolling motion occurs on a flat surface, so the balloon rolls itself into more-or-less a cylinder shape.

Imagine, if you will, that the liquid sand mixture inside is a temperature sensitive material. It starts "freezing" at room temperature. It freezes (like many things) from the outside surface inwards. By rolling it on a colder surface (such as the marver) - it freezes the skin even quicker, but it also shapes the skin (of the balloon) into a cylinder. That pretty much describes what is occurring to a hot glass bubble during the marvering process.

Now, depending on which angle you roll the molten glass on the surface of the marver, it will determine the shape of the bubble. So, instead of tilting the board (as in our example), you're tilting the liquid sand bag/balloon, a.k.a. the bubble on the end of your blowpipe. There's yet one more force at work here: GRAVITY ~ your friend...

If you marver with your hands down low (below the surface of the marver) it will keep the form squat. This technique helps stabilizes the neck area which in turn offers you a firm (and hopefully symmetrical) base to work from.

Fig. M₁

If you marver horizontally - parallel with the surface of the marver - you can shape the sidewalls into a cylinder - very useful if you're shooting for a tumbler form. WATCH IT! Excessive marvering in this position may cause your bubble to 'weenie' out-of-control!

Fig. M₂

It is subtle changes in the angle of the pipe in relation to the marver which dictate what shape your bubble will be, that plus the glass temperature, and speed at which you rotate the pipe. If the glass is already cool or cold, not much will happen except chilling the outside surface. If the glass is "smokin' hot" - the effect can be quite dramatic.

YOU CAN COUNTERACT THE FORCE OF GRAVITY BY POINTING UP THE TIP OF THE GLASS AND MARVERING AT A STEEP ANGLE.

THIS IS A CHALLENGING TECHNIQUE TO MASTER. IF THE GLASS IS HOT, YOU'LL HAVE LITTLE OR NO STRUCTURE IN THE BUBBLE TO MARVER WITH. YOU MUST FULLY SUPPORT THE WEIGHT OF THE PIPE AND THE WEIGHT OF THE GLASS. PLUS YOU MUST KEEP THE PIPE ROTATING EVENLY TO MAINTAIN SYMMETRY AND KEEP THINGS ON CENTER.

IF THE GLASS IS REALLY HOT — THE FORM WILL WANT TO STRETCH AND ELONGATE WHILE YOU MARVER IN THIS POSITION. YOU CAN PREVENT IT FROM GETTING TOO LONG BY MARVERING IN JUST THE OPPOSITE POSITION (FIG. M_1 PREVIOUS PAGE) OR YOU CAN ALLOW THE WEIGHT OF THE PIPE TO PUSH YOUR FORM A LITTLE MORE COMPACT WHILE MARVERING.

FIG. M_3

WHEN YOU WATCH PROFESSIONAL GLASSBLOWERS MARVER — YOU'LL NOTICE HOW QUICKLY THEY CHANGE AXIS (THE ANGLE AT WHICH THEY MARVER). EACH TIME THEY ROLL THE GLASS ON THE MARVER, THEY ARE EITHER CHILLING A SURFACE (TO BLOW AGAINST) OR REINFORCING THE FORM TO MAINTAIN SYMMETRY. YOU WILL ALSO NOTICE THAT THEY DON'T ALWAYS HAVE THE GLASS ON THE MARVER, THAT OCCASSIONALLY THEY LIFT THE ENTIRE PIECE OFF OF THE MARVER AND SHAPE IT IN THE AIR. THIS IS REFERRED TO AS "AIR MARVERING".

AIR MARVERING (LIKE IT SOUNDS,) IS A VERY VALUABLE SHAPING TECHNIQUE TO LEARN. IT ALLOWS YOU A CHANCE TO ASSESS THE BEHAVIOR OF YOUR BUBBLE AND GIVES YOU AN OPPORTUNITY TO DECIDE WHAT TO DO NEXT. THE MORE YOU CAN SHAPE YOUR GLASS WITHOUT ACTUALLY TOUCHING IT [WITH TOOLS] THE HOTTER YOUR GLASS WILL BE, THE EASIER IT IS TO BLOW, AND ULTIMATELY THE BETTER GLASSBLOWER YOU WILL BECOME. (REFER BACK TO PAGE 19 FOR VISUAL CLUES).

SO ... GETTING BACK TO OUR TUMBLER EXAMPLE. LET'S SAY YOU'VE TAKEN A GOOD SOLID REHEAT IN THE GLORY HOLE. THE WHOLE PIECE IS MOVING NICE N' GOOEY-LIKE. YOU'LL FIRST WANT TO SET-UP THE NECK AREA WITH A QUICK PASS DOWN THE MARVER (AS IN FIG. M_1, PREVIOUS PAGE). THEN, AIR MARVER FOR A MOMENT. NEXT, GIVE THE PIECE A QUICK PASS HORIZONTALLY OVER THE MARVER (AS IN FIG. M_2), TO SET UP THE SIDE WALLS... ANOTHER AIR MARVER ~ AND THEN POINT-UP THE TIP (AS IN FIG. M_3 ABOVE). THE PIECE SHOULD BE MORE OR LESS SYMMETRICAL AT THIS POINT. NOW, YOU CAN HANG THE PIECE OVER THE BACK EDGE OF THE MARVER AND B L O W!

AGAIN, WATCH FOR SIGNS OF EXPASION.

KEEP YOUR EYE ON THE BUBBLE. IF IT STARTS TO EXPAND TOO THIN WHERE YOU DON'T WANT IT TO — QUICKLY MARVER THAT AREA TO CHILL IT OUT, FREEZE IT UP, AND PREVENT IT FROM BLOWING OUT ANY FURTHER THERE.

ALSO, IF YOU ACCIDENTALLY MARVER YOUR PIECE INCOMPLETELY OR MAKE IT LOP-SIDED — YOU CAN HANG IT OVER THE BACK EDGE OF THE MARVER AND GIVE THE PIECE A QUICK PUFF TO GET IT ROUND AGAIN.

REMEMBER: TAKE IT IN STEPS ...

BLOW A LITTLE, MARVER A LITTLE. MARVER A BIT MORE, BLOW A BIT MORE... KEEP WATCHING WHAT YOUR BUBBLE IS DOING. IF IT'S NOT BLOWING OUT MUCH, EITHER BLOW HARDER, OR MORE SIMPLY ~ REHEAT IT, AND THEN BLOW IT **HOT·N'·E·-Z!** BUT... DON'T BLOW IT TOO THIN! YOU'LL NEED SOME THICKNESS IN YOUR BUBBLE (STRUCTURE) IN ORDER TO GET THROUGH THE NEXT STEP WHICH IS **NECKING**.

FIG. M4

DO TRY TO DEVELOP A WORKING RHYTHM. ITS' TIMING, TEMPO; ONE MOVEMENT FLOWS INTO THE NEXT...

... LIKE **MUSIC!**

INDEED, THE SIMILARITIES BETWEEN GLASSBLOWING AND MUSIC ARE STRIKING: USUALLY THERE'S SOME KIND OF PLAN TO FOLLOW: DESIGN/SCORE, AN ORCHESTRATOR OR GAFFER TO WATCH, AND THE PIECE OCCURS START-TO-FINISH AS ONE CONTINUOUS MOVEMENT. SOMETIMES THERE'S ROOM FOR IMPROVISATION, SOLO'S, AND ALMIGHTY CRESCENDOS!

SOME PEOPLE MAY REFER TO IT AS A DANCE, OTHERS (less enthused) MAY CALL IT SIMPLY "TURNING POLE". WHATEVER YOU WISH TO CALL IT — USUALLY YOU ONLY GET ONE SHOT AT EACH PIECE, SO DO TRY AND MAKE YOUR BEST EFFORT.

<u>FOR PRACTICE</u>: TAKE A TWO GATHER BUBBLE. GET IT AS HOT AS YOU DARE. USING EITHER THE MARVER OR WET NEWSPAPER — SHAPE IT IN AS MANY DIFFERENT WAYS AS YOU CAN. MAKE 'EM SHORT N' SQUAT, OR LONG AND NARROW. REHEAT THEM AGAIN. CHANGE IT'S SHAPE AGAIN. IF THE BUBBLE GETS HORRIBLY DISTORTED,... WHO CARES? TRASH IT AND START OVER AGAIN.

TRY TO BUILD UP A 'VOCABULARY' OF SHAPES THROUGH THIS EXERCISE. CHALLENGE YOURSELF TO BLOW FORMS YOU WOULDN'T NORMALLY THINK OF, OR WORK WITH. THIS WILL HELP DIVERSIFY YOUR SKILLS AS A GLASSBLOWER AND MAKE YOU A BETTER GAFFER. ALSO, TRY TO WORK AS HOT AS YOU CAN AND BE AS FLUID WITH YOUR MOVEMENTS AS POSSIBLE. IT'S TIME WELL SPENT.

THE TUMBLER BUBBLE

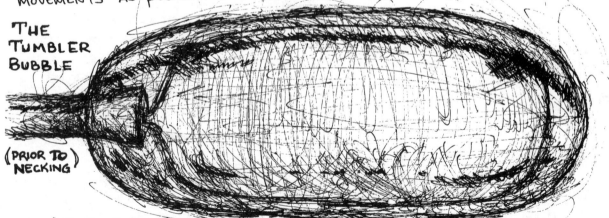

(PRIOR TO NECKING)

AT THIS POINT THE BUBBLE SHOULD BE UNIFORMLY BLOWN-OUT → WITH EVEN WALL-THICKNESS AND RELATIVELY ON-CENTER. FROM HERE, YOU NEED TO INITIATE A NECKLINE (A.K.A. A JACKLINE) IN ORDER TO BE ABLE TO **TRANSFER** YOUR VESSEL.

AFTER THAT,... SOME FINAL SHAPING AND BLOWING, AND THEN IT'S TIME TO PUNTY-UP, (the TRANSFER) AND LASTLY OPEN UP YOUR TUMBLER INTO IT'S FINAL SHAPE.

Necking

NO, THIS PROCEDURE DOESN'T INVOLVE OLD CHEVY'S, YOUNG HORMONES, AND SUBMARINE RACES, RATHER IT DEALS WITH SHAPING YOUR BUBBLE SO THAT A CLEAN, BREAK-OFF LINE IS CREATED ⟿ FURTHERING THE SUCCESSFUL VESSEL-MAKING PROCESS.

SO, PICKING UP WHERE WE LEFT OFF, WE HAVE A SITUATION SIMILAR TO THE IMAGE DRAWN IN FIG. N_1, ⟶ A TWO OR THREE GATHER BUBBLE WITH EVEN WALL-THICKNESS THROUGHOUT IS ON-CENTER AND READY TO BE NECKED.

FIRST, REHEAT THE WHOLE THING IN THE GLORY HOLE. CONCENTRATE ON HEATING THE NECK AREA. KEEP THE PIECE TURNING, AND HORIZONTAL AT ALL TIMES. RETURN TO THE BENCH.

Fig. N_1

NECK THE PIECE BY USING THE JACKS TO GENTLY SQUEEZE THE BLADES AGAINST THE **GLASS** - JUST ABOUT AS CLOSE TO THE END OF THE BLOWPIPE AS YOU CAN. MAKE CERTAIN THAT THE LINE YOU'RE CUTTING IS <u>OFF</u> THE END OF THE BLOWPIPE, OTHERWISE YOU'LL FIND IT VERY DIFFICULT TO TRANSFER THE PIECE LATER. FIG. N_2

FIG. N_2 SHOWS THE INITIAL NECKLINE BEING CUT IN.

MORE-THAN-LIKELY IT WILL TAKE AN ADDITIONAL REHEAT AND NECKING TO ACHIEVE AN ADEQUATE NECKLINE. AGAIN, TAKE IT IN STEPS!

BY ANGLING THE JACKS OUTWARDS, AS SHOWN IN FIG. N_3, YOU CAN AID THE NECKING PROCESS BY STRETCHING THE GLASS AND CONSEQUENTLY THINNING THE WALL-THICKNESS THERE. THIS TECHNIQUE MAY ALSO HELP YOU LATER IF YOU DISCOVER ALL YOUR PIECES COME OUT WITH THICK LIPS.

Fig. N_3

GO BACK IN FOR A FINAL REHEAT ON THE NECK, AND CUT-IN A NICE CRISP LINE WITH THE JACKS (FIG. N_4). THIS WILL HOPEFULLY PROVIDE YOU WITH A CLEAN AND PREDICTABLE BREAK-OFF POINT.

CAUTION: LIKE EVERYTHING IN GLASSBLOWING, (OR LIFE FOR THAT MATTER) THERE EXISTS THE POSSIBILITY THAT YOU CAN OVERDO IT. YOU CAN SQUEEZE A LINE SO TIGHT AS TO CUT-OFF THE HOLE COMPLETELY ⇒ THEREBY THE PROSPECT OF MAKING

Fig. N_4

34 A VESSEL OUT OF THE OBJECT A GREAT DEAL MORE CHALLENGING!!

THE REVERSE IS ALSO TRUE: FORGETTING TO NECK THE PIECE, OR ONLY DOING A HALF-ASSED ATTEMPT WILL MAKE THE TRANSFER VERY DIFFICULT OR MESSY. SAVE YOURSELF UNNECESSARY ANGUISH, AND ELIMINATE THE ARDUOUS TASK OF TRIMMING — DO IT RIGHT IN THE FIRST PLACE.

SOME SIMPLE FACTS ABOUT NECKING:

○ NECKING IS ONE OF THE MOST CHALLENGING OF ALL HOT GLASS TECHNIQUES TO GET USED-TO. IT TAKES CONCENTRATION, COORDINATION AND PRACTICE, PRACTICE, PRACTICE.

○ SQUAT FORMS ARE EASIER TO NECK THAN LONG ONES:

○ THICKER FORMS ARE EASIER TO NECK THAN THIN ONES, THEY HOLD THEIR HEAT BETTER AND ARE LESS LIKELY TO COLLAPSE DURING DEEP REHEATS.

○ FULL REVOLUTIONS ARE A MUST! USE THE WHOLE BENCH WHILE NECKING, NOT JUST THREE OR FOUR INCHES!

○ DON'T BE TOO AGGRESSIVE! YOU CAN EASILY SQUEEZE TOO HARD AND CUT AN ASYMMETRICAL CREASE IN THE NECK INSTEAD OF A NICE SMOOTH LINE.

○ KEEP YOUR JACKS LUBED WITH WAX, IF YOU NOTICE SOME SCREECHING SOUNDS EMANATING FROM YOUR JACKS WHILE NECKING — STOP AND GET SOME WAX ON 'EM. OTHERWISE, YOU'LL DAMAGE THE TOOL BY GRINDING THE METAL OFF - WHICH RESULTS IN A CURIOUS BLACK BUILD-UP ON THE MOUTH OF YOUR GLASS PIECE.

○ NECKING IS FAIRLY EASY IF THE GLASS IS HOT AND ON-CENTER. IF THE GLASS IS COLD OR FLOPPING ALL OVER — IT'LL BE A STRUGGLE AND A FIGHT TO ESTABLISH AN ACCEPTABLE NECKLINE.

SQUAT FORMS

E·Z TO CONTROL, & KEEP ON-CENTER

LONG FORMS

TENDENCY TO FLOP ALL-OVER!

FOR PRACTICE:

GATHER SOME GLASS ON A LARGE PUNTY. MARVER IT INTO A CYLINDER. SIT DOWN AT THE BENCH AND PRACTICE NECKING IT INTO A SERIES OF SPHERES.

SEE HOW MANY YOU CAN MAKE IN A HALF HOUR. THEN TRY IT WITH AN ADDITIONAL GATHER OF GLASS. ONCE YOU'VE GOT THE KNACK OF IT, TRY IT WITH A BUBBLE IN IT. THE JACKS CAN BE USED TO NECK LINES IN ANYWHERE ALONG THE LENGTH OF THE BUBBLE, CONSEQUENTLY MAKING THEM A VERY VALUABLE SHAPING TOOL AS WELL.

AGAIN, REMEMBER TO WORK FROM THE PIPE (OR PUNTY) SIDE ON OUT. THIS HELPS MAINTAIN SOME STABILITY WITHIN THE PIECE AND MAKES IT EASIER TO NECK THE WORK, WITH GREATER ACCURACY.

FLAttening The Bottom

THE NEXT TASK IS TO FINISH BLOWING AND SHAPING THE TUMBLER FORM.
SINCE THE NECKING PROCESS IS DONE, YOU NEEDN'T HEAT THAT AREA TOO MUCH MORE.
TRY TO GET THE BOTTOM HOT (BY REHEATING IN THE GLORY HOLE). SHAPE THE
BOTTOM AT THE MARVER OR WITH THE WET NEWSPAPER ↘ , BLOW THE BOTTOM OUT
A BIT FURTHER — WITHOUT BLOWING IT TOO
THIN ~ SO WATCH IT! TAKE IT EASY!

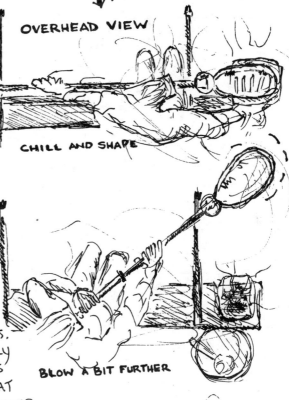

OVERHEAD VIEW

CHILL AND SHAPE

IF YOU STILL HAVE ENOUGH HEAT LEFT IN YOUR
PIECE, YOU CAN TRY PADDLING-IN THE <u>BOTTOM</u>.
USE FULL REVOLUTIONS OF THE BLOWPIPE TO
COVER THE WHOLE SURFACE AND GENTLY PRESS
AGAINST THE GLASS WITH A PADDLE. SOME PEOPLE
USE THE BACK OF THEIR JACKS TO DO THIS TOO, IF
THE SURFACE ISN'T TOO LARGE.

IF THE GLASS IS VERY HOT OR VERY THIN
THE BOTTOM MAY CAVE-IN SOMEWHAT — CREATING
A "KICK-FOOT" — AN INDENTATION IN THE BOTTOM
OF THE VESSEL. SOME GLASSBLOWERS LIKE THIS
EFFECT, AND OTHERS DON'T. IF YOU DON'T LIKE IT,
YOU CAN ALWAYS PUFF IT OUT AND TRY TO PADDLE
IT SMOOTH.

BLOW A BIT FURTHER

BE CAREFUL WHEN PADDLING-IN THE BOTTOMS.
IF YOU ATTACK IT TOO AGGRESSIVELY, YOU'RE LIKELY
TO DISTORT YOUR OVERALL FORM AND PUSH THINGS
OFF-CENTER. YOU MAY END-UP HAVING TO REHEAT
AND RESHAPE EVERYTHING ALL OVER AGAIN IN ORDER
TO GET IT LOOKING RIGHT.

ALSO, TO INSURE THE LIKELIHOOD OF SUCCESS
YOUR FIRST TIME OUT — KEEP THE BOTTOM OF
THE VESSEL ON THE "THICK-SIDE"
(IF AT ALL POSSIBLE)... THE EXTRA
GLASS WILL OFFER MORE STRENGTH AND
RESILIENCE DURING SOME OF THE UPCOMING
"TRICKY MOMENTS".

PADDLE THE BOTTOM FLAT.

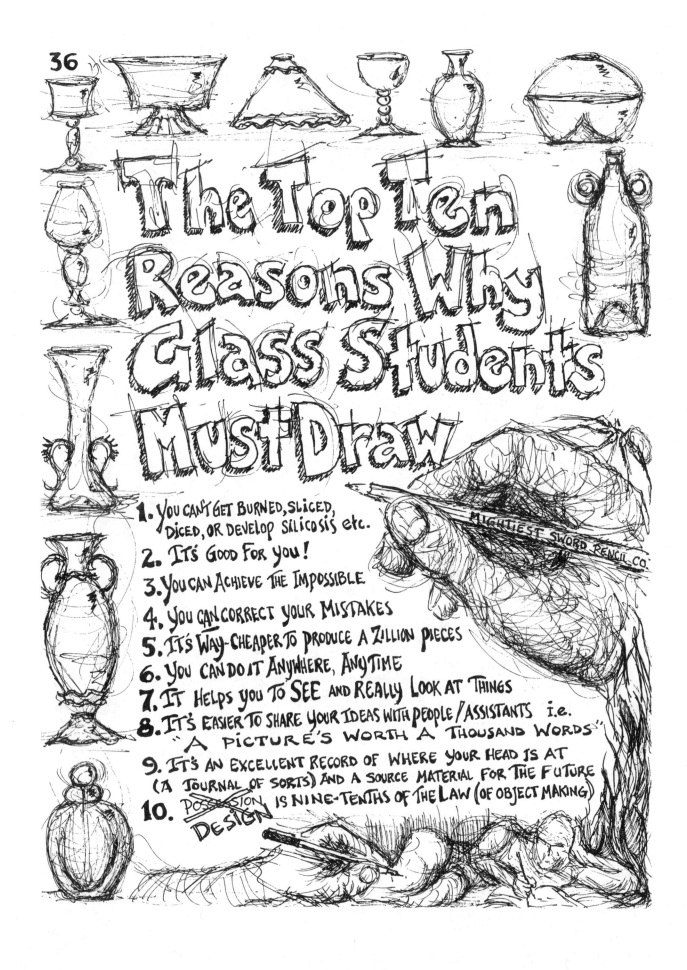

The Top Ten Reasons Why Glass Students Must Draw

1. YOU CAN'T GET BURNED, SLICED, DICED, OR DEVELOP SILICOSIS etc.

2. IT'S GOOD FOR YOU!

3. YOU CAN ACHIEVE THE IMPOSSIBLE

4. YOU CAN CORRECT YOUR MISTAKES

5. IT'S WAY-CHEAPER TO PRODUCE A ZILLION PIECES

6. YOU CAN DO IT ANYWHERE, ANYTIME

7. IT HELPS YOU TO SEE AND REALLY LOOK AT THINGS

8. IT'S EASIER TO SHARE YOUR IDEAS WITH PEOPLE/ASSISTANTS i.e. "A PICTURE'S WORTH A THOUSAND WORDS"

9. IT'S AN EXCELLENT RECORD OF WHERE YOUR HEAD IS AT (A JOURNAL OF SORTS) AND A SOURCE MATERIAL FOR THE FUTURE

10. ~~POSSESSION~~ DESIGN IS NINE-TENTHS OF THE LAW (OF OBJECT MAKING)

MIGHTIEST SWORD PENCIL CO.

Punty Time

THE **TRANSFER** IS A VITAL STEP IN THE FORMATION OF BLOWN GLASS OBJECTS. ESSENTIALLY YOU ARE REVERSING THE AXIS OF THE PIECE BY ATTACHING A PUNTY TO THE BOTTOM OF THE PIECE AND BREAKING IT FREE FROM THE BLOWPIPE.

THERE ARE A FEW IMPORTANT THINGS YOU NEED TO KEEP IN MIND WHILE "PUNTYING UP":

#1. THE PIECE YOU'RE PUNTYING-UP TO SHOULD:

    A. BE "ON-CENTER"

    B. BE BLOWN OUT THE WAY YOU WANT IT TO BE.- YOU WON'T GET ANOTHER CHANCE.

    C. HAVE A CLEAN, CLEARLY-DEFINED NECKLINE.

    D. BE COOL (TEMPERATURE-WISE), AND NOT MOVING AROUND ON YOU.

#2. THE ACTUAL PUNTY ROD SHOULD BE THE CORRECT DIAMETER (OR THICKNESS) TO HANDLE THE WEIGHT AND SIZE OF THE PIECE WHICH YOU'RE TRANSFERRING. IN OTHER WORDS: BIG PIECES REQUIRE BIG PUNTIES!

#3. TIMING IS EVERYTHING! BE SWIFT WITH YOUR MOVEMENTS DURING THE TRANSFER PROCESS. YOUR PIECE'S SURVIVAL MAY DEPEND ON IT.

#4. THE PUNTY SHOULD BE ATTACHED TO THE DEAD CENTER OF THE BOTTOM OF THE PIECE. IT'S THE ONLY CHANCE YOU'LL GET, SO TRY TO TARGET IT ON CENTER AS CLOSE AS YOU CAN GET IT.

THERE ARE TWO WAYS YOU CAN GO ABOUT COMPLETING THE TRANSFER: SOLO (BY YOURSELF) OR ASSISTED (WITH TEAMWORK). IN METHOD ONE, YOU HAVE TO DO EVERYTHING ON YOUR OWN. IN METHOD TWO, YOU HAVE AN ASSISTANT PREPARE THE PUNTY FOR YOU, CONSEQUENTLY IT IS A LITTLE EASIER TO DO.

METHOD ONE - SOLO.

YOU MAY TRANSFER THE BUBBLE FROM THE BLOWPIPE TO THE PUNTY IN THE FOLLOWING FASHION: 1ST - **FLASH** THE ENTIRE PIECE IN THE GLORY HOLE (FOR A "COUNT" OF FIVE), THEN SET THE PIPE ON THE BENCH OR HANG IT UP IF THERE'S A VERTICAL (OR "HANGING") YOKE NEARBY. GRAB A PREHEATED PUNTY FROM THE PIPEWARMER AND GATHER UP A SMALL BLOB OF GLASS ON IT'S RED-TIPPED END.

MARVER THE GLASS HORIZONTALLY INTO A CYLINDER SHAPE. THEN, BY ANGLING YOUR HANDS UPWARDS, POINT-UP THE TIP OF THE GLASS ～ ROLLING AND PUSHING SLIGHTLY FORWARDS AS YOU DO SO ➘

① ② ③

38 NOTE AVOID OVERCHILLING THE VERY TIP OF YOUR PUNTY (BY EXCESSIVE MARVERING) – IT NEEDS TO BE -HOT- IN ORDER TO STICK TO THE BOTTOM OF YOUR TUMBLER.

BACK AT THE BENCH, PICK UP YOUR TWEEZERS AND USE THEM TO GUIDE THE PUNTY AS CLOSE TO DEAD CENTER AS YOU CAN GET IT. TOUCH UP LIGHTLY AT FIRST... THEN, ROTATE THE PUNTY (WHICH IN TURN ROTATES THE WHOLE PIECE) AND CHECK TO SEE IF YOU'RE "ON CENTER."

ATTACH THE PUNTY

IF YOU'RE A LITTLE OFF, GO AHEAD AND TRY TO PUSH THE PUNTY A BIT MORE ON CENTER. IT'S THE ONLY CHANCE YOU'LL GET! BE CERTAIN TO MAKE **FULL** REVOLUTIONS DOWN THE RAILS OF THE BENCH TO CHECK YOUR SYMMETRY.

NOW, DIP YOUR WHOLE HAND -TWEEZERS AND ALL, IN THE BUCKET OF WATER AND CHILL THE NECKLINE BY DIRECTING THE FLOW OF DROPLETS WITH THE TIPS OF THE TWEEZERS TO CASCADE PRECISELY ONTO THE NECKLINE.

CHECK AND CENTER.

AVOID DRIPPING WATER ONTO THE PIECE ITSELF!

NOTE: IT IS THE WATER – NOT THE TOOL – WHICH IS CHILLING THE NECK. THE WATER DISRUPTS THE SURFACE TENSION OF THE GLASS, IN ADDITION TO RAPIDLY CHILLING THE GLASS AND SETS UP A STRESS POINT WHERE THE GLASS WANTS TO BREAK AT.

WHEN THE PUNTY FEELS STIFF, i.e. THERE IS LIMITED MOVEMENT WHEN YOU LIFT THE PUNTY UP AND DOWN, YOU'RE READY TO TAP THE BLOWPIPE TO RELEASE THE PIECE. WITH THE BACK END OF YOUR TWEEZERS BONK THE BLOWPIPE JUST ABOVE THE MOILE – FIRM AND SQUARE. THE PIECE SHOULD BREAK FREE-CLEAN AND EASY. IF IT FAILS TO RELEASE – TRY TAPPING IT AGAIN. IF IT STILL DOESN'T COME OFF ~ USE A LITTLE MORE WATER AND TRY AGAIN (SOME NECKS ARE MORE THICKER AND MORE STUBBORN THAN OTHERS... ...).

CHILL THE NECK WITH SOME WATER

WHEN YOU FREE THE PIECE, PLACE THE PIPE IN THE APPROPRIATE PIPE BUCKET AND TAKE YOUR PUNTY-UPED VESSEL TO THE GLORY HOLE AS QUICKLY AS YOU CAN.

SINCE TEAMWORK CAN GREATLY EASE THE PREVIOUS PROCEDURE BY A FACTOR OF FOUR LET'S SEE HOW THAT METHOD WORKS:

=BONK=

TAP THE PIECE FREE.

GATHERING AND SHAPING THE PUNTY IS IDENTICAL TO THE FIRST METHOD, EXCEPT AS "GAFFER" YOU GET TO HANG OUT AT THE BENCH WHILE YOUR ASSISTANT PREPARES IT.

C'MON, SOMETIME THIS CENTURY WOULD BE NICE...

IN THE MEANTIME, YOU CAN PRE-CHILL THE NECKLINE WITH THE JACKS BY NECKING IT THERE. JUST A FEW FULL REVOLUTIONS SHOULD DO THE TRICK.

NEXT, INSPECT THE PUNTY BEFORE YOU ATTACH IT TO THE BOTTOM OF YOUR PIECE. IF IT'S NOT RIGHT, SEND IT BACK OR HAVE YOUR ASSISTANT MAKE ANOTHER ONE.

THERE'S NO EXCUSE FOR ACCEPTING A BAD PUNTY! TAKE THE TIME TO TRAIN YOUR ASSISTANT IN THE FIRST PLACE ~ IT'LL PAY OFF IN THE FUTURE!

STICK UP THE PUNTY TO THE BOTTOM – GENTLY AT FIRST, ROTATE THE BLOWPIPE AND GUIDE THE PUNTY ON-CENTER PUSHING IT A BIT FURTHER ON.

[AS ASSISTANT: YOU'LL HAVE TO KEEP YOUR HANDS LOOSE, ACTING AS SUPPORT FOR THE PUNTY AND ALLOWING THE GAFFER TO DO THE MOVES...]

MAKE A FEW MORE TURNS DOWN THE BENCH TO DOUBLE CHECK THAT THE PUNTY IS ON-CENTER. THIS ALSO GIVES THE PUNTY A CHANCE TO SET-UP.

"HOWZIT FEEL?"

ALMOST THERE.

FINALLY, DUNK YOUR WHOLE HAND ((WITH THE TWEEZERS IN THEM)) IN YOUR BLOCKBUCKET AND LET GRAVITY PULL THOSE WATER DROPLETS ON THE NECKLINE ((NOT ON YOUR PIECE!)).

COMPLETING
THE TRANSFER...

AGAIN, USE THE BACK END OF THE TWEEZERS TO TAP THE PIECE OFF. MANY GAFFERS NOWADAYS LIFT THEIR ENTIRE BLOWPIPE OFF OF THE RAILS BEFORE THEY STRIKE THE PIECE FREE. THIS WAY NO SHOCK IS ABSORBED BY THE BENCH AND THE BRUNT OF THE FORCE IS FELT BY THE PRE-STRESSED NECKLINE. THE PIECE SHOULD COME OFF NICE AND CLEAN-LIKE.

HAVE YOUR ASSISTANT TAKE THE PIECE IMMEDIATELY UP TO THE GLORY HOLE FOR A RE-HEAT WHILE YOU PLACE YOUR PIPE IN THE APPROPRIATE BUCKET. NOTE: IF THE PIECE IS FLOPPING AROUND BECAUSE THE PUNTY IS TOO HOT, TRY HOLDING THE WORK DOWN (YOU MAY EVEN SET THE PIECE DOWN ON IT'S LIP) AND PUSH THE PUNTY AGAINST THE BASE. GIVE IT A FEW SECONDS TO SET-UP AND TRY IT AGAIN, IT SHOULD BE STABLE.

IT'S A GOOD IDEA TO FLASH THE WHOLE PIECE WITHIN THE GLORY HOLE AS QUICK AS YOU CAN. THIS WILL REDUCE THERMAL SHOCK AND SUBSEQUENT CRACKING BY THERMALLY STABALIZING THE PIECE. WHEN FLASHING THE PIECE HOWEVER, BE AWARE THAT THE PUNTY IS STILL RELATIVELY HOT IN COMPARISON TO THE REST OF THE PIECE. BECAUSE OF IT'S SMALL SIZE, IT WILL HEAT UP FASTER THAN ANYTHING ELSE. LIKEWISE, IT COOLS VERY RAPIDLY AND CONSEQUENTLY REQUIRES CONSTANT ATTENTION AND NUMEROUS REHEATS.

A FINE LINE EXISTS BETWEEN TOO HOT N' FLOPPY OF A PUNTY AND ONE WHICH IS TOO COLD—AND WHERE THE SLIGHTEST JARRING OF THE PUNTY RESULTS IN A NEW FLOOR MODEL. PRACTICE, TRIAL & ERROR ARE THE BEST WAYS IN WHICH TO BECOME FAMILIAR WITH THE LIMITATIONS OF CERTAIN PUNTIES (PLEASE REFER TO APPENDIX A FOR ADDITIONAL PUNTY STYLES).

THE CURE FOR FLOPPY PUNTIES

FOR PRACTICE:
BLOW A SPHERE. NECK IT DOWN AS TIGHT AS YOU CAN. PRACTICE PUNTYING IT UP. ONCE YOU TRANSFER IT SUCCESSFULLY, SEAL UP THE HOLE ON THE OTHER END, THEN PUNTY UP TO THAT POINT AND TRANSFER IT AGAIN. KEEP TRANSFERRING IT AGAIN N' AGAIN. USE A FRESH PUNTY EACH TIME. THIS KIND OF REPETITIVE DRILL WILL HOPEFULLY TRAIN YOU HOW TO MAKE PUNTIES QUICKLY AND MORE EFFICIENTLY. IF THE SPHERE DROPS AND CRASHES—WHO CARES? MAKE AN-OTHER.

THIS IS ALSO GOOD PRACTICE FOR ASSISTED TRANSFERS. PLAY "PASS THE BALL" AS MANY TIMES AS YOU CAN TOLERATE WITH YOUR ASSISTANT. SWITCH ROLES AND LET YOUR ASSISTANT BE THE GAFFER AND TRY IT THAT WAY FOR A WHILE.

YOU CAN ALWAYS TRY MAKING DIFFERENT STYLES OF PUNTIES DURING THIS TYPE OF EXERCISE TO SEE HOW EACH ONE PERFORMS FOR YOU. (SEE APPENDIX A pgs 91-3)

Finishing the Tumbler

AFTER FLASHING THE WHOLE PIECE IN THE GLORY HOLE, CONCENTRATE ON HEATING JUST THE LIP OF THE WORK — THAT AREA WHERE IT BROKE FREE FROM THE BLOWPIPE. SINCE IT'S REALLY THE COLDEST PART OF THE PIECE, IT WILL NATURALLY TAKE A WHILE LONGER TO HEAT-UP AND BECOME "PLASTIC".

BE PATIENT. ALSO, BE SURE TO FLASH THAT PUNTY OCCASSIONALLY — OR YOUR PIECE MAY ELECT TO JUMP-OFF AND COMMIT SUICIDE. **NOTE:** YOU SHOULD ALWAYS FLASH THE PUNTY AND WHOLE PIECE BEFORE LEAVING THE GLORY HOLE AND IMMEDIATELY UPON RETURN → IT'S VITAL THAT YOU MAINTAIN THERMAL STABILITY THROUGHOUT.

WHEN THE LIP NO LONGER APPEARS JAGGED AND EXHIBITS SOME ORANGE/RED COLOR THERE, RETURN TO THE BENCH AND PREPARE TO OPEN UP THE LIP OF THE VESSEL.

Q? "HOW CAN I TELL IF THE LIP IS HOT ENOUGH TO WORK WHILE REHEATING IN THE GLORY HOLE? IT'S SO BRIGHT I CAN BARELY SEE ANYTHING...".

A. PRACTICE AND EXPERIENCE... YOU WILL EVENTUALLY DEVOLOP A FEEL FOR REHEATING PIECES AND HOW LONG IT TAKES TO GET SOMETHING HOT. YOU CAN ALSO TRY PULLING THE WHOLE PIECE OUT OF THE GLORY HOLE AND MOVE IT TO THE SIDE TO CHECK ON IT. THE ORANGE/RED GLOW OF THE GLASS SHOULD BE APPARENT ENOUGH IF THE GLASS IS HOT ENOUGH. YOU ALSO MAY NOTICE SOME MOVEMENT IN THE GLASS → IT MAY SAG A LITTLE IF YOU STOP THE PIPE ROTATION MOMENTARILY. IF THERE'S NO MOVEMENT OR COLOR — GET THE GLASS HOTTER!

OPENING THE LIP OF THE VESSEL TENDS TO BE ONE OF THE TRICKIEST TECHNIQUES TO BECOME FAMILIAR WITH FOR MOST BEGINNERS. IT LOOKS REALLY EASY, YET THERE ARE SUBTLE FORCES AT WORK AND IT REQUIRES A BIT OF FINESSE TO PULL OFF.

OPENING THE TUMBLER WITH THE JACKS

GRAB THE JACKS IN THE PALM OF YOUR HAND — (PALM SIDE-UP), AND SQUEEZE THE BLADES GENTLY TOGETHER SO THAT THE TIPS TOUCH TOGETHER. INSERT THE TIPS JUST INSIDE THE LIP OF YOUR TUMBLER 【 IF BOTH TIPS WON'T FIT BECAUSE THE HOLE IS TOO SMALL — TRY JUST ONE BLADE OF THE JACKS. IF THAT IS STILL TOO BIG, YOU MAY HAVE TO REAM THE HOLE LARGER WITH THE POINT OF YOUR TWEEZERS 】.

USE FULL REVOLUTIONS OF THE PUNTY UP AND DOWN THE LENGTHS OF THE RAILS COMBINED WITH MOVEMENTS OF YOUR JACKS TO FLARE THE LIP OPEN. YOUR HANDS HAVE TO WORK IN UNISON, YET THEY PERFORM DISTINCTIVELY DIFFERENT OPERATIONS. IT'S ALOT LIKE PATTING YOUR HEAD AND RUBBING YOUR BELLY AT THE SAME TIME!

ONCE THE TIPS OF YOUR JACKS FIT WELL ENOUGH INSIDE THE MOUTH OF THE VESSEL — YOU CAN GO AHEAD AND ALLOW THEM TO S L O W L Y SPRING OPEN. THEY SHOULD BE EQUALLY TOUCHING BOTH SIDES OF THE LIP.

IF YOU ARE TOO AGGRESSIVE WITH THE SPRING ACTION — YOU MAY END-UP MAKING A "DUCK BILL" AND THROWING EVERYTHING OUT-OF-ROUND. IT'S BETTER TOO LITTLE THAN TOO MUCH AT THIS STAGE. YOU MAY FIND THAT IT TAKES TWO OR THREE OR TWENTY REHEATS TO GET THE LIP IN THE SHAPE THAT YOU WANT IT, BUT CONSIDERING HOW MUCH TIME IT'S TAKEN YOU TO GET TO THIS STAGE, YOU'LL FIND IT'S WORTH THE EFFORT TO GET IT RIGHT.

ALLOW THE SPRING OF THE JACKS TO GENTLY RIDE AGAINST THE INNER LIP OF THE VESSEL, COMBINED WITH THE CONSTANT ROTATIONS TO OPEN IT UP.

IF YOU OPEN UP THE LIP BEYOND THE SPRING OF THE JACKS (i.e. THEY'RE ALL THE WAY OPEN BUT THEY FAIL TO TOUCH BOTH OF THE OPPOSING WALLS), YOU MAY HAVE TO MOVE THE BLADES TO THE TOP OR BOTTOM THIRD OF THE VESSEL AND WORK FROM THERE.

OVERHEAD VIEW-OPENING THE VESSEL

KEEP THE JACKS PARALLEL WITH THE PUNTY AND ALWAYS MOVING AT THE SAME SPEED. TRY TO USE AS MUCH OF THE BENCH AS YOU CAN TO INSURE THAT YOU MAKE COMPLETE REVOLUTIONS AND THAT YOU TOUCH ALL BASES.

IF YOU NOTICE SOME SQUEELING OR SCREECHING SOUNDS EMINATING FROM THE PIECE OR JACKS — STOP! WHAT YOU'RE DOING! EITHER YOUR JACKS NEED MORE WAX (AS A LUBRICANT) OR MORE-THAN-LIKELY THE GLASS IS TOO COLD AND IS SCREAMING IN PAIN (OR BOTH!)! REMEMBER, HOT GOOD, COLD BAD. THE JACKS ARE MADE OF METAL AND (LIKE THE MARVER) CAN SUCK THE HEAT OUTTA YER PIECE QUICKER THAN YOU CAN SAY LICKETY-SPLIT. THIS IS WHY YOU CAN ONLY OPEN THE VESSEL SO MUCH BEFORE THE GLASS FREEZES UP AND YOU HAVE TO TAKE ANOTHER REHEAT.

YOU HAVE THE OPPORTUNITY TO DRAMATICALLY ALTER THE SHAPE OF YOUR VESSEL AT THIS POINT SIMPLY BY CHANGING THE ANGLE AT WHICH YOU SHAPE WITH THE JACKS. IF YOU KEEP THE BLADES PARALLEL WITH THE PIECE, YOU'LL WIND UP WITH A PIECE THAT HAS STRAIGHT SIDEWALLS. IF YOU ANGLE THE JACKS SLOWLY UPWARD YOU CAN FLARE THE LIP. THE MORE ANGLE YOU GIVE IT — THE WIDER THE FLARE WILL BECOME. YOU CAN EVEN FLARE IT SO FAR AS TO FOLD THE LIP COMPLETELY OVER! SEE NEXT PAGE...

WHEN OPENING VESSELS...

KEEP THE JACKS PARALLEL FOR STRAIGHT-WALLED VESSELS...

ANGLE THE JACKS FOR FLARED LIPS

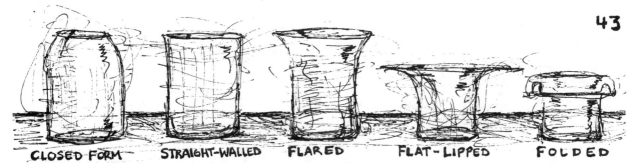

| CLOSED FORM | STRAIGHT-WALLED | FLARED | FLAT-LIPPED | FOLDED |

FIVE VARIATIONS ON THE TUMBLER FORM
COMPLETED ON THE PUNTY AFTER THE TRANSFER.

AGAIN, IT IS IMPORTANT TO REMEMBER TO BE ESPECIALLY CAREFUL WHEN YOU'RE MOVING AROUND THE HOT SHOP WITH YOUR PIECE ON THE END OF THE PUNTY. BE GENTLE EACH TIME YOU SET THE PUNTY ON THE YOKE OR ON THE BENCH. ABRUPT JARRING OR UNNECESSARY FORCE MAY CAUSE YOUR PIECE TO BREAK FREE FROM THE PUNTIES BRITTLE GRIP AND SEND IT (IN WHAT APPEARS TO BE SLOW MOTION) CASCADING TO THE WELCOME FLOOR BELOW (AND NEAR CERTAIN DEATH!).

BOX IT!

THERE ARE A FEW DIFFERENT WAYS TO GET YOUR PIECE OFF THE PUNTY AND INTO THE ANNEALER. YOU CAN TAP IT OFF DIRECTLY INTO THE ANNEALER, OR ONTO A "KNOCK-OFF" TRAY AND USE SPECIAL GLOVES TO LOAD IT IN THE ANNEALER. OR, IF YOU HAVE AN ASSISTANT HANDY → YOU MAY TAP THE PIECE OFF INTO THE GLOVES AND HAVE THEM LOAD IT FOR YOU.

THE FIRST THING YOU NEED TO DO IS MAKE SURE THAT THE PIECE IS STABILIZED ENOUGH BEFORE YOU KNOCK IT OFF. YOU DON'T WANT IT MOVING AROUND ON YOU! MAKE SURE THERE'S NO COLOR IN THE PIECE (INDICATING THAT IT IS STILL HOT).

MOST GAFFERS WILL DO A QUICK FLASH ON THE WHOLE PIECE BEFORE BOXING IT.

THE NEXT THING YOU NEED TO DO IS TO CHILL THE PUNTY AT EXACTLY THE POINT WHERE IT IS ATTACHED TO THE PIECE. MOST EVERY GLASSBLOWER HAS A METHOD WHICH WORKS BEST FOR THEM. AMONGST THE MOST POPULAR TECHNIQUES ARE : CHILLING THE JOINT BY REPEATED TAPS WITH A BUTTERKNIFE OR SIMILAR TOOL.

OR: USING A DROP OR THREE OF WATER EXACTLY ON THE JOINT TO HELP RAPIDLY CHILL THE PUNTY.

THE 'TAP N' CHILL METHOD SEEMS TO WORK WELL FOR MOST SMALL PIECES. ESSENTIALLY YOU TAP THE CONTACT POINT BY REPEATEDLY CHILLING IT WITH THE POINT OF A BUTTERKNIFE. SET THE PUNTY INTO THE NOTCH OF A BREAK-OFF TRAY. ROTATE IT SLOWLY AS YOU GENTLY TAP AT THE JOINT. TWO REVOLUTIONS, OR SO, SHOULD BE ENOUGH.

"TAP" "TAP" "TAP"

BREAK OFF

44 GRAB A WOODEN PADDLE OR "BONKING TOOL" AND STRIKE THE PUNTY FIRMLY CLOSE TO THE PIECE ((NOT TO BE CONFUSED WITH A "WHACK!")). THIS SHOULD BE ENOUGH SHOCK TO POP THE PIECE OFF INTO THE BREAK-OFF TRAY, AND THEN YOU CAN GLOVE IT INTO THE OVEN.

FOR LARGER PIECES, OR STUBBORN PUNTIES, USE WATER TO HELP IT BREAK OFF EASY. AVOID DRIPPING WATER ON THE PIECE! IT CAN CAUSE YOUR PIECE TO CRACK OR AT THE VERY LEAST - CAUSE UNSIGHTLY QUENCH MARKS.

TILT YOUR PUNTY - HANDLE END DOWN, TO GAIN EASY ACCESS TO THE PUNTY AREA. GRAB YOUR TWEEZERS AND DIP YOUR WHOLE HAND IN A BUCKET OF WATER. USE THE POINTS OF THE TWEEZERS TO GUIDE A DROP OR TWO OF WATER ON THE PUNTY AS CLOSE TO THE BOTTOM OF THE PIECE AS YOU CAN GET IT!

IF YOU HAVE AN ASSISTANT, THEY MAY PUT ON THE GLOVES AND PRE-HEAT THEM BY EXPOSING THEM TO THE HEAT FROM THE GLORY HOLE FOR 3- to 5 SECONDS. THEN, YOUR ASSISTANT MAY SUPPORT / CRADLE THE PIECE FROM UNDERNEATH (WITH THE GLOVES) AND YOU CAN TAP THE PUNTY TO RELEASE THE TUMBLER.

DON'T DELAY — PUT IT AWAY!

AVOID HOLDING THE PIECE ANY LONGER THAN NECESSARY, AS THE RESULTING BLACK BURN MARKS AND CURIOUS SMOKING KEVLAR GLOVE ODOR UPSETS SHOPMATES AND INSTRUCTORS. ALSO, BESIDES BEING VERY EXPENSIVE, THOSE GLOVES ARE EXTREMELY COLD IN COMPARISON TO YOUR HOT GLASS OBJECT ~ AND YOU DON'T WANT TO RISK THERMAL SHOCKING IT BY ADMIRING IT'S BEAUTY... WAIT UNTIL IT'S ANNEALED.

TAKE CARE IN LOADING ANNEALERS. KNOW BEFOREHAND WHICH ONE YOU'LL BY GOING IN TO. HAVE TOOLS, GLOVES, AND PROTECTIVE CLOTHING ETC. READY AND WAITING. TRY TO MAKE THE BEST USE OF ANNEALING SPACE. COMMON PRACTICE IS TO LOAD LEFT - TO - RIGHT, BACK-TO-FRONT. BE AWARE OF OTHER PEOPLE'S WORK, AND OTHER WORKERS AS WELL.

NOTE: WHEN PUTTING STUFF AWAY ⇒ PROTECT YOURSELF!

ANOTHER CURIOUS SMELL YOU MIGHT DETECT MAY BE YOUR ARM HAIR, HEAD OF HAIR, OR FACIAL HAIR BURNING AWAY! WEAR LONG SLEEVES, GLOVES, A HAT OR BANDANA FOR YOUR HEAD, AND A FACE SHIELD WHEN LOADING ANNEALERS. ALSO, SPEND AS LITTLE TIME AS POSSIBLE IN THE ANNEALER — TO CUT DOWN ON YOUR EXPOSURE. **IN and OUT!**

Basic Annealing Tips

TOP LOADER

FRONT LOADER

COMMON ANNEALER STYLES

RULE NUMBER ONE: IF YOU ARE UNFAMILIAR WITH THE OPERATION OF AN ANNEALER → ASK FIRST! DON'T TOUCH ANYTHING!

RULE NUMBER TWO: NEVER, EVER OPEN AN ANNEALER WITHOUT CHECKING IT'S STATUS FIRST → EITHER BY CHECKING THE PYROMETER FOR THAT OVEN OR BY ASKING SOMEONE "INFORMED" (e.g. THE INSTRUCTOR, SHOP TECH. OR CO-WORKER).

IF YOU ACCIDENTLY OPEN AN ANNEALER WHEN IT'S "COMING DOWN" YOU MAY RISK CRACKING (AND DESTROYING) EACH AND EVERY PIECE INSIDE! DON'T DO IT!

THE PROCESS OF ANNEALING IS CALCULATED COOLING OF THE GLASS TO SUFFICIENTLY RELIEVE STRAIN WITHIN THE GLASS AS IT DROPS IN TEMPERATURE.

MANY PUBLICATIONS ALREADY EXIST WHICH EXPLAIN THE WHOLE PROCESS OF ANNEALING (e.g. SEE HENRY HALEM'S GLASS NOTES FOR MORE INFORMATION). BASICALLY, THE THICKER THE GLASS, THE LONGER THE ANNEALING AND COOLING CYCLE WILL BE.

MOST ANNEALERS WILL BE "HELD" AROUND 880°F to 950°F (FOR MOST SODA-LIME GLASS) WHILE LOADING. A COMPUTER OR MANUALLY ACTIVATED CONTROLLER WILL THEN BE SET TO COOL THE GLASS THROUGH TEMPERATURE STAGES — GENERALLY WITHIN A TWELVE TO TWENTY FOUR HOUR PERIOD — TO ROOM TEMPERATURE.

AVOID OPENING AND CLOSING THE ANNEALER (WHILE LOADING) ANY MORE THAN ABSOLUTELY NECESSARY. DON'T KEEP PEEKING IN THERE TO CHECK ON YOUR PIECE (IT'S NOT GOING ANYWHERE) AND, EXPOSING THE GLASS TO COOL DRAFTS CAN CAUSE IT TO CRACK! SO, BE PATIENT AND WAIT... ... ...

IT'S BEST NOT TO 'CRACK' (OPEN) THE ANNEALER UNTIL THE PYROMETER READS BELOW 200°F. WORK SHOULD NOT BE HANDLED UNTIL IT IS COOL-TO-TOUCH. ALSO, IT IS RECOMMENDED THAT YOU WAIT ABOUT TWENTY-FOUR HOURS AFTER THE PIECE COMES OUT TO DO ANY COLDWORKING TO IT. IT ALLOWS THE GLASS A CHANCE TO FULLY STABILIZE THERMALLY, AND OFFERS YOU A CHANCE TO VISUALIZE WHAT TYPE OF GRINDING, POLISHING, SANDBLASTING etc. YOU WANT TO DO TO IT.

YOU'LL BE AMAZED AT HOW MUCH YOUR PIECE SEEMS TO SHRINK DURING IT'S 'REST' IN THE ANNEALER. WHEN WHAT SEEMED QUITE GIGANTIC ON THE PUNTY THE DAY BEFORE ~> COMES OUT NO LARGER THAN AN OVERSIZED SHOT GLASS TODAY, THE SENSE OF AWESOME ACCOMPLISHMENT WANES A LITTLE BIT. C'est la vie!

MOST ANNEALERS ARE CONSTRUCTED OF INSULATED BRICK OR FIBER. SOME ARE "TOP LOADERS" WHILE OTHERS MAY BE "FRONT LOADERS." THEY ALL WORK PRETTY MUCH THE SAME ~ ELECTRIC ELEMENTS KEEP THE OVEN HOT. SOME ANNEALERS ARE EQUIPPED WITH KILL SWITCHES WHICH CUT THE POWER TO THE ELEMENTS WHEN THE DOOR IS OPENED. SOME DON'T (they ALL SHOULD) SO, FOR SAFETY'S SAKE - NEVER EVER TOUCH YOUR PIPE OR PUNTY AGAINST THE ELEMENTS WHEN LOADING WORK. YOU MAY GET ELECTROCUTED ϟ! IT IS ALWAYS BEST AND SAFEST TO LOAD ALL WORK INTO THE ANNEALERS WITH THE PROTECTIVE GLOVES. period.

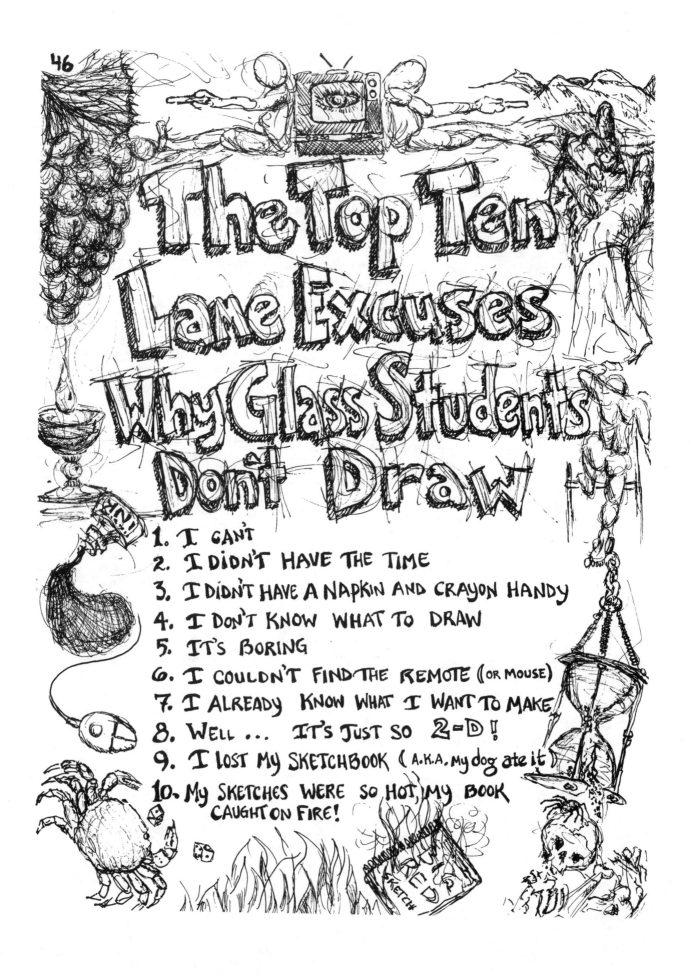

The Top Ten Lame Excuses Why Glass Students Don't Draw

1. I CAN'T
2. I DIDN'T HAVE THE TIME
3. I DIDN'T HAVE A NAPKIN AND CRAYON HANDY
4. I DON'T KNOW WHAT TO DRAW
5. IT'S BORING
6. I COULDN'T FIND THE REMOTE (OR MOUSE)
7. I ALREADY KNOW WHAT I WANT TO MAKE
8. WELL... IT'S JUST SO 2=D !
9. I LOST MY SKETCHBOOK (A.K.A. My dog ate it
10. My SKETCHES WERE SO HOT, MY BOOK CAUGHT ON FIRE!

IS THERE LIFE AFTER TUMBLERS? DEPT.

WHAT'S NEXT?

Now that you've made the ultimate object of desire, it's time to move on to BIGGER and BETTER things. UNLESS, of course, the **TUMBLER** completely satisfies your aesthetic needs and utilitarian wants, then it's time for you to quit. But for those of you who simply can't get enough ~ READ ON...

First, a thing or two about SCALE...

IS BIGGER BETTER?

MAYBE? DID YA' EVER WONDER? ¿ HOWZIT ? DO YOU KNOW? HOW COME? WHY?

No, not necessarily, However it IS more NOTICEABLE. Someone once said, " IF YOU CAN'T MAKE IT GOOD, MAKE IT BIG!" Another person mused, "IF you can't make it BIG, MAKE it BLUE !" Whatever the case may be, keep in mind that blowing larger works in glass requires more skill, more material (therefore it's hotter and harder to move), more time, and more than-likely assistants. Just about everything else is the same. Understand also that if you're having difficulty in achieving a

48 PARTICULAR FORM, THAT THAT PROBLEM WILL FOLLOW YOU EVEN IF YOU DECIDE THAT " OH , IT'LL BE EASIER IF I MAKE THE PIECE A LITTLE LARGER".

GET THE SKILLS AND PROCESS DOWN PAT IN THE FIRST PLACE. THE TECHNIQUES FOR BLOWING JUMBO PIECES ARE VIRTUALLY THE SAME AS ANY TWO GATHER BUBBLE, IT JUST TAKES A LITTLE MORE TORQUE , A BIT MORE SWEAT &, AND THE WISDOM TO KNOW WHAT YOU'RE MAKING , WHY AND HOW.

NOTE : REGARDLESS OF WHAT YOU'RE ATTEMPTING TO MAKE, TEAMWORK WILL GREATLY ENHANCE YOUR ABILITY TO ACHIEVE IT. NO LIE. FIND SOMEBODY TO WORK WITH YOU, AND MAKE YOUR LIFE EASIER. WAITA MINUTE...

A FEW WORDS ON TEAMWORK

?Q? ? "WHOSE PIECE IS IT ANYWAY? WHEN I MAKE SOMETHING THAT INVOLVES OTHER PEOPLE, HOW DO I GET AWAY WITH SAYING THAT IT'S MINE?"

A. IT IS UP TO THE INDIVIDUAL ARTIST TO DECIDE HOW MUCH CREDIT THE TEAM RECEIVES. WITHOUT A DOUBT THE FINEST WORKS IN GLASS TODAY ARE ACCOMPLISHED VIA A WELL-HONED TEAM, ONE THAT OPERATES WITH SURGICAL PRECISION AND TIMING.

NOTHING IS LEFT TO GUESSWORK. ORCHESTRATION, NOT UNLIKE A QUINTET OF FIRST-CHAIR MUSICIANS JAMMING TOGETHER, IS THE KEY TO TEAM BLOWING. EVERYONE KNOWS WHAT IS EXPECTED OF THEM, AND WHAT DUTIES THEY ARE TO PERFORM.

IN THE PAST THIRTY-SOMETHING YEARS OF "AMERICAN STUDIO GLASS" WE'VE EVOLVED FROM SMALL GARAGE-SIZED SOLO EXPERIMENTATIONS TO FULL-BLOWN HARDCORE rock N' roll CREWS PUSHING THE ENVELOPE IN SCALE, SKILLS/TECHNIQUES AND VISUAL VOCABULARY.

IT APPEARS AS THOUGH THE PREVIOUS LIMITATIONS REGARDING WHAT MAY BE MADE OUT OF THIS PRECOCIOUS MATERIAL HAVE ALL BUT DISOLVED........

WORKING ON A TEAM CAN BE EXTREMELY REWARDING, ESPECIALLY WHEN THE WORK MAKES IT IN THE BOX! IT REMAINS ONE OF THE FASTEST WAYS TO LEARN ABOUT GLASSBLOWING. EVEN IF YOUR ONLY FUNCTION ON THE TEAM IS TO OPEN DOORS OR SHIELD THE GAFFER, YOU WILL LEARN WHAT IT TAKES. BUT BACK TO THE QUESTION THAT START-ED THIS MONOLOGUE ."WHOSE WORK IS IT ANYWAY?"

SOME WILL SAY;"IT'S WHOEVER DESIGNED IT."

SOME WILL SAY;"IT'S WHOEVER MADE IT."

SOME WILL SAY; "CAN WE TALK ABOUT SOMETHING ELSE?"...

I'M INCLINED TO AGREE. GIVE CREDIT WHERE IT IS DUE, AND ALLOW ART HISTORIANS TO SOLVE THAT PARTICULAR PUZZEL.

LIFE'S KINDA SHORT, LET'S BLOW GLASS...

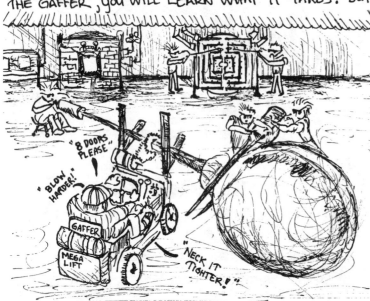

"8 DOORS PLEASE"

"BLOW HARDER!"

GAFFER

MEGA LIFT

"NECK IT TIGHTER!"

BLOWING GLASS IN TEAMS HAS MANY ADVANTAGES OVER BLOWING GLASS SOLO. SIMPLY BY HAVING AN EXTRA PAIR OF HANDS AROUND TO OPEN DOORS OR ACCESS TOOLS FOR YOU CAN BE A BIG HELP. PLUS THE CHALLENGING TASK OF COMPLETING A SUCCESS- FUL TRANSFER IS UMPTEEN TIMES E A S I E R IF YOU HAVE SOMEONE TO PREPARE THE PUNTY FOR YOU.

ASSISTANTS CAN ALSO DELIVER HANDLES, BITS, AND THINGS WHICH YOU CAN APPLY TO YOUR GLASS TO ENHANCE YOUR VESSEL'S OVERALL APPEARANCE.

YOU CAN ALSO BLOW AND SHAPE GLASS AT THE SAME TIME VERY ACCURATELY USING AN ASSISTANT. THIS ENABLES YOU TO ACHIEVE MORE COMPLICATED FORMS WITH LESS EFFORT, AND, IN A SHORTER PERIOD OF TIME.

BESIDES BEING A TIMESAVER, TEAM BLOWING CAN BE A LIFESAVER. BLOWING GLASS ALONE, ALL BY YOURSELF, ISN'T NECESSARILY THE SAFEST ACTIVITY IN THE WORLD. ACCIDENTS HAPPEN. YOU NEVER KNOW WHAT MIGHT GO WRONG... "SAFETY IN NUMBERS," THAT KIND OF THING. ALSO, IF YOU ALLOW YOUR ASSISTANT(S) TO DO REHEATS FOR YOU, YOU WON'T GET AS EXHAUSTED AS QUICK AS YOU WOULD WORKING SOLO. SAVE YOUR BODY FOR THE REALLY IMPORTANT STUFF.

FINALLY, WHEN WORKING ON A TEAM, **REMEMBER:** IT IS THE GAFFER WHO CALLS ALL THE SHOTS. IT IS A RESPECTED AND HONORED POSITION TO HAVE. THE GAFFER'S COMMANDS ARE TO BE OBEYED AND CARRIED OUT WITHOUT QUESTION. EVEN IF WHAT THEY MIGHT REQUEST IS NOT EXACTLY THE WAY YOU'D DO IT — TRY YOUR BEST TO GET THEM WHAT THEY WANT. WHY?... BECAUSE SOMEDAY, SOMETIME, YOU'LL GET THE HOT SEAT, BE THE GAFFER AND HAVE EVERYBODY TO WAIT ON YOU HAND AND FOOT. AND THEN YOU'LL FIND OUT "HOW SWEET IT IS!"...

SEE ALSO PAGES 97 to 99 – APPENDIX D FOR ADDITIONAL HINTS ON HOW TO "ASSIST THE GAFFER".

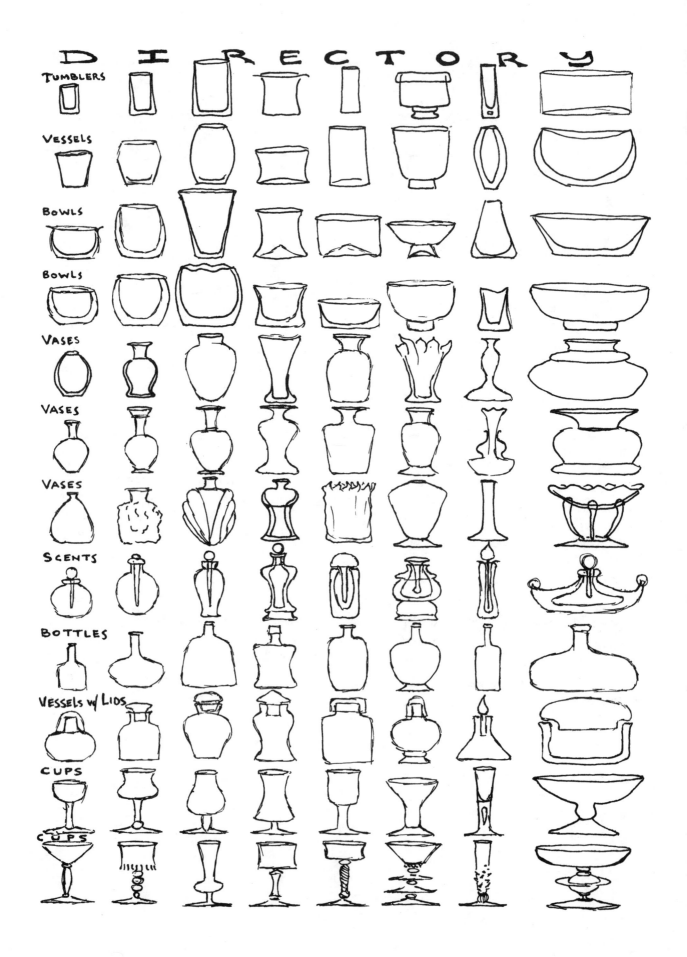

DIRECTORY

TUMBLERS

VESSELS

BOWLS

BOWLS

VASES

VASES

VASES

SCENTS

BOTTLES

VESSELS w/ LIDS

CUPS

CUPS

52 ← LOOKING AT THE **DIRECTORY OF FORMS**, YOU CAN SEE THE WIDE VARIETY OF SHAPES THAT ARE POSSIBLE WITH BLOWN GLASS. MANY ARE VERY BASIC FORMS. THAT DOES NOT IMPLY OR MEAN THAT THEY'RE EASY TO DO! A TIGHT, SHALLOW BOWL WITH STRAIGHT SIDEWALLS IS A VERY CHALLENGING FORM TO BLOW. JUST TRY IT! YOU'LL SEE WHAT I MEAN....

IF YOU WANT TO BE A WELL-ROUNDED GLASSBLOWER, AND ASPIRE TO BE A "MAESTRO" OR "MAESTRA" IN YOUR OWN RIGHT ~ YOU SHOULD PRACTICE AS MANY OF THESE FORMS AS YOU CAN. CALL IT DEVELOPING YOUR GAFFER VOCABULARY. ONCE YOU GET THE HANG OF IT ~ YOU CAN THEN ADVANCE ON TO MAKING MORE COMPLICATED FORMS.

START WITH A SKETCH. DRAW FIRST WHAT YOU ENVISION THE COMPLETED OBJECT WILL (HOPEFULLY) LOOK LIKE. NEXT, DRAW THE STEPS NECESSARY TO GET YOU TO THAT STAGE. MAKE AN IMAGE OF THE OBJECT WHILE IT IS STILL ON THE BLOWPIPE- JUST BEFORE THE TRANSFER.

THIS PROCESS HELPS YOU VISUALIZE THE WHOLE PROCESS - FROM START-TO-FINISH. IT IS AN EXCELLENT EXERCISE FOR BEGINNERS TO BECOME MORE FAMILIAR WITH ALL THE STEPS INVOLVED, AS IT TRAINS YOU TO THINK LIKE A GLASSBLOWER.

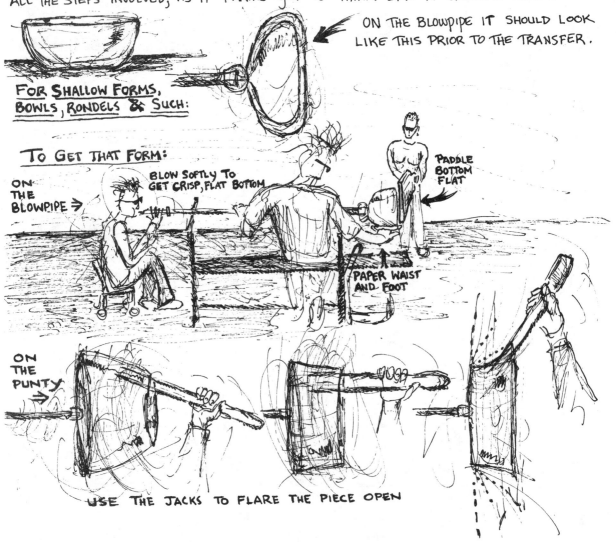

ON THE BLOWPIPE IT SHOULD LOOK LIKE THIS PRIOR TO THE TRANSFER.

FOR SHALLOW FORMS, BOWLS, RONDELS & SUCH:

TO GET THAT FORM:

ON THE BLOWPIPE →

BLOW SOFTLY TO GET CRISP, FLAT BOTTOM

PADDLE BOTTOM FLAT

PAPER WAIST AND FOOT

ON THE PUNTY →

USE THE JACKS TO FLARE THE PIECE OPEN

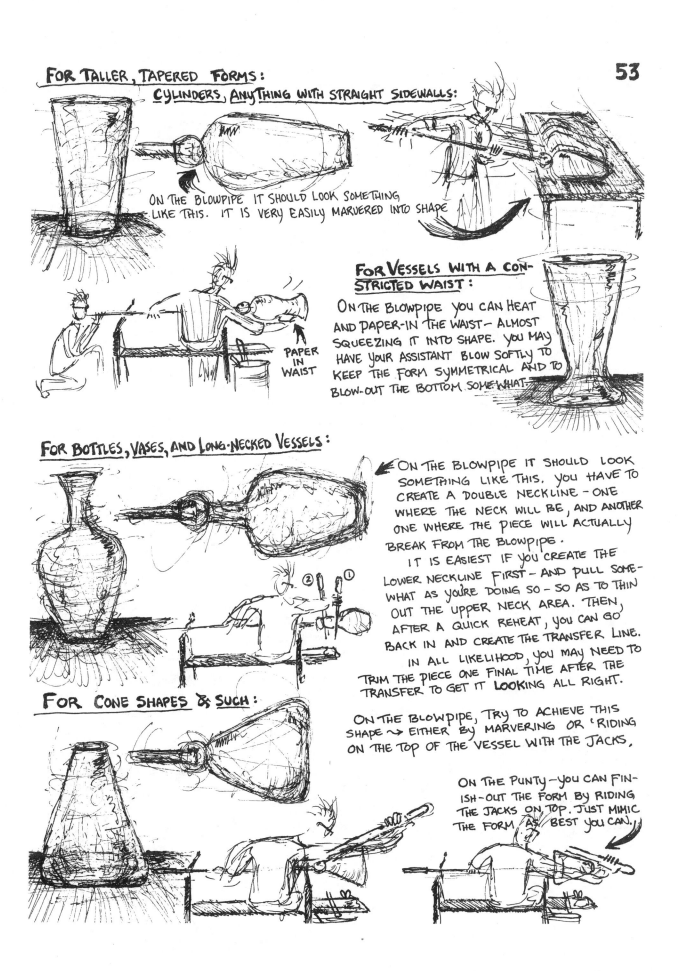

FOR TALLER, TAPERED FORMS:

CYLINDERS, ANYTHING WITH STRAIGHT SIDEWALLS:

ON THE BLOWPIPE IT SHOULD LOOK SOMETHING LIKE THIS. IT IS VERY EASILY MARVERED INTO SHAPE

PAPER IN WAIST

FOR VESSELS WITH A CONSTRICTED WAIST:

ON THE BLOWPIPE YOU CAN HEAT AND PAPER-IN THE WAIST — ALMOST SQUEEZING IT INTO SHAPE. YOU MAY HAVE YOUR ASSISTANT BLOW SOFTLY TO KEEP THE FORM SYMMETRICAL AND TO BLOW-OUT THE BOTTOM SOMEWHAT.

FOR BOTTLES, VASES, AND LONG-NECKED VESSELS:

ON THE BLOWPIPE IT SHOULD LOOK SOMETHING LIKE THIS. YOU HAVE TO CREATE A DOUBLE NECKLINE — ONE WHERE THE NECK WILL BE, AND ANOTHER ONE WHERE THE PIECE WILL ACTUALLY BREAK FROM THE BLOWPIPE.

IT IS EASIEST IF YOU CREATE THE LOWER NECKLINE FIRST — AND PULL SOMEWHAT AS YOU'RE DOING SO — SO AS TO THIN OUT THE UPPER NECK AREA. THEN, AFTER A QUICK REHEAT, YOU CAN GO BACK IN AND CREATE THE TRANSFER LINE.

IN ALL LIKELIHOOD, YOU MAY NEED TO TRIM THE PIECE ONE FINAL TIME AFTER THE TRANSFER TO GET IT **LOOKING** ALL RIGHT.

ON THE BLOWPIPE, TRY TO ACHIEVE THIS SHAPE ↝ EITHER BY MARVERING OR 'RIDING ON THE TOP OF THE VESSEL WITH THE JACKS,

FOR CONE SHAPES & SUCH:

ON THE PUNTY — YOU CAN FINISH-OUT THE FORM BY RIDING THE JACKS ON TOP. JUST MIMIC THE FORM AS BEST YOU CAN.

Handles, Prunts and Hot Bits other of information

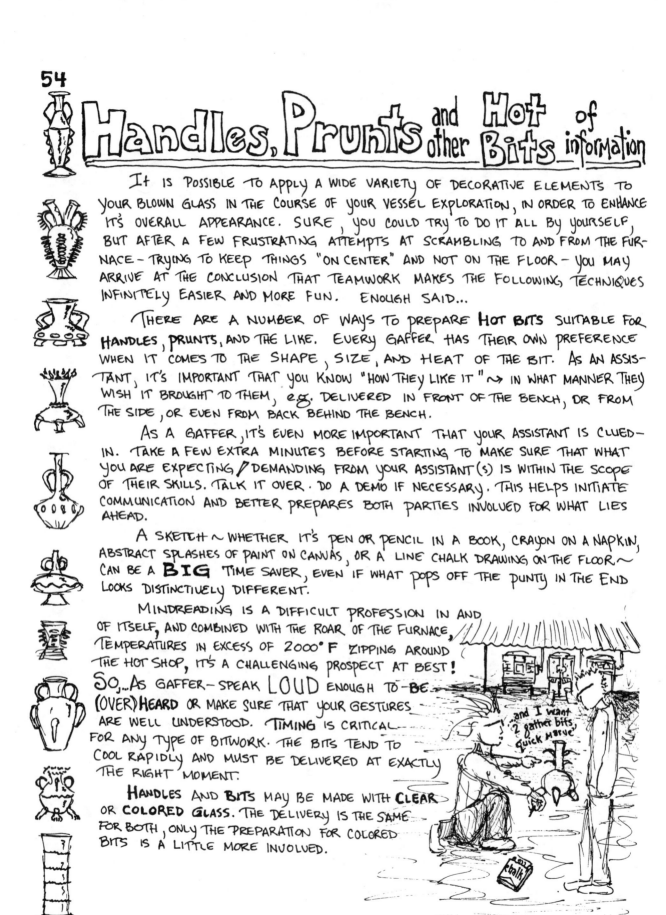

It is possible to apply a wide variety of decorative elements to your blown glass in the course of your vessel exploration, in order to enhance it's overall appearance. Sure, you could try to do it all by yourself, but after a few frustrating attempts at scrambling to and from the furnace — trying to keep things "on center" and not on the floor — you may arrive at the conclusion that teamwork makes the following techniques infinitely easier and more fun. Enough said...

There are a number of ways to prepare **HOT BITS** suitable for **HANDLES, PRUNTS,** and the like. Every gaffer has their own preference when it comes to the shape, size, and heat of the bit. As an assistant, it's important that you know "how they like it" ⤳ in what manner they wish it brought to them, e.g. delivered in front of the bench, or from the side, or even from back behind the bench.

As a gaffer, it's even more important that your assistant is clued-in. Take a few extra minutes before starting to make sure that what you are expecting / demanding from your assistant(s) is within the scope of their skills. Talk it over. Do a demo if necessary. This helps initiate communication and better prepares both parties involved for what lies ahead.

A sketch ∼ whether it's pen or pencil in a book, crayon on a napkin, abstract splashes of paint on canvas, or a line chalk drawing on the floor ∼ can be a **BIG** time saver, even if what pops off the punty in the end looks distinctively different.

Mindreading is a difficult profession in and of itself, and combined with the roar of the furnace, temperatures in excess of 2000° F zipping around the hot shop, it's a challenging prospect at best! So,...as gaffer — speak **LOUD** enough to be (over)heard or make sure that your gestures are well understood. Timing is critical for any type of bitwork. The bits tend to cool rapidly and must be delivered at exactly the right moment.

HANDLES and **BITS** may be made with **CLEAR** or **COLORED GLASS.** The delivery is the same for both, only the preparation for colored bits is a little more involved.

and I want 2 gather bits, Quick Marue

chalk

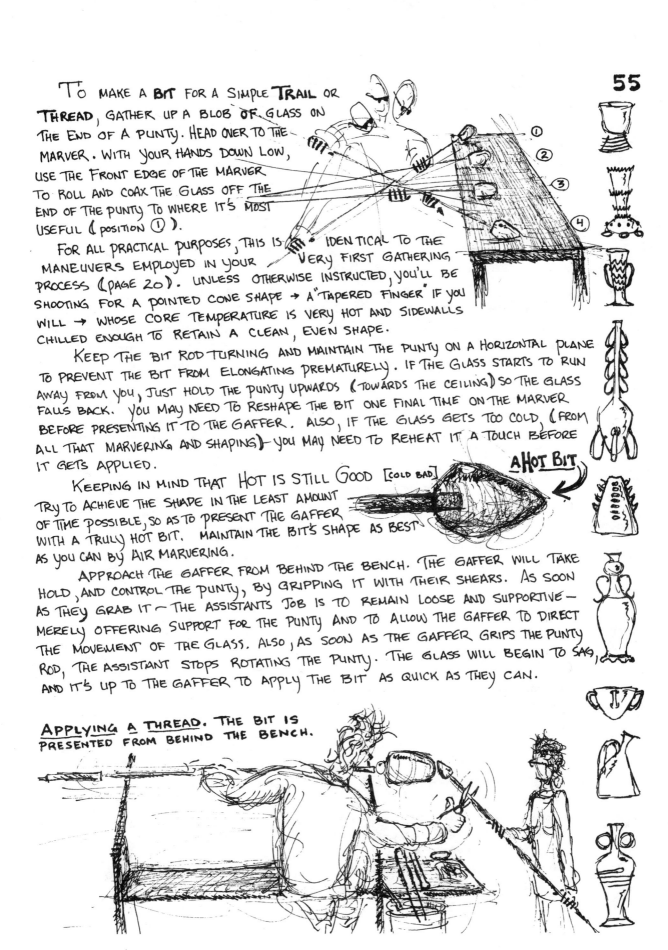

To make a **BIT** for a simple **TRAIL** or **THREAD**, gather up a blob of glass on the end of a punty. Head over to the marver. With your hands down low, use the front edge of the marver to roll and coax the glass off the end of the punty to where it's most useful (position ①).

For all practical purposes, this is identical to the maneuvers employed in your very first gathering process (page 20). Unless otherwise instructed, you'll be shooting for a pointed cone shape → a "tapered finger" if you will → whose core temperature is very hot and sidewalls chilled enough to retain a clean, even shape.

Keep the bit rod turning and maintain the punty on a horizontal plane to prevent the bit from elongating prematurely. If the glass starts to run away from you, just hold the punty upwards (towards the ceiling) so the glass falls back. You may need to reshape the bit one final time on the marver before presenting it to the gaffer. Also, if the glass gets too cold (from all that marvering and shaping) you may need to reheat it a touch before it gets applied.

Keeping in mind that HOT IS STILL GOOD [COLD BAD] try to achieve the shape in the least amount of time possible, so as to present the gaffer with a truly hot bit. Maintain the bit's shape as best as you can by air marvering.

A HOT BIT

Approach the gaffer from behind the bench. The gaffer will take hold, and control the punty, by gripping it with their shears. As soon as they grab it → the assistants job is to remain loose and supportive — merely offering support for the punty and to allow the gaffer to direct the movement of the glass. Also, as soon as the gaffer grips the punty rod, the assistant stops rotating the punty. The glass will begin to sag, and it's up to the gaffer to apply the bit as quick as they can.

APPLYING A THREAD. THE BIT IS PRESENTED FROM BEHIND THE BENCH.

FOR **BODY WRAPS**, YOU CAN EITHER ATTACH THE BIT TO THE MOILE AND WORK YOUR WAY OUT TOWARDS THE BOTTOM OF THE PIECE, OR START AT THE BOTTOM AND WRAP UPWARDS TO THE NECK OF THE PIECE. OR START ANYPLACE YOU LIKE! IT'S A GAFFERS CHOICE.

ONCE THE BIT IS TOUCHED-UP, IT IS PULLED BACK AWAY FROM THE PIECE AN INCH OR TWO. THE PIPE IS ROTATED AWAY FROM THE GAFFER TOWARDS THE END OF THE RAILS, CAUSING THE GLASS BIT TO BE WOUND AROUND THE BODY OF THE PIECE.

TURN

OVERHEAD VIEW
BASIC BODY WRAP.

START HERE

THE GAFFER CONTROLS EVERYTHING; FROM THE SPEED OF THE PIPE ROTATION TO THE DIRECTION OF THE BIT & PUNTY.

VARIATIONS IN THE SPEED OF ROTATION, IN ADDITION THE BIT'S TEMPERATURE — HAVE A TREMENDOUS INFLUENCE ON THE OUTCOME OF THE WRAP. SLOWER ROTATIONS AND COOLER TEMP'S WILL PRODUCE LARGER, THICKER THREADS, WHEREAS QUICK TURNS COMBINED WITH HOT BITS MAY YIELD THINNER THREADS.

THE BEST WAY TO GAUGE THE THICKNESS OF THE THREADS IS TO PAY SPECIAL ATTENTION TO HOW THICK THE GLASS IS AS IT GOES ON TO THE PIECE. LOOK AT THE GLASS THREAD IN THAT SPACE BETWEEN THE PIECE AND THE BIT PUNTY. IF YOU PULL THE PUNTY BACK FURTHER AWAY FROM THE PIECE (SAY ABOUT 4" to 6") THE THREADS WILL GET THINNER. IF YOU MOVE THE BIT CLOSER TO THE PIECE, THE THICKER THE THREADS WILL GET. AGAIN, IT IS CONTINGENT ON THE TEMPERATURE OF THE BIT AND THE SPEED AT WHICH THE PIECE IS TURNED.

WHEN YOU REACH THE END OF YOUR PIECE AND WANT TO COMPLETE THE WRAP, YOU CAN EITHER CUT THE BIT FREE WITH THE SHEARS (ALREADY IN YOUR HAND – ISN'T THAT CONVENIENT?) OR YANK BACK HARD AWAY FROM THE PIECE TO TRY AND BREAK THE THREAD FREE. IF THE BIT'S STILL HOT ENOUGH, IT SHOULD COME OFF CLEANLY, OTHERWISE YOU MIGHT STILL HAVE TO SNIP IT FREE.

MUCH OF THE SUCCESS IN THE THREADING PROCESS IS DEPENDENT ON THE PIECE'S TEMPERATURE AS WELL AS THE HOT BIT. IF THE GAFFER'S PIECE IS TOO HOT – IT MAY BE VERY DIFFICULT TO CONTROL AND MAINTAIN ON-CENTER. LIKEWISE, IF THE BIT IS TOO HOT – IT MAY ALSO LOSE SHAPE AND BE DIFFICULT TO CONTROL ~ MUCH LESS GET A NICE, EVEN WRAP FROM. CONVERSELY, IF BOTH THE BIT AND THE PIECE ARE TOO COLD, THEY MAY NOT STICK AT ALL AND YOU'LL BE FORCED TO DO IT ALL OVER AGAIN...

YES, THERE ARE ALOT OF VARIABLES GOVERNING THE THREADING PROCESS, WHICH IS WHY IT TAKES A FAIR AMOUNT OF PRACTICE, FOR BOTH THE ASSISTANT AND GAFFER, TO GET THE HANG OF IT. AND IF THAT ISN'T ENOUGH, THERE ARE THE OPTIONS...

AS STATED EARLIER, YOU CAN ADD **COLOR** TO YOUR WRAPS TO SPICE UP YOUR PIECES. SEE THE CHAPTER ON COLOR FOR QUICK AND EASY METHODS OF PREPARING COLORED BITS (PAGES 76-80). ALSO, FOR MORE EVEN, MACHINE-LIKE THREADS — MANY GLASSBLOWERS WILL USE A SET OF ROLLERS TO TURN THEIR PIPE ON AND THREAD THE PARISON WITH PRECISION. BY ADJUSTING THE ANGLE OF THE ROLLERS SLIGHTLY, YOU CAN MAKE THE BLOWPIPE TRACK

FROM RIGHT-TO-LEFT (OR LEFT-TO-RIGHT DEPENDING ON WHICH DIRECTION YOU ARE TURNING IT) WITH PREDICTABLE RESULTS. THE ROLLERS MAY BE CLAMPED TO THE RAILS OF THE BENCH OR BOLTED TO SOME OTHER UNIT FOR STABILITY. A YOKE MAY BE SET-UP NEAR THE ROLLERS TO SUPPORT THE ASSISTANT'S PUNTY DURING APPLICATION.

THE GAFFER IS RESPONSIBLE FOR GETTING THE PIECE ON-CENTER AND KEEPING IT THAT WAY DURING THE THREADING PROCESS. THEY WILL CONTROL THE SPEED OF ROTATION, AND SUBSEQUENTLY HOW FAST THE PIECE WILL TRACK.

IT IS UP TO THE ASSISTANT TO APPLY THE BIT, PULL BACK A TOUCH AND CONTROL THE THICKNESS OF THE THREAD BY MAINTAINING THEIR POSITION RELATIVE TO THE PIECE. IT IS TRULY A TEAM EFFORT AND TAKES A BIT OF CONCENTRATION, (NOT-TOO-MENTION YOU-KNOW-WHAT!). IT IS VERY EASY TO LAY IT ON TOO-THICK AT FIRST AND RUN OUT OF GLASS BY THE TIME YOU REACH THE BOTTOM. OR, NOT ATTACH THE BIT WELL-ENOUGH IN THE FIRST PLACE AND WIND-UP WITH A THIN MONO-FILAMENT THREAD THAT BARELY MAKES A DENT, OR ONE WHICH MYSTERIOUSLY COMES OFF IN A BIG LUMPY SLUG SHAPE AND PERMANENTLY GLUES ITSELF TO THE SIDE OF YOUR PIECE. **Yuck!**

A WELL-THREADED PIECE CAN BE A THING OF BEAUTY IN AND OF ITSELF. YOU CAN TAKE IT ONE STEP FURTHER AND ADD COLOR TO THOSE THREADS, AS STATED EARLIER. FROM THERE, YOU HAVE THE OPTION OF AUGMENTING THE THREADED PATTERN BY **RAKING** OR **COMBING** THE THREADS WITH A POINTED 'HOOKING' TOOL. THIS MAY YIELD A FEATHER PATTERN SIMILAR TO THE TURN-OF-THE CENTURY **ART NOUVEAU** PIECES MADE POPULAR BY DESIGNERS LIKE **TIFFANY, GALLE,** AND **CARTER.**

THE **HOOKING TOOL** CAN BE A SCRATCH AWL, OR THE POINT OF A FILE WITH A A SMALL HOOK BENT AT IT'S TIP, OR WHATEVER SIMILAR TOOL YOU CAN SCROUNGE-UP AROUND THE SHOP.

SIMPLY THREAD THE PIECE WITH YOUR FAVORITE COLOR. THEN TAKE A GOOD SOLID REHEAT IN THE GLORY HOLE. THE THREADS SHOULD BE GLOWING BRIGHT ORANGE WHEN THEY'RE HOT ENOUGH.

HAVE A SEAT AT THE BENCH, STOP THE PIPE ROTATION AND LET THE PIECE SAG. PICK UP THE HOOKING TOOL IN YOUR RIGHT HAND, FLIP THE GLASS PIECE WITH YOUR LEFT AND BEGIN TO DRAW THROUGH THE SURFACE OF THE GLASS — RAKING THE THREADS WITH THE CURVE OF THE HOOK. THE HOTTER THE GLASS IS, THE EASIER THIS IS TO DO.

YOU CAN EITHER START AT THE NECK AND WORK YOUR WAY DOWN THE PIECE, OR START AT THE BOTTOM AND PULL UP TOWARDS THE NECK (AS ILLUSTRATED) — IT DOESN'T MATTER.

YOU CAN THEN FLIP THE PIECE **180°** AND COMB THE OTHER SIDE. YOU MIGHT EVEN DO IT ONCE OR TWICE MORE FOR ADDED EFFECT, OR COMB THE PATTERN IN THE OPPOSITE DIRECTION.

IN ALL LIKELIHOOD, YOUR PIECE WILL NEED TO BE REHEATED AFTER EACH RAKE OR COMB BECAUSE THE THREADS COOL-OFF SO RAPIDLY. ALSO, IT IS LIKELY

YES. THIS ONE HAS ONE.

BLOWPIPE TRACKS THIS WAY.

: OVERHEAD VIEW
THREADING WITH ROLLERS

BIT IS ATTACHED TO THE MOILE.

YOKE FOR STABILITY

A HOOKING TOOL

THREAD.

HOOK.

REPEAT.

58 THAT YOUR BUBBLE WILL BECOME HORRIBLY DISTORTED IN THE COURSE OF THE PROCESS, NOT-TO-WORRY, THOUGH. IF YOU KEEP YOUR BUBBLES ON THE THICK-SIDE, YOU SHOULD BE ABLE TO REHEAT AND REWORK THEM FAIRLY SYMMETRICAL EVEN AFTER THE MOST AGGRESSIVE AMOUNT OF 'FEATHERING'.

FOR PRACTICE:

I WOULD RECOMMEND TRYING TO THREAD SOME BASIC SHAPES WITH CLEAR GLASS AT FIRST. THIS WAY, YOU AND YOUR ASSISTANT CAN WORK OUT THE BUGS WITHOUT WASTING EXPENSIVE COLOR. TRY TO GET THE THREADS TO GO ON EVENLY AND SMOOTHLY. ONCE YOU BECOME PROFICIENT AT LAYIN' 'EM ON IN CLEAR, YOU CAN MOVE ON TO COLORS. EXPERIMENT WITH DIFFERENT COMBINATIONS OF COLORS. TRY JUST THREADING THE TOP THIRD OR BOTTOM THIRD OF THE PIECE. SEE WHAT EFFECT COMBING THE THREADS IN VARIOUS DIRECTIONS DOES FOR YOU.

EVEN THOUGH TRAILED GLASS DESIGNS HAVE BEEN AROUND SINCE ANCIENT EGYPT AND BEFORE THE INVENTION OF THE BLOW-PIPE, THERE'S STILL ROOM LEFT FOR MORE. WHO KNOWS, YOU MAY HIT UPON A COLOR AND DESIGN COMBINATION THAT IS TRULY UNIQUE AND INNOVATIVE!

VASE w/ COMBED TRAILS OR "FEATHER PATTERN"

HANDLES

AT ONE POINT OR ANOTHER IN YOU GLASSBLOWING "CAREER" YOU'LL PROBABLY WANT TO PUT A HANDLE ON A PIECE.

HANDLES CAN BE DECORATIVE, FUNCTIONAL, OR BOTH. THEY CAN BE LARGE, SMALL, BLOWN, SOLID, COLORED OR CLEAR. THEY DO TAKE A FAIR AMOUNT OF PRACTICE TO GET USED TO.

HANDLES CAN BE PREPARED (BY YOUR ASSISTANT) IN A SIMILAR FASHION TO HOT BITS, EXCEPT YOU MAY WANT A LITTLE MORE GLASS → DEPENDING ON THE SIZE OF THE HANDLE. ALSO, THE SHAPE IS A LITTLE BIT DIFFERENT.

YOU'LL WANT A VERY HOT CORE TEMPERATURE FOR GREATER EASE IN APPLICATION AND CUTTING. AVOID MARVERING THE GLASS BETWEEN GATHERS. A CHILLED OUTSIDE WALL SURFACE HELPS MAINTAIN THE BIT'S SHAPE AND OFFERS SOME STABILITY IN HANDLING. THE ASSISTANT SHOULD JUST MARVER THE BIT HORIZONTALLY ON THE MARVER INTO A LARGE THUMB SHAPE. (AIR MARVER BETWEEN PASSES DOWN THE STEEL TO HELP MAINTAIN THE SHAPE AND HEAT OF THE BIT.)

AGAIN, THE BIT IS KEPT HORIZONTAL UNTIL IT'S PRESENTED TO THE GAFFER

THE GAFFER INSPECTS THE HANDLE-BIT BEFORE ADDING IT.

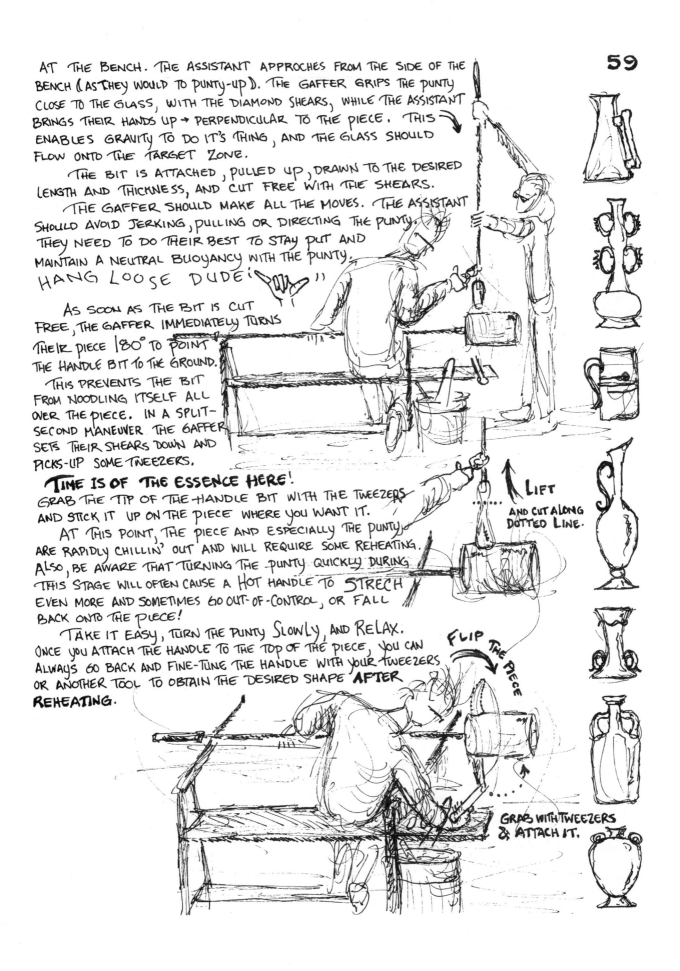

AT THE BENCH. THE ASSISTANT APPROCHES FROM THE SIDE OF THE BENCH (AS THEY WOULD TO PUNTY-UP). THE GAFFER GRIPS THE PUNTY CLOSE TO THE GLASS, WITH THE DIAMOND SHEARS, WHILE THE ASSISTANT BRINGS THEIR HANDS UP → PERPENDICULAR TO THE PIECE. THIS ENABLES GRAVITY TO DO IT'S THING, AND THE GLASS SHOULD FLOW ONTO THE TARGET ZONE.

THE BIT IS ATTACHED, PULLED UP, DRAWN TO THE DESIRED LENGTH AND THICKNESS, AND CUT FREE WITH THE SHEARS.

THE GAFFER SHOULD MAKE ALL THE MOVES. THE ASSISTANT SHOULD AVOID JERKING, PULLING OR DIRECTING THE PUNTY. THEY NEED TO DO THEIR BEST TO STAY PUT AND MAINTAIN A NEUTRAL BUOYANCY WITH THE PUNTY. HANG LOOSE DUDE!

AS SOON AS THE BIT IS CUT FREE, THE GAFFER IMMEDIATELY TURNS THEIR PIECE 180° TO POINT THE HANDLE BIT TO THE GROUND.

THIS PREVENTS THE BIT FROM NOODLING ITSELF ALL OVER THE PIECE. IN A SPLIT-SECOND MANEUVER THE GAFFER SETS THEIR SHEARS DOWN AND PICKS-UP SOME TWEEZERS.

TIME IS OF THE ESSENCE HERE!
GRAB THE TIP OF THE HANDLE BIT WITH THE TWEEZERS AND STICK IT UP ON THE PIECE WHERE YOU WANT IT.

AT THIS POINT, THE PIECE AND ESPECIALLY THE PUNTY ARE RAPIDLY CHILLIN' OUT AND WILL REQUIRE SOME REHEATING. ALSO, BE AWARE THAT TURNING THE PUNTY QUICKLY DURING THIS STAGE WILL OFTEN CAUSE A HOT HANDLE TO STRECH EVEN MORE AND SOMETIMES GO OUT-OF-CONTROL, OR FALL BACK ONTO THE PIECE!

TAKE IT EASY, TURN THE PUNTY SLOWLY, AND RELAX. ONCE YOU ATTACH THE HANDLE TO THE TOP OF THE PIECE, YOU CAN ALWAYS GO BACK AND FINE-TUNE THE HANDLE WITH YOUR TWEEZERS OR ANOTHER TOOL TO OBTAIN THE DESIRED SHAPE **AFTER REHEATING.**

LIFT
AND CUT ALONG DOTTED LINE.

FLIP THE PIECE

GRAB WITH TWEEZERS & ATTACH IT.

SO, WHEN YOU COME OUT OF THE GLORY HOLE, THE HANDLE SHOULD BE STILL PRETTY WARM. THIS EXTRA BIT OF HEAT CAN ALLOW YOU TO STRETCH THE HANDLE FURTHER OR SIMPLY SMOOTH OUT THE CURVE OF ITS SHAPE.

YOU CAN USE THE ROUNDED EDGE OF YOUR TWEEZERS TO DO THIS, OR SOME GAFFERS WILL USE A WOODEN DOWEL OR STICK OF GRAPHITE. AVOID **GRIPPING** OR **CRIMPING** THE HANDLE ANY MORE THAN NECESSARY AS IT CAN EASILY LEAVE PERMANENT, IRREPARABLE MARKS. 'COURSE, THERE MIGHT BE SOME PEOPLE OUT THERE THAT _LIKE_ LUMPY HANDLES...

YOU CAN ALSO DO A FINE-TUNE TO THE HANDLE TO POSITION IT CORRECTLY ON THE PIECE BY GENTLY SQUEEZING IT BETWEEN THE BLADES OF YOUR TWEEZERS. THIS CAN HELP YOU ALIGN THE HANDLE SO IT WON'T APPEAR TOO CROOKED WHEN VIEWED FROM THE SIDE (OR STRAIGHT-ON).

→ SMOOTH IT OUT ←

OVERHEAD VIEW
ALIGNING THE HANDLE WITH TWEEZERS

NOTE: HANDLES SHOULD GO ON LAST. THE PIECE SHOULD BE PUNTIED, THE LIPS OF THE VESSEL FULLY OPENED etc... THE PIECE NEEDS TO BE FULLY STABALIZED AND NOT MOVING AROUND ON YOU. OTHERWISE EVERYTHING CAN GET PRETTY WHACKY AND **GROTESQUELY DISTORTED.**

THERE ARE MANY DIFFERENT STYLES OF HANDLES TO CHOOSE FROM. TAKE A LOOK AT IMPORT STORES WHICH CARRY GLASS AND SEE (& _FEEL_) WHAT'S AVAILABLE IN THE COMMERCIAL REALM. EXAMINE HOW THE HANDLE IS ATTACHED. WAS IT STUCK-UP FIRST AT THE BOTTOM OR TOP OF THE VESSEL? DOES THE HANDLE CURVE IN OR OUT? DOES IT FUNCTION WELL? WHY?

ALSO - LOOK AT CERAMIC FORMS AS WELL. QUITE OFTEN YOU MIGHT FIND SOME INTERESTING INTERPRETATIONS OF THE HANDLE IDEA ~ WHICH MAY BE TOTALLY ADAPTED INTO HOT GLASS.

THERE IS ULTIMATELY ONLY ONE WAY I KNOW HOW TO GET BETTER AT DOING HANDLES, AND THAT'S BY MAKING THEM.

FOR PRACTICE: MAKE A BASIC FORM, SUCH AS A TUMBLER. PRACTICE PUTTING TWO, FOUR OR FIFTY HANDLES ON IT. AS MANY AS YOU CAN. TRY VARIATIONS - SUCH AS ATTACHING THEM FROM THE TOP VS. THE BOTTOM. TRY CUTTING WITH THE STRAIGHT SHEARS INSTEAD OF THE DIAMOND SHEARS AND SEEING WHAT THAT DOES FOR YOU.

IT'S TRULY THROUGH REPETITION THAT WE DEVOLOP SKILLS, PLUS MAKE MISTAKES, AND hopefully LEARN SOMETHING (NEW) FROM THEM.

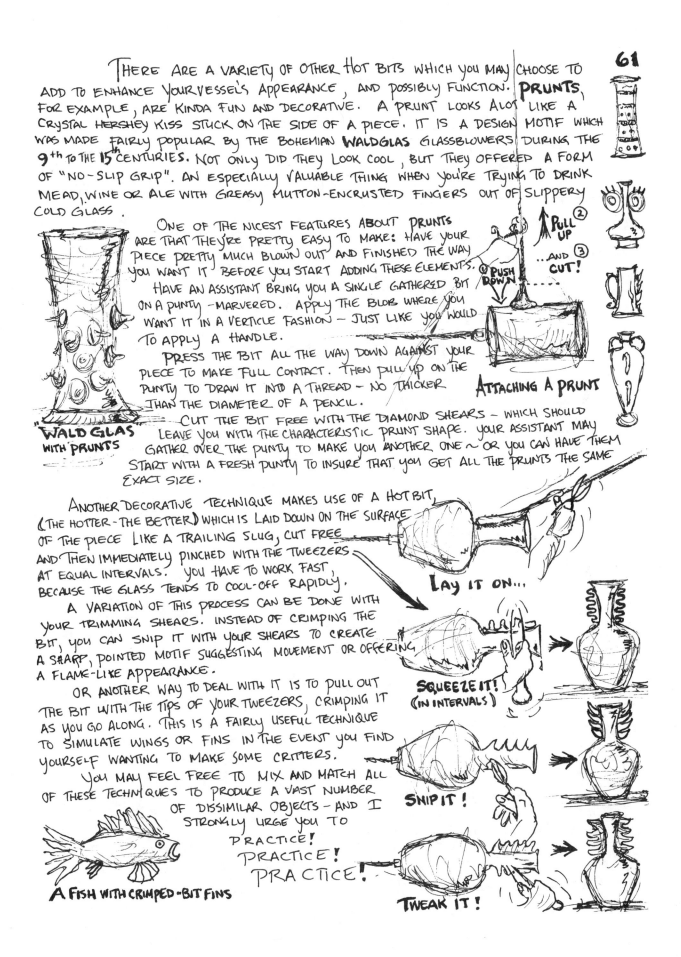

THERE ARE A VARIETY OF OTHER HOT BITS WHICH YOU MAY CHOOSE TO ADD TO ENHANCE YOUR VESSEL'S APPEARANCE, AND POSSIBLY FUNCTION. **PRUNTS**, FOR EXAMPLE, ARE KINDA FUN AND DECORATIVE. A PRUNT LOOKS ALOT LIKE A CRYSTAL HERSHEY KISS STUCK ON THE SIDE OF A PIECE. IT IS A DESIGN MOTIF WHICH WAS MADE FAIRLY POPULAR BY THE BOHEMIAN **WALDGLAS** GLASSBLOWERS DURING THE 9th TO THE 15th CENTURIES. NOT ONLY DID THEY LOOK COOL, BUT THEY OFFERED A FORM OF "NO-SLIP GRIP". AN ESPECIALLY VALUABLE THING WHEN YOU'RE TRYING TO DRINK MEAD, WINE OR ALE WITH GREASY MUTTON-ENCRUSTED FINGERS OUT OF SLIPPERY COLD GLASS.

ONE OF THE NICEST FEATURES ABOUT PRUNTS ARE THAT THEY'RE PRETTY EASY TO MAKE: HAVE YOUR PIECE PRETTY MUCH BLOWN OUT AND FINISHED THE WAY YOU WANT IT BEFORE YOU START ADDING THESE ELEMENTS.

HAVE AN ASSISTANT BRING YOU A SINGLE GATHERED BIT ON A PUNTY - MARVERED. APPLY THE BLOB WHERE YOU WANT IT IN A VERTICLE FASHION - JUST LIKE YOU WOULD TO APPLY A HANDLE.

PRESS THE BIT ALL THE WAY DOWN AGAINST YOUR PIECE TO MAKE FULL CONTACT. THEN PULL UP ON THE PUNTY TO DRAW IT INTO A THREAD - NO THICKER THAN THE DIAMETER OF A PENCIL.

CUT THE BIT FREE WITH THE DIAMOND SHEARS - WHICH SHOULD LEAVE YOU WITH THE CHARACTERISTIC PRUNT SHAPE. YOUR ASSISTANT MAY GATHER OVER THE PUNTY TO MAKE YOU ANOTHER ONE ~ OR YOU CAN HAVE THEM START WITH A FRESH PUNTY TO INSURE THAT YOU GET ALL THE PRUNTS THE SAME EXACT SIZE.

① PUSH DOWN
↑ PULL ② UP
...AND ③ CUT!

ATTACHING A PRUNT

"WALD GLAS" WITH PRUNTS

ANOTHER DECORATIVE TECHNIQUE MAKES USE OF A HOT BIT, (THE HOTTER - THE BETTER) WHICH IS LAID DOWN ON THE SURFACE OF THE PIECE LIKE A TRAILING SLUG, CUT FREE AND THEN IMMEDIATELY PINCHED WITH THE TWEEZERS AT EQUAL INTERVALS. YOU HAVE TO WORK FAST, BECAUSE THE GLASS TENDS TO COOL-OFF RAPIDLY.

A VARIATION OF THIS PROCESS CAN BE DONE WITH YOUR TRIMMING SHEARS. INSTEAD OF CRIMPING THE BIT, YOU CAN SNIP IT WITH YOUR SHEARS TO CREATE A SHARP, POINTED MOTIF SUGGESTING MOVEMENT OR OFFERING A FLAME-LIKE APPEARANCE.

OR ANOTHER WAY TO DEAL WITH IT IS TO PULL OUT THE BIT WITH THE TIPS OF YOUR TWEEZERS, CRIMPING IT AS YOU GO ALONG. THIS IS A FAIRLY USEFUL TECHNIQUE TO SIMULATE WINGS OR FINS IN THE EVENT YOU FIND YOURSELF WANTING TO MAKE SOME CRITTERS.

YOU MAY FEEL FREE TO MIX AND MATCH ALL OF THESE TECHNIQUES TO PRODUCE A VAST NUMBER OF DISSIMILAR OBJECTS - AND I STRONGLY URGE YOU TO PRACTICE! PRACTICE! PRACTICE!

LAY IT ON...

SQUEEZE IT! (IN INTERVALS)

SNIP IT!

TWEAK IT!

A FISH WITH CRIMPED-BIT FINS

62

IN THE FOLLOWING PAGES YOU'LL SEE ILLUSTRATED SOME ADDITIONAL METHODS TO THIS MADNESS. THESE TECHNIQUES INVOLVE EVEN MORE PATIENCE AND PRACTICE TO 'MASTER'. THEY WILL UNDOUBTEDLY CLAIM MORE THAN THEIR FAIR SHARE OF VICTIMS FROM YOU DURING THE COURSE OF THE ADVENTURE, BUT THEY OFFER SO MUCH VARIETY IN RETURN.

THE IDEA HERE IS TO PROVIDE YOU WITH AS MUCH INFORMATION REGARDING BASIC GLASSFORMING TECHNIQUES AS POSSIBLE IN SUCH A FORMAT. THIS, IN TURN, WILL FURNISH YOU WITH THE SKILLS NECESSARY TO ACCOMPLISH YOUR ARTISTIC VISION THROUGH THIS DIVERSE, LIMITLESS MEDIUM.

MOST OF THE PROCEDURES ARE VARIATIONS OF TECHNIQUES THAT YOU ARE ALREADY FAMILIAR WITH. (UNLESS, OF COURSE, YOU ARE JUMPING AROUND IN THIS BOOK AND SCOPING AHEAD TO SEE HOW IT ENDS...). I INVITE YOU TO REVIEW AND PRACTICE THEM. THEY CAN ONLY SERVE TO INCREASE YOUR GLASSBLOWING VOCABULARY.

SUBTEXT A — HOW TO MAKE YOUR VERY 1ST OWN GOBLET — by I.B. INSANE

ONE OF THE BIGGEST CHALLENGES IN GLASSBLOWING IS THE EXECUTION OF A WELL MADE GOBLET (NO, I DON'T MEAN YOU KILL THE THING...). AGAIN, THIS IS ONE OF THOSE PROCESSES WHICH LOOK MUCH EASIER TO DO THAN THEY ACTUALLY ARE, 'CAUSE THERE'S A WHOLE HOST OF ELEMENTS INVOLVED (ACTUALLY ONLY THREE), AND IF YOU MESS UP ON JUST ONE OF THEM THE RESULTS CAN BE: DISASTEROUS, DISENCHANTING, OR SIMPLY DYSFUNCTIONAL.

MANY A FRIEND AND RELATIVE OF MINE CONTINUE TO THIS DAY TO ENJOY DRINKING OUT OF MY "BLOBLETS" — THOSE VESSELS (WHICH I MADE OVER A DECADE AGO) THAT SERVE AS A TESTAMENT TO MY EDUCATIONAL EXPERIENCE. HOWEVER, THE SAD-BUT-TRUE THING IS THAT I'VE PRETTY MUCH DESTROYED ALL OF "MY BEST GOBLET(S) EVER" USUALLY DURING THE COURSE OF MAKING THEM — JUST BEFORE THEY'RE S'POSE TO BE BOXED - Y'KNOW THAT "FISH-THAT-GOT-AWAY" ANALOGY. IT REALLY SINKS IN....

SPEAKING OF SINKS — WATCH OUT FOR THEM! I SWEAR, THEY HAVE SOME MYSTERIOUS POWER WHICH CAUSES YOU TO LOSE HOLD OF THE REMAINING NICE GOBLETS THAT YOU HAD, (DURING THE WASHING PROCESS,) AND SMASH IT INTO PIECES.

OR PERHAPS THERE'S SOME SUBCONSCIOUS DESIRE TO PUNISH MYSELF. BY MAKING MORE, I MUST DESTROY MORE. THUS, CREATING THE NEED... THE WANT...

SUPPLY . DEMAND AND ALL THAT STUFF... I DIGRESS... EXCUSE ME...

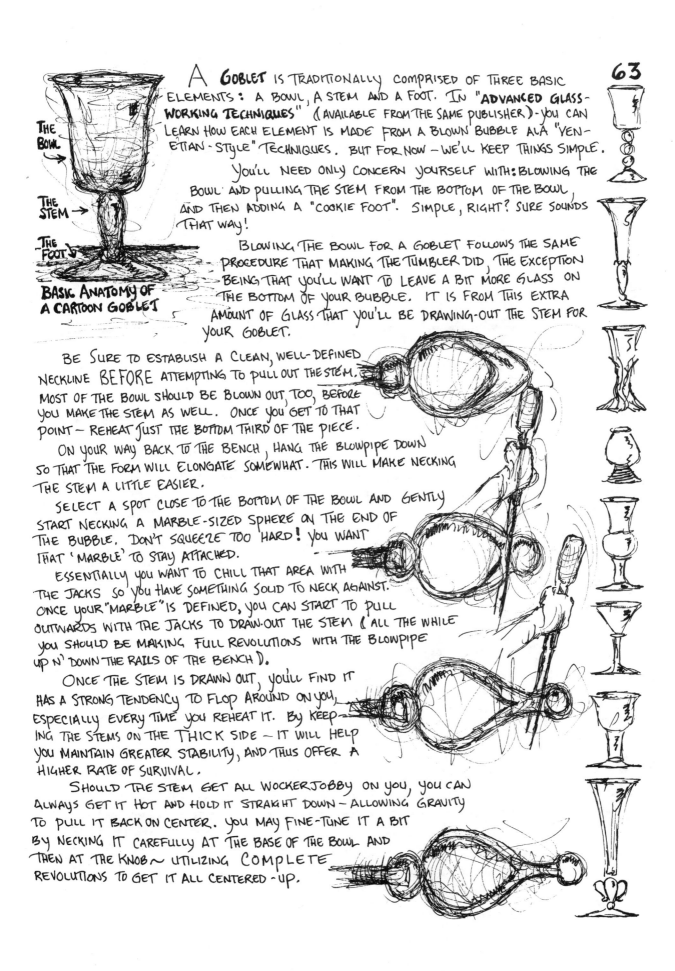

A **GOBLET** IS TRADITIONALLY COMPRISED OF THREE BASIC ELEMENTS: A BOWL, A STEM AND A FOOT. IN "**ADVANCED GLASS-WORKING TECHNIQUES**" (AVAILABLE FROM THE SAME PUBLISHER) — YOU CAN LEARN HOW EACH ELEMENT IS MADE FROM A BLOWN BUBBLE ALA "VENETIAN-STYLE" TECHNIQUES. BUT FOR NOW — WE'LL KEEP THINGS SIMPLE.

YOU'LL NEED ONLY CONCERN YOURSELF WITH: BLOWING THE BOWL AND PULLING THE STEM FROM THE BOTTOM OF THE BOWL, AND THEN ADDING A "COOKIE FOOT". SIMPLE, RIGHT? SURE SOUNDS THAT WAY!

BLOWING THE BOWL FOR A GOBLET FOLLOWS THE SAME PROCEDURE THAT MAKING THE TUMBLER DID, THE EXCEPTION BEING THAT YOU'LL WANT TO LEAVE A BIT MORE GLASS ON THE BOTTOM OF YOUR BUBBLE. IT IS FROM THIS EXTRA AMOUNT OF GLASS THAT YOU'LL BE DRAWING-OUT THE STEM FOR YOUR GOBLET.

THE BOWL

THE STEM →

THE FOOT ↘

BASIC ANATOMY OF A CARTOON GOBLET

BE SURE TO ESTABLISH A CLEAN, WELL-DEFINED NECKLINE BEFORE ATTEMPTING TO PULL OUT THE STEM. MOST OF THE BOWL SHOULD BE BLOWN OUT, TOO, BEFORE YOU MAKE THE STEM AS WELL. ONCE YOU GET TO THAT POINT — REHEAT JUST THE BOTTOM THIRD OF THE PIECE.

ON YOUR WAY BACK TO THE BENCH, HANG THE BLOWPIPE DOWN SO THAT THE FORM WILL ELONGATE SOMEWHAT. THIS WILL MAKE NECKING THE STEM A LITTLE EASIER.

SELECT A SPOT CLOSE TO THE BOTTOM OF THE BOWL AND GENTLY START NECKING A MARBLE-SIZED SPHERE ON THE END OF THE BUBBLE. DON'T SQUEEZE TOO HARD! YOU WANT THAT 'MARBLE' TO STAY ATTACHED.

ESSENTIALLY YOU WANT TO CHILL THAT AREA WITH THE JACKS SO YOU HAVE SOMETHING SOLID TO NECK AGAINST. ONCE YOUR "MARBLE" IS DEFINED, YOU CAN START TO PULL OUTWARDS WITH THE JACKS TO DRAW-OUT THE STEM (ALL THE WHILE YOU SHOULD BE MAKING FULL REVOLUTIONS WITH THE BLOWPIPE UP N' DOWN THE RAILS OF THE BENCH).

ONCE THE STEM IS DRAWN OUT, YOU'LL FIND IT HAS A STRONG TENDENCY TO FLOP AROUND ON YOU, ESPECIALLY EVERY TIME YOU REHEAT IT. BY KEEPING THE STEMS ON THE **THICK** SIDE — IT WILL HELP YOU MAINTAIN GREATER STABILITY, AND THUS OFFER A HIGHER RATE OF SURVIVAL.

SHOULD THE STEM GET ALL WOCKERJOBBY ON YOU, YOU CAN ALWAYS GET IT HOT AND HOLD IT STRAIGHT DOWN — ALLOWING GRAVITY TO PULL IT BACK ON CENTER. YOU MAY FINE-TUNE IT A BIT BY NECKING IT CAREFULLY AT THE BASE OF THE BOWL AND THEN AT THE KNOB ~ UTILIZING **COMPLETE** REVOLUTIONS TO GET IT ALL CENTERED-UP.

ONCE THE BOWL AND THE STEM ARE TO YOUR SATISFACTION, YOUR ASSISTANT MAY GATHER UP GLASS FOR THE FOOT. THE FOOT USUALLY REQUIRES TWO GATHERS, AND IS BEST ACCOMPLISHED BY TAKING THE FIRST GATHER AND NOT MARVERING IT. JUST HANG OUT, AIR MARVER IT, AND LET THE AIR COOL THE OUTSIDE SKIN ENOUGH SO YOU CAN GET THE SECOND GATHER ON TOP OF IT. THIS ALLOWS THE CORE TO RETAIN IT'S HEAT AND FOR THE GLASS TO FLOW WITH GREATER EASE.

THE GLASS MAY BE FAIRLY FLOPPY AND SOMEWHAT DIFFICULT TO CONTROL, SO DO YOUR BEST TO GET TO THE MARVER AS QUICK AS POSSIBLE. TRY TO AIR MARVER THE GLASS INTO A BALL-SHAPE ON YOUR WAY OVER.

LET IT BALL UP...

DROP IT.

CUT IT FREE

POSITION THE PUNTY A COUPLE OF INCHES OFF THE SURFACE OF THE MARVER AND THEN HOLD THE PUNTY STRAIGHT UP N' DOWN TO GET THE GLASS TO FLOW ONTO THE MARVER. IT SHOULD START TO PUDDLE-UP INTO A COOKIE-SHAPE. YOU CAN USE THE DIAMOND SHEARS TO GUIDE AND SUPPORT THE PUNTY AND ALSO DIRECT THE FLOW OF GLASS.

ONCE YOU GET A GOOD-SIZED COOKIE - CUT THE GLASS FREE WITH THE DIAMOND SHEARS. IF, FOR WHATEVER REASON, THE COOKIE GETS MESSED-UP, OR IS LESS-THAN-ROUND - TRASH IT AND MAKE ANOTHER. THERE'S NO REASON TO ACCEPT A GOOFY FOOT, OR ONE THAT LOOKS ANYTHING LESS THAN 'PERFECT'.

& PICK IT UP!

AS SOON AS THE COOKIE IS CUT FREE - THE GAFFER COMES OVER WITH THE REST OF THE GOBLET AND POSITIONS IT DIRECTLY OVER THE FOOT. YOU CAN USE THE DIAMOND SHEARS TO GRIP THE BLOWPIPE AND HELP GUIDE IT INTO POSITION.

YOU'LL WANT TO HIT DEAD CENTER AS BEST AS YOU CAN. I RECOMMEND THAT YOU JUST LIGHTLY TOUCH-UP THE STEM TO THE FOOT AT FIRST, AND THEN TURN THE BLOWPIPE 180° TO THE RIGHT, AND THEN 180° TO THE LEFT (WHICH IN TURN ROTATES THE COOKIE) TO CHECK AND MAKE SURE THAT YOU'RE ON-CENTER. YOU CAN COR-RECT MOST IRREGULARITIES BY PUSHING THE GLASS FURTHER ON WHERE YOU NEED IT. YOU REALLY ONLY GET ONE SHOT AT THIS - SO TRY AND MAKE IT COUNT. YOU CAN, HOWEVER, ALWAYS CUT OFF THE FOOT (WITH THE DIAMOND SHEARS) IF YOU SCREW IT UP AND HAVE YOUR ASSISTANT MAKE YOU ANOTHER...

NEXT, GIVE THE WHOLE PIECE A QUICK FLASH IN THE GLORY HOLE. THEN, POSITION THE GOBLET SO THAT THE FOOT IS JUST INSIDE OF THE GLORY HOLE DOOR. YOU WANT TO HEAT THE FOOT SO THAT THE CHILL MARKS (FROM THE MARVER) DISAP-PEAR. WATCH IT! THAT STEM LIKES TO GET HOT TOO! BUT YOU'LL WANT TO HAVE SOME STABILITY THERE, SO AVOID OVERHEATING IT!

THE PIECE IS BROUGHT BACK TO THE BENCH AND PADDLED TO FLATTEN THE BOTTOM. IT HELPS TO ACTUALLY PUSH THE FOOT BACK TOWARDS THE

STEM TO ADHERE IT BETTER AND KEEP IT FROM COMING OFF LATER. YOU CAN USE A WOODEN PADDLE OR THE BACK OF YOUR JACKS TO DO THIS.

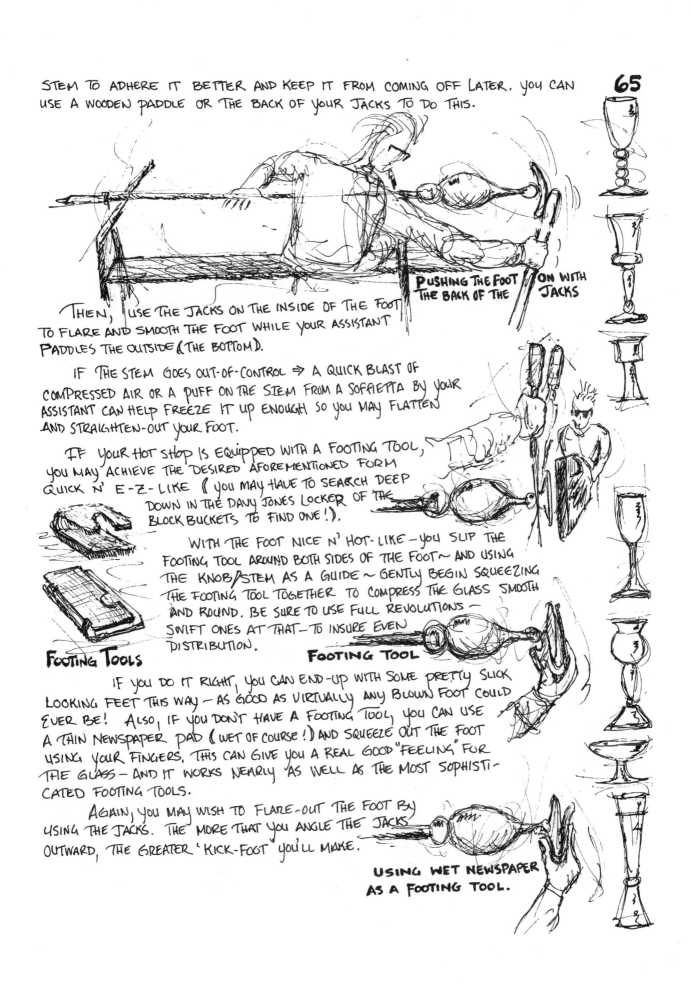

PUSHING THE FOOT ON WITH THE BACK OF THE JACKS

THEN, USE THE JACKS ON THE INSIDE OF THE FOOT TO FLARE AND SMOOTH THE FOOT WHILE YOUR ASSISTANT PADDLES THE OUTSIDE (THE BOTTOM).

IF THE STEM GOES OUT-OF-CONTROL ⇒ A QUICK BLAST OF COMPRESSED AIR OR A PUFF ON THE STEM FROM A SOFFIETTA BY YOUR ASSISTANT CAN HELP FREEZE IT UP ENOUGH SO YOU MAY FLATTEN AND STRAIGHTEN-OUT YOUR FOOT.

IF YOUR HOT SHOP IS EQUIPPED WITH A FOOTING TOOL, YOU MAY ACHIEVE THE DESIRED AFOREMENTIONED FORM QUICK N' E-Z-LIKE (YOU MAY HAVE TO SEARCH DEEP DOWN IN THE DAVY JONES LOCKER OF THE BLOCK BUCKETS TO FIND ONE!).

WITH THE FOOT NICE N' HOT-LIKE — YOU SLIP THE FOOTING TOOL AROUND BOTH SIDES OF THE FOOT — AND USING THE KNOB/STEM AS A GUIDE — GENTLY BEGIN SQUEEZING THE FOOTING TOOL TOGETHER TO COMPRESS THE GLASS SMOOTH AND ROUND. BE SURE TO USE FULL REVOLUTIONS — SWIFT ONES AT THAT — TO INSURE EVEN DISTRIBUTION.

FOOTING TOOLS

FOOTING TOOL

IF YOU DO IT RIGHT, YOU CAN END-UP WITH SOME PRETTY SLICK LOOKING FEET THIS WAY — AS GOOD AS VIRTUALLY ANY BLOWN FOOT COULD EVER BE! ALSO, IF YOU DON'T HAVE A FOOTING TOOL, YOU CAN USE A THIN NEWSPAPER PAD (WET OF COURSE!) AND SQUEEZE OUT THE FOOT USING YOUR FINGERS. THIS CAN GIVE YOU A REAL GOOD "FEELING" FOR THE GLASS — AND IT WORKS NEARLY AS WELL AS THE MOST SOPHISTI-CATED FOOTING TOOLS.

AGAIN, YOU MAY WISH TO FLARE-OUT THE FOOT BY USING THE JACKS. THE MORE THAT YOU ANGLE THE JACKS OUTWARD, THE GREATER 'KICK-FOOT' YOU'LL MAKE.

USING WET NEWSPAPER AS A FOOTING TOOL.

WHEN ALL THREE ELEMENTS APPEAR IN ORDER, YOU MAY PROCEED TO PUNTY IT UP. WHILE YOU HAVE YOUR ASSISTANT PREPARE THE PUNTY FOR YOU, TAKE A GOOD LAST FLASH IN THE GLORY HOLE AND THEN HAVE A SEAT AT THE BENCH.

USE A PADDLE OR THE BACK OF THE JACKS TO SMOOTH AND CENTER THE FOOT ONE FINAL TIME BEFORE YOU PUNTY IT. IT'S ABOUT THE LAST CHANCE YOU'LL GET TO MAKE SURE THAT YOUR GOBLET WILL STAND UP STRAIGHT.

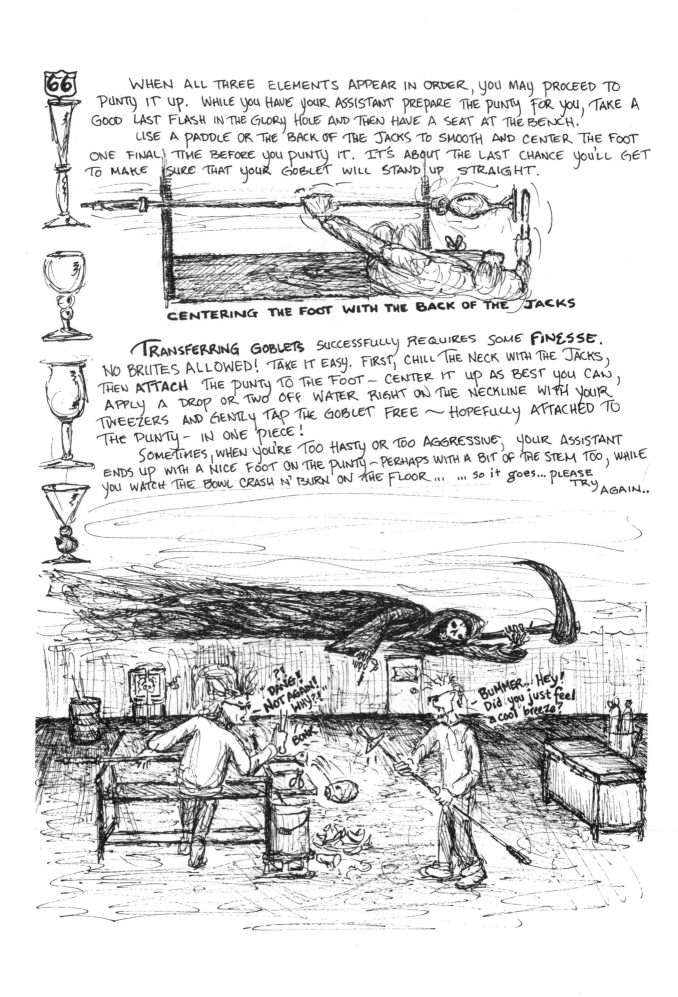

CENTERING THE FOOT WITH THE BACK OF THE JACKS

TRANSFERRING GOBLETS SUCCESSFULLY REQUIRES SOME **FINESSE**. NO BRUTES ALLOWED! TAKE IT EASY. FIRST, CHILL THE NECK WITH THE JACKS, THEN **ATTACH** THE PUNTY TO THE FOOT — CENTER IT UP AS BEST YOU CAN, APPLY A DROP OR TWO OFF WATER RIGHT ON THE NECKLINE WITH YOUR TWEEZERS AND GENTLY TAP THE GOBLET FREE ~ HOPEFULLY ATTACHED TO THE PUNTY — IN ONE PIECE!

SOMETIMES, WHEN YOU'RE TOO HASTY OR TOO AGGRESSIVE, YOUR ASSISTANT ENDS UP WITH A NICE FOOT ON THE PUNTY — PERHAPS WITH A BIT OF THE STEM TOO, WHILE YOU WATCH THE BOWL CRASH N' BURN ON THE FLOOR... ... so it goes... PLEASE TRY AGAIN..

ADDING STEMS

ANOTHER WAY TO CREATE STEMS FOR YOUR GOBLETS IS TO ADD THEM ON TO THE BOTTOM OF YOUR BOWL. IT IS NOT TOO DISSIMILAR FROM ATTACHING HANDLES ON A PIECE. THERE ARE TWO COMMON METHODS FOR DOING IT → ATTACHING THE STEM HORIZONTALLY ~ LIKE YOU WOULD A PUNTY ~ OR VIA AN OVERHEAD DROP.

ADDING A STEM - HORIZONALLY.

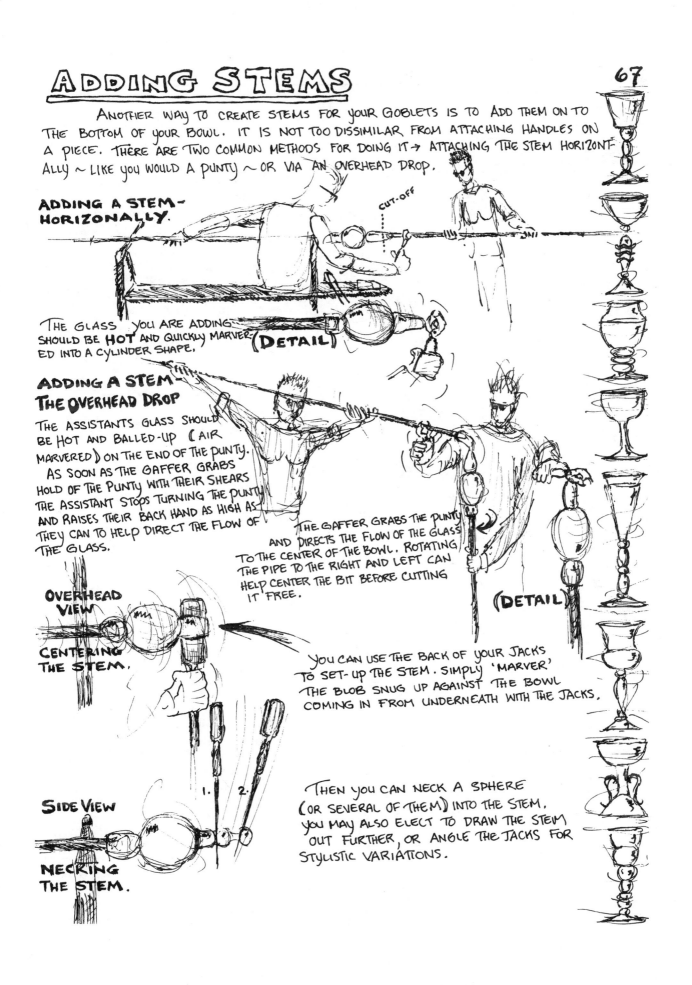

CUT-OFF

THE GLASS YOU ARE ADDING SHOULD BE **HOT** AND QUICKLY MARVERED INTO A CYLINDER SHAPE.

(DETAIL)

ADDING A STEM - THE OVERHEAD DROP

THE ASSISTANTS GLASS SHOULD BE HOT AND BALLED-UP (AIR MARVERED) ON THE END OF THE PUNTY.
AS SOON AS THE GAFFER GRABS HOLD OF THE PUNTY WITH THEIR SHEARS THE ASSISTANT STOPS TURNING THE PUNTY AND RAISES THEIR BACK HAND AS HIGH AS THEY CAN TO HELP DIRECT THE FLOW OF THE GLASS.

THE GAFFER GRABS THE PUNTY AND DIRECTS THE FLOW OF THE GLASS TO THE CENTER OF THE BOWL. ROTATING THE PIPE TO THE RIGHT AND LEFT CAN HELP CENTER THE BIT BEFORE CUTTING IT FREE.

(DETAIL)

OVERHEAD VIEW

CENTERING THE STEM.

1.   2.

YOU CAN USE THE BACK OF YOUR JACKS TO SET-UP THE STEM. SIMPLY 'MARVER' THE BLOB SNUG UP AGAINST THE BOWL COMING IN FROM UNDERNEATH WITH THE JACKS.

SIDE VIEW

NECKING THE STEM.

THEN YOU CAN NECK A SPHERE (OR SEVERAL OF THEM) INTO THE STEM. YOU MAY ALSO ELECT TO DRAW THE STEM OUT FURTHER, OR ANGLE THE JACKS FOR STYLISTIC VARIATIONS.

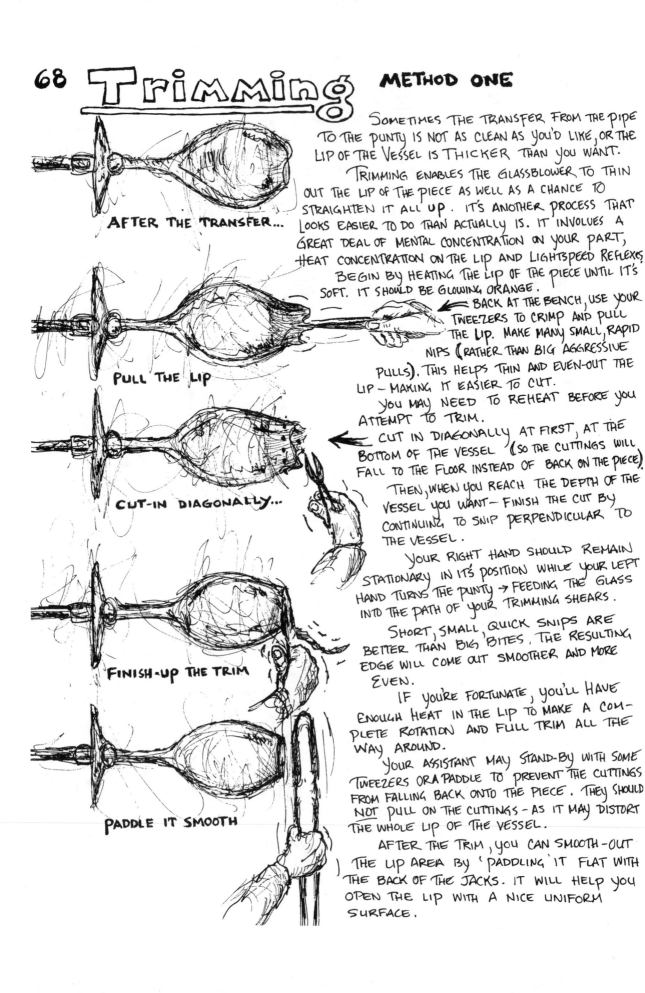

68 Trimming

SOMETIMES THE TRANSFER FROM THE PIPE TO THE PUNTY IS NOT AS CLEAN AS YOU'D LIKE, OR THE LIP OF THE VESSEL IS THICKER THAN YOU WANT.

TRIMMING ENABLES THE GLASSBLOWER TO THIN OUT THE LIP OF THE PIECE AS WELL AS A CHANCE TO STRAIGHTEN IT ALL UP. IT'S ANOTHER PROCESS THAT LOOKS EASIER TO DO THAN ACTUALLY IS. IT INVOLVES A GREAT DEAL OF MENTAL CONCENTRATION ON YOUR PART, HEAT CONCENTRATION ON THE LIP AND LIGHTSPEED REFLEXES.

BEGIN BY HEATING THE LIP OF THE PIECE UNTIL IT'S SOFT. IT SHOULD BE GLOWING ORANGE.

BACK AT THE BENCH, USE YOUR TWEEZERS TO CRIMP AND PULL THE LIP. MAKE MANY SMALL, RAPID NIPS (RATHER THAN BIG AGGRESSIVE PULLS). THIS HELPS THIN AND EVEN-OUT THE LIP – MAKING IT EASIER TO CUT.

YOU MAY NEED TO REHEAT BEFORE YOU ATTEMPT TO TRIM.

CUT IN DIAGONALLY AT FIRST, AT THE BOTTOM OF THE VESSEL (SO THE CUTTINGS WILL FALL TO THE FLOOR INSTEAD OF BACK ON THE PIECE).

THEN, WHEN YOU REACH THE DEPTH OF THE VESSEL YOU WANT – FINISH THE CUT BY CONTINUING TO SNIP PERPENDICULAR TO THE VESSEL.

YOUR RIGHT HAND SHOULD REMAIN STATIONARY IN ITS POSITION WHILE YOUR LEFT HAND TURNS THE PUNTY → FEEDING THE GLASS INTO THE PATH OF YOUR TRIMMING SHEARS.

SHORT, SMALL, QUICK SNIPS ARE BETTER THAN BIG BITES. THE RESULTING EDGE WILL COME OUT SMOOTHER AND MORE EVEN.

IF YOU'RE FORTUNATE, YOU'LL HAVE ENOUGH HEAT IN THE LIP TO MAKE A COMPLETE ROTATION AND FULL TRIM ALL THE WAY AROUND.

YOUR ASSISTANT MAY STAND-BY WITH SOME TWEEZERS OR A PADDLE TO PREVENT THE CUTTINGS FROM FALLING BACK ONTO THE PIECE. THEY SHOULD NOT PULL ON THE CUTTINGS – AS IT MAY DISTORT THE WHOLE LIP OF THE VESSEL.

AFTER THE TRIM, YOU CAN SMOOTH-OUT THE LIP AREA BY 'PADDLING' IT FLAT WITH THE BACK OF THE JACKS. IT WILL HELP YOU OPEN THE LIP WITH A NICE UNIFORM SURFACE.

AFTER THE TRANSFER...

PULL THE LIP

CUT-IN DIAGONALLY...

FINISH-UP THE TRIM

PADDLE IT SMOOTH

AFTER A GOOD QUICK REHEAT, YOU HAVE THE OPTION OF PUFFING-OUT THE BOWL. YOU CAN INCREASE THE VOLUME OF YOUR GOBLET AND THIN IT OUT SOMEWHAT BY DOING THIS - EITHER WITH A STEAMSTICK (LEFT) OR USING AN ASSISTANT WITH A SOFFIETTA.

WITH A STEAMSTICK, YOU SIMPLY STICK THE WET, POINTED END IN THE LIP OF THE VESSEL — MAKING A COMPLETE SEAL. THE MOISTURE FROM THE WOOD WILL VAPORIZE AND INFLATE THE BUBBLE.

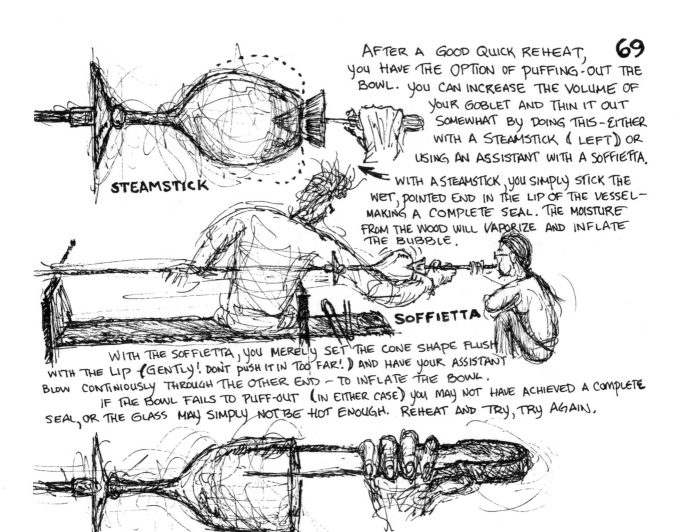

STEAMSTICK

SOFFIETTA

WITH THE SOFFIETTA, YOU MERELY SET THE CONE SHAPE FLUSH WITH THE LIP (GENTLY! DON'T PUSH IT IN TOO FAR!) AND HAVE YOUR ASSISTANT BLOW CONTINIOUSLY THROUGH THE OTHER END — TO INFLATE THE BOWL.

IF THE BOWL FAILS TO PUFF-OUT (IN EITHER CASE) YOU MAY NOT HAVE ACHIEVED A COMPLETE SEAL, OR THE GLASS MAY SIMPLY NOT BE HOT ENOUGH. REHEAT AND TRY, TRY AGAIN.

AT LONG LAST, YOU CAN TAKE YOUR FINAL REHEAT(S) AND OPEN UP THE LIP OF THE VESSEL TO COMPLETE YOUR FORM.

AGAIN, BE CAREFUL WHEN OPENING GOBLETS WITH THE JACKS. IT IS VERY EASY TO OVERDO IT AND FLARE THE LIP SO MUCH AS TO MAKE THE GOBLET USELESS AS A DRINKING VESSEL. INDEED, THE DEGREE TO WHICH YOU OPEN THE BOWL CAN DRAMATICALLY EFFECT IT'S OVERALL PRESENTATION AND FUNCTION.

THIS METHOD OF TRIMMING WORKS WELL FOR VIRTUALLY ANY TYPE OF PIECE WHERE YOU'RE ONLY CONCERNED WITH "CLEANING-UP" THE LIP AREA. IT'S APPROPRIATE FOR SMALL AND LARGE PIECES ALIKE. ANOTHER METHOD OF TRIMMING IS DEPICTED ON THE FOLLOWING PAGE.

FINISHED GOBLET

Trimming
METHOD TWO

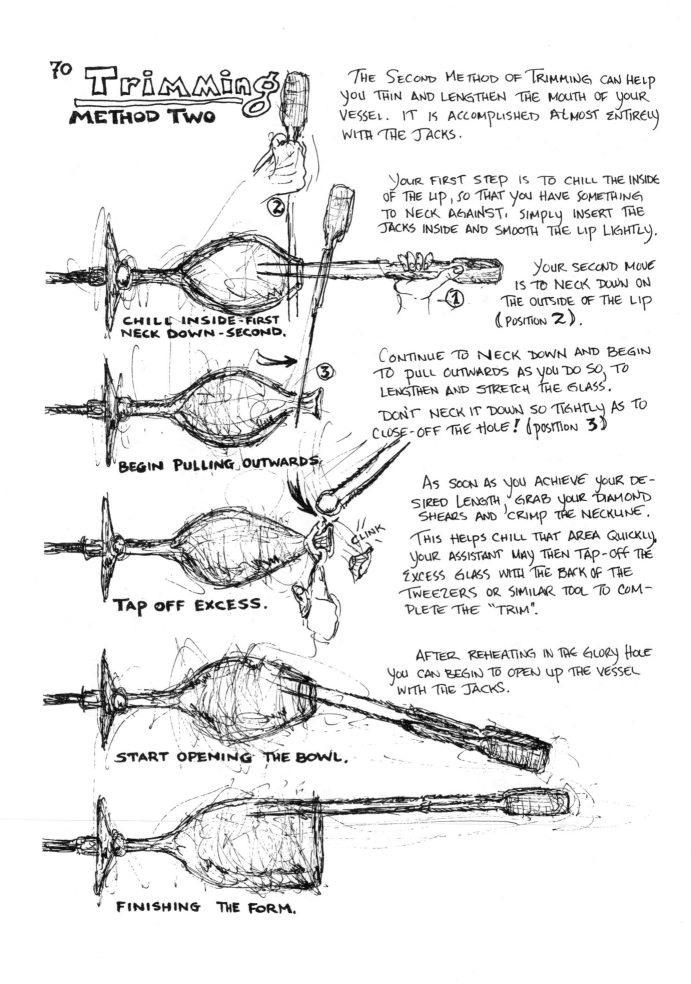

THE SECOND METHOD OF TRIMMING CAN HELP YOU THIN AND LENGTHEN THE MOUTH OF YOUR VESSEL. IT IS ACCOMPLISHED ALMOST ENTIRELY WITH THE JACKS.

YOUR FIRST STEP IS TO CHILL THE INSIDE OF THE LIP, SO THAT YOU HAVE SOMETHING TO NECK AGAINST. SIMPLY INSERT THE JACKS INSIDE AND SMOOTH THE LIP LIGHTLY.

YOUR SECOND MOVE IS TO NECK DOWN ON THE OUTSIDE OF THE LIP (POSITION 2).

CONTINUE TO NECK DOWN AND BEGIN TO PULL OUTWARDS AS YOU DO SO, TO LENGTHEN AND STRETCH THE GLASS.

DON'T NECK IT DOWN SO TIGHTLY AS TO CLOSE-OFF THE HOLE! (POSITION 3)

AS SOON AS YOU ACHIEVE YOUR DESIRED LENGTH, GRAB YOUR DIAMOND SHEARS AND CRIMP THE NECKLINE.

THIS HELPS CHILL THAT AREA QUICKLY. YOUR ASSISTANT MAY THEN TAP-OFF THE EXCESS GLASS WITH THE BACK OF THE TWEEZERS OR SIMILAR TOOL TO COMPLETE THE "TRIM".

AFTER REHEATING IN THE GLORY HOLE YOU CAN BEGIN TO OPEN UP THE VESSEL WITH THE JACKS.

CHILL INSIDE - FIRST NECK DOWN - SECOND.

BEGIN PULLING OUTWARDS.

CLINK

TAP OFF EXCESS.

START OPENING THE BOWL.

FINISHING THE FORM.

OVERHEAD VIEW
PADDLING THE LIP SMOOTH

GOBLET-MAKING IS INDEED AN ART IN AND OF ITSELF. AS STATED EARLIER, IT IS ONE OF THE MOST DIFFICULT TECHNIQUES IN ALL OF GLASSBLOWING TO MASTER. IT TEMPERS YOUR SOUL. YOU MUST F O C U S. IT TEACHES YOU DISCIPLINE. YOU LEARN HUMILITY, AND GAIN TREMENDOUS APPRECIATION FOR THOSE BLOWERS THAT MAKE GOBLETS SO WELL (AND MAKE IT LOOK SO EASY!).

FORTUNATELY, STYLISTIC VARIATIONS ABOUND ~ AND THERE'S A VAST NUMBER OF GOBLETS THAT HAVE YET TO BE MADE ~ OR EVEN BEEN DREAMT OF!

FOR PRACTICE: THE ONLY WAY I KNOW HOW TO GET PROFICIENT AT MAKING GOB-LETS IS BY DOING THEM. TAKE IT STEP BY STEP. ~ ESPECIALLY IF YOU CAN DEVOTE SOME TIME AND GLASS TO PRACTICING EACH ELEMENT.

SPEND A BLOWSLOT JUST TRYING TO MAKE A DECENT BOWL FORM. ONCE YOU GET THAT PART DOWN — TRY ADDING A STEM. TRY THEM HORIZONTALLY, AND THEN TRY THE OVERHEAD DROP METHOD. SEE HOW MANY VARIATIONS OF GOBLET STEMS YOU CAN COME UP WITH.

FINALLY — SPEND ANOTHER BLOWSLOT JUST PICKING-UP FEET. PRACTICE IT UNTIL YOU CAN DO IT IN YOUR SLEEP. ALSO, TRY TO WORK WITH THE SAME ASSISTANT EACH TIME YOU BLOW. THAT WAY, YOU BOTH BENEFIT FROM THE REPITITION AND PRACTICE. TRY SWITCHING POSITIONS (GAFFER / ASSISTANT) — SO YOU ALLOW THE OTHER PERSON A CHANCE TO SCREW THINGS UP ONCE IN A WHILE...

HAND ME THOSE SHEARS-PLEASE, DEAR GOD.

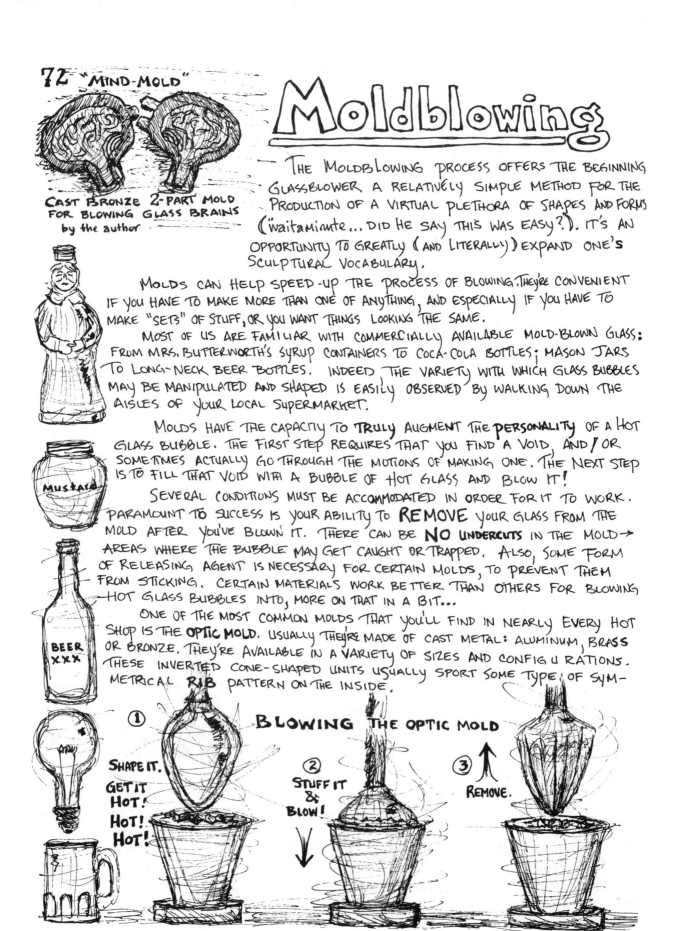

"MIND-MOLD"

CAST BRONZE 2-PART MOLD
FOR BLOWING GLASS BRAINS
by the author

Moldblowing

THE MOLDBLOWING PROCESS OFFERS THE BEGINNING GLASSBLOWER A RELATIVELY SIMPLE METHOD FOR THE PRODUCTION OF A VIRTUAL PLETHORA OF SHAPES AND FORMS ("waitaminute... DID HE SAY THIS WAS EASY?"). IT'S AN OPPORTUNITY TO GREATLY (AND LITERALLY) EXPAND ONE'S SCULPTURAL VOCABULARY.

MOLDS CAN HELP SPEED-UP THE PROCESS OF BLOWING. THEY'RE CONVENIENT IF YOU HAVE TO MAKE MORE THAN ONE OF ANYTHING, AND ESPECIALLY IF YOU HAVE TO MAKE "SETS" OF STUFF, OR YOU WANT THINGS LOOKING THE SAME.

MOST OF US ARE FAMILIAR WITH COMMERCIALLY AVAILABLE MOLD-BLOWN GLASS: FROM MRS. BUTTERWORTH'S SYRUP CONTAINERS TO COCA-COLA BOTTLES; MASON JARS TO LONG-NECK BEER BOTTLES. INDEED THE VARIETY WITH WHICH GLASS BUBBLES MAY BE MANIPULATED AND SHAPED IS EASILY OBSERVED BY WALKING DOWN THE AISLES OF YOUR LOCAL SUPERMARKET.

MOLDS HAVE THE CAPACITY TO **TRULY** AUGMENT THE **PERSONALITY** OF A HOT GLASS BUBBLE. THE FIRST STEP REQUIRES THAT YOU FIND A VOID, AND / OR SOMETIMES ACTUALLY GO THROUGH THE MOTIONS OF MAKING ONE. THE NEXT STEP IS TO FILL THAT VOID WITH A BUBBLE OF HOT GLASS AND BLOW IT!

SEVERAL CONDITIONS MUST BE ACCOMMODATED IN ORDER FOR IT TO WORK. PARAMOUNT TO SUCCESS IS YOUR ABILITY TO **REMOVE** YOUR GLASS FROM THE MOLD AFTER YOU'VE BLOWN IT. THERE CAN BE **NO UNDERCUTS** IN THE MOLD→ AREAS WHERE THE BUBBLE MAY GET CAUGHT OR TRAPPED. ALSO, SOME FORM OF RELEASING AGENT IS NECESSARY FOR CERTAIN MOLDS, TO PREVENT THEM FROM STICKING. CERTAIN MATERIALS WORK BETTER THAN OTHERS FOR BLOWING HOT GLASS BUBBLES INTO, MORE ON THAT IN A BIT...

ONE OF THE MOST COMMON MOLDS THAT YOU'LL FIND IN NEARLY EVERY HOT SHOP IS THE **OPTIC MOLD**. USUALLY THEY'RE MADE OF CAST METAL: ALUMINUM, BRASS OR BRONZE. THEY'RE AVAILABLE IN A VARIETY OF SIZES AND CONFIGURATIONS. THESE INVERTED CONE-SHAPED UNITS USUALLY SPORT SOME TYPE OF SYMMETRICAL RIB PATTERN ON THE INSIDE.

Mustard

BEER
XXX

① SHAPE IT. GET IT HOT! HOT! HOT!

BLOWING THE OPTIC MOLD

② STUFF IT & BLOW!

③ REMOVE.

THE KEY TO SUCCESSFUL MOLDBLOWING, REGARDLESS OF WHAT TYPE OF **73**
MOLD IT IS, IS TO **SHAPE** YOUR BUBBLE AS CLOSE TO THE MOLD'S INTERIOR SHAPE AS POSSIBLE,
AND **BLOW IT** AS HOT AS YOU CAN. THIS HELPS YOU MAINTAIN AN EVEN-WALL THICKNESS IN YOUR PIECE,
AND THUS MAKES THE BEST USE OUT OF YOUR GLASS. IT ALSO PREVENTS THE GLASS FROM BLOWING
OUT TOO THIN AT ANY ONE SPOT.

FOR OPTIC MOLDS: YOU'LL WANT YOUR BUBBLE BLOWN ALL THE WAY DOWN TO THE BOTTOM,
AND IN A TAPERED SHAPE. YOU CAN MARVER, AND BLOW YOUR BUBBLE INTO THAT SHAPE. THEN,
JUST BEFORE YOU BLOW INTO THE MOLD, YOU'LL WANT TO GET THE BUBBLE SCREAMIN' HOT IN THE
GLORY HOLE.

NEXT, DROP THE BUBBLE STRAIGHT INTO THE MOLD. TRY TO GET THE GLASS ALL THE WAY
IN•UNTIL IT REACHES THE BOTTOM OF THE MOLD. NEVER FORCE IT! IF YOU'RE HEIGHT-CHALLENGED
YOU MAY NEED TO JUMP-UP ON A BOX OR CINDER BLOCK TO HAVE ENOUGH CLEARANCE TO BLOW
THE MOLD. TRY TO HIT THE CENTER OF THE MOLD WITH YOUR BUBBLE. BLOW IT AS SOON AS
YOU HAVE IT LINED-UP. BLOW HARD, OR **BLOW N' CAP** TO GET FULL **EXPANSION**
AND THE CRISPIEST DETAIL POSSIBLE. AFTER A FEW SECONDS AND A FINAL PUFF,
REMOVE THE GLASS FROM THE MOLD AND CHECK IT OUT.

IF IT ALL BLOWS OUT OK, YOU CAN CONTINUE-ON, AND FINISH SHAPING
AND BLOWING THE PIECE TO IT'S FINAL FORM... **NOTE:** THE MORE THAT YOU
HAVE TO HEAT AND REHEAT THE PIECE, THE LESS C R I S P YOUR OPTIC PATTERN
WILL APPEAR. ALSO, THE MORE THAT YOU BLOW OUT THE FORM, THE LESS DETAIL
AND **OPTICAL EFFECT** YOU WILL RETAIN.

YOU ALSO HAVE THE OPTION OF **THE OPTIC TWIST:**

BLOW IT!

IMMEDIATELY AFTER BLOWING
THE OPTIC MOLD, NECK DOWN
A SMALL KNOB ON THE BOTTOM OF
THE BUBBLE WITH THE JACKS.

NECK DOWN A KNOB...

THEN QUENCH THE KNOB
IN A BUCKET OF WATER.
THIS SHOULD FREEZE-UP THE BOTTOM,
GIVING YOU SOMETHING 'SOLID' TO GRIP
ON TO, TO CREATE THE TWIST PATTERN.

TSSS

QUENCH IT.

YOU MAY OR MAY NOT NEED TO REHEAT
BEFORE ATTEMPTING TO TWIST, DE-
PENDING ON HOW HOT YOUR BUBBLE
IS. IF IT'S STILL GOOD N' HOT,
GO AHEAD AND GRIP THE KNOB
WITH THE DIAMOND SHEARS - AND HOLD
IT TIGHT WHILE TURNING THE PIPE
WITH YOUR OTHER HAND.

GRIP THE KNOB

THE PATTERN SHOULD START SPIRALING
AND TWISTING. THE HOTTER YOUR BUBBLE IS,
THE EASIER IT IS TO DO.

TURN THE PIPE

TWIST IT UP!

THE MORE THAT YOU TWIST IT, THE
TIGHTER THE OPTIC PATTERN WILL BE.

ONCE YOU GET THE EFFECT THAT YOU
LIKE, CUT OFF THE EXCESS KNOB (OR
TAP IT OFF) AND REHEAT.

74 AFTER A GOOD REHEAT, YOU CAN PROCEED TO NECK, BLOW AND SHAPE THE PIECE INTO IT'S FINAL FORM.

? Q ? HOW COME WHEN I TRY TO GET A GOOD TWIST IN MY BUBBLE — ONLY THE BOTTOM PART GETS TWISTED AND NOT THE WHOLE THING?

A. YOU'RE PROBABLY NOT GETTING THE BUBBLE HOT ENOUGH TO BEGIN WITH. AND THEN IT'S LIKELY THAT YOU'RE WORKING TOO COLD, OR NOT REHEATING DEEP ENOUGH IN THE GLORY HOLE. **HOT GOOD, COLD BAD!**

OPTIC MOLDS TEND TO BE SOMEWHAT FORGIVING IN TERMS OF WHAT KIND OF BUBBLE YOU STUFF IN THEM (i.e. THEY NEEDN'T BE PERFECT) AND WHAT YOU GET OUT OF THEM — THAT IS, SOMETHING WITH THE APPEARANCE OF BEING ON-CENTER. THEY SEEM TO BE ESPECIALLY CONVENIENT FOR THE GOBLET-MAKING PROCESS BECAUSE OF THEIR OPTIC QUALITIES AND CAPABILITIES. THIS DOES NOT MEAN, HOWEVER, THAT YOU CAN BE LAZY AND STUFF WHATEVER BUBBLE YOU FEEL LIKE INTO THE MOLD. OPTIC MOLDS, LIKE ALL MOLDS, TAKE SOME PRACTICE GETTING USED-TO. GETTING YOUR BUBBLE IN THE RIGHT SHAPE AND WITH THE CORRECT THICKNESS PRIOR TO BLOWING THE MOLD IS THE MOST CRITICAL PART OF THE PROCESS. IT IS A TECHNIQUE WHICH YOU DEVOLOP THROUGH TIME AND WITH EXPERIENCE,

STICKING WITH THE MOTTO, "KEEP IT SIMPLE!"

YOU COULD FINISH YOUR OPTIC MOLD-BLOWN BUBBLE INTO A PILSNER-STYLE CUP (AS DRAWN BELOW). ALL YOU WOULD NEED TO DO WOULD BE TO: NECK-IN YOUR TRANSFER LINE (①) AND SHAPE THE BOTTOM OF THE BOWL (② – YOUR ASSISTANT MAY BLOW AT THE SAME TIME TO INCREASE VOLUME IN THE BOWL), AND PICK-UP A COOKIE FOOT (NOT DRAWN). THEN IT'S THE USUAL, TRANSFER, REHEAT AND OPEN-UP THE CUP etc. etc...

FOR PRACTICE:

THE OPTIC CUP PICTURED AT THE RIGHT IS A SEEMINGLY STRAIGHT—FORWARD KINDA-FORM. THIS DOES NOT IMPLY THAT IT IS EASY TO MAKE. IT IS, HOWEVER, A GOOD FORM TO PRACTICE YOUR OPTIC TWIST SKILLS AS WELL AS AN OPPORTUNITY FOR YOU TO INCREASE YOUR SPEED IN BLOWING (THUS, INCREASING YOUR POTENTIAL OUTPUT!).

SHOOT FOR MAKING FOUR OF THESE CUPS IN A HOUR'S TIME. ONCE YOU GET THAT DOWN, SHOOT FOR SIX. OR EVEN EIGHT per HOUR! TRY TO BLOW THEM THINNER too!

IF THERE ARE SOME OTHER OPTIC MOLDS AROUND, TRY YOUR HAND AT BLOWING THEM TOO. NOTICE THE DIFFERENCES BETWEEN THE MOLDS AND THE RESULTS OF THEIR INFLUENCES ON THE BUBBLES WHICH YOU BLOW INTO THEM!

FINISHED CUP

AS MENTIONED EARLIER, MANY OTHER POSSIBILITES EXIST IN THE REALM OF MOLDBLOWING. VIRTUALLY ANY FIRE-PROOF SUBSTANCE MAY BE USED FOR A MOLD. PERHAPS THE MOST COMMON MATERIAL UTILIZED BY MOLD-MAKERS IS WOOD. BLOCKS ARE A SIMPLE EXAMPLE OF A WET WOOD-OPEN-FACE MOLD.

IF FOR EXAMPLE YOU WERE TO PUT TWO BLOCKS TOGETHER (A "RIGHTY" AND A "LEFTY") AND BLOW A BUBBLE INTO THE CAVITY ~ YOU WOULD HAVE **A BASIC** TWO-PART BLOW MOLD. INDEED, MANY WOOD MOLDS USED IN **PRODUCTION** ARE JUST VARIATIONS ON THIS IDEA. THE MOLDS ARE USUALLY HINGED

ON ONE SIDE ~ WITH TWO HANDLES MOUNTED ON IT SOMEWHERE ~ ENABLING THE ASSISTANT TO OPEN AND CLOSE THE MOLD AS NEEDED. SOME MOLDS MUST BE CLAMPED SHUT DURING THE BLOW TO PREVENT THEM FROM OPENING FROM THE EXPANDING PRESSURE.

EVEN WITH THE MOST PRIMITIVE WOODWORKING SKILLS AND/OR EQUIPMENT, YOU CAN COME-UP WITH SOME PRETTY INTERESTING MOLDS FOR BLOWING HOT GLASS INTO. FIRST, A FEW TIPS: ▪HARDWOODS LAST THE LONGEST (ESPECIALLY CHERRY, APPLE OR OTHER FRUIT WOODS).   ▪AVOID USING PLYWOOD, PARTICLE-BOARD OR ANY OTHER RESIN-BONDED WOOD PRODUCT AS THE GLUES WHICH BIND THEM ARE FLAMMABLE AND TOXIC TO BREATHE WHEN THEY ARE BURNED.   ▪THE WOOD WILL LAST LONGER IF YOU PRE-SOAK IT IN WATER BEFORE BLOWING INTO IT.   ▪ IF YOUR GLASS FORMS ARE HAVING TROUBLE BLOWING ALL-THE-WAY-OUT IN THE MOLD — IT MAY BE THAT YOU NEED SOME VENT HOLES DRILLED NEAR THE BOTTOM OF YOUR MOLD. THE HOLES WILL ALLOW ANY AIR THAT IS TRAPPED IN THERE A CHANCE TO ESCAPE, (PLUS THEY WORK WELL FOR LETTING THE WATER DRAIN-OUT AS WELL!).

PERHAPS THE SIMPLEST WOOD MOLD YOU CAN MAKE IS THE BOX MOLD: SIMPLY NAIL SOME BOARDS TOGETHER TO CREATE A FOUR-SIDED (PLUS A BOTTOM) BOX SHAPE. KEEP IT ON THE SMALL-SIDE AT FIRST ~ JUST TO GET A FEELING FOR THE PROCESS.

YOUR NEXT STEP IS TO SOAK THE MOLD IN WATER ~ FIFTEEN MINUTES tu A HALF HOUR (to OVERNIGHT) OR SO. WHILE IT'S SOAKING, GO AHEAD AND PREPARE YOUR BUBBLE. TRY TO GUESSTIMATE HOW MUCH GLASS YOU'LL NEED TO FILL THEN MOLD ~ AND THEN SOME. AGAIN, DO YOUR BEST TO SHAPE YOUR BUBBLE AS CLOSE TO THE INSIDE OF YOUR MOLD AS YOU CAN GET IT (YES! IN THIS CASE IT'S OKAY TO STICK A ROUND SHAPE INTO A SQUARE HOLE!). YOU MAY WANT TO NECK-IN A TRANSFER-LINE AT THIS TIME AS WELL...

WHEN EVERYTHING'S LOOKING RIGHT — YANK THE MOLD OUT OF THE WATER (YOUR ASSISTANT CAN HELP YOU OUT WITH THAT) AND SLAP YOUR HOT BUBBLE IN THE MOLD AND BLOW IT! BLOW IT HARD, CAP IT, BLOW IT AGAIN ~ ALLOW THE FORM TO SET-UP FOR A FEW SECONDS, MAYBE PUFF IT ONE FINAL TIME AND THEN REMOVE IT FROM THE MOLD. CHECK IT OUT.

IF THE PIECE LOOKS GOOD ~ FLASH IT AND BOX IT, OR IF YOU CARE TO — PUNTY IT UP AND FINISH IT HOW YOU LIKE.

IF THE PIECE LOOKS CRAPPY OR BLEW OUT TOO THIN, TRASH IT AND TRY, TRY AGAIN! SUCH IS THE NATURE OF MOLDBLOWING!

FOR VARIATIONS ~ RESHAPE THE INTERIOR OF YOUR BOX WITH WET NEWSPAPER, OR TWIGS, OR DOWEL RODS etc. TO CREATE UNIQUE, INDIVIDUAL PIECES BASED ON A COMMON FORM.

A SIMPLE BOX MOLD

FINISHED FORM

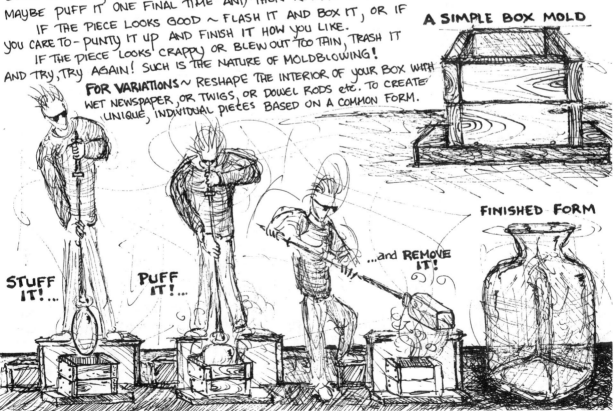

STUFF IT!...

PUFF IT!...

...and **REMOVE IT!**

SOME THINGS YOU MIGHT WANNA KNOW ABOUT

Color (AS DESCRIBED IN BLACK & WHITE)

FIRST OFF, WHAT IS COLOR? RATHER THAN DISCUSS THE PHYSICAL, NOT-TOO-MENTION THE PHILOSOPHICAL ASPECTS OF THIS RATHER OPEN-ENDED QUESTION, WHICH WOULD SURELY DOUBLE THE THICKNESS OF THIS ALREADY LONG-WINDED MANUAL, WE'LL STICK TO IT'S APPLICATIONS IN HOT GLASS.

MOST STUDIOS MELT A CLEAR BATCH OR CULLET (A.KA. "CRYSTAL"), AND INTRODUCE COLOR AT VARIOUS STAGES OF THE BLOWING PROCESS. THIS COLOR IS MANUFACTURED BY FACTORIES (SUCH AS "KUGLER", "ZIMMERMANN" AND "REICHENBACH") WHOSE SOLE PURPOSE IS TO CREATE COMPATIBLE COLORED GLASSES FOR INDUSTRY AND STUDIO GLASSMAKERS.

TO PRODUCE OR ACHIEVE COLORED GLASS, A VARIETY OF CHEMICAL FORMULAS MUST BE PAIN-STAKINGLY FOLLOWED. THE INTRODUCTION OF METALS & METALLIC OXIDES INTO THE MELTING FURNACE WITH THE INITIAL BATCH WILL YIELD A LARGE QUANTITY OF ONE (HOPEFULLY) PREDICTABLE COLOR. COBALT OXIDE FOR EXAMPLE, WILL CONTRIBUTE A BLUISH COLOR. COPPER MAY PRODUCE ANY-THING FROM A RED TO A GREEN, AND GOLD IS RESPONSIBLE FOR ACHIEVING THOSE LUSCIOUS REDS AND ORANGES (CONSEQUENTLY THEY ARE MORE EXPENSIVE!).

THE METALLIC OXIDES MUST BE MIXED AND MELTED-IN PROPERLY, ACCORDING TO SPECIFIC FORMULAS, WHICH WILL DICTATE BOTH THE DENSITY OF THE COLOR AND IT'S COEFFICENT OF EXPANSION OR "COMPATIBILITY".

COMPATIBILITY IS VITALLY IMPORTANT TO THE SUCCESS OF YOUR COLOR MASTERPIECE. IF THE COLOR COOLS MORE RAPIDLY, OR SIGNIFICANTLY LESS, THAN THAT OF YOUR CRYSTAL DURING ANNEALING, — SOME INTERNAL STRESS (DUE TO THERMAL INBALANCES) WILL ARISE AND QUITE OFTEN CRACK, CHECK OR FRACTURE THE WORK.

WHAT CAN YOU DO ABOUT THIS?... ASK OTHER GLASSWORKERS (WHO ARE FAMILIAR WITH THE CRYSTAL OR BATCH THAT YOU'RE USING) ABOUT THE PARTICULAR PALETTE OF COLORS THAT YOU INTEND TO USE. IT IS THE EASIEST METHOD OF CHECKING COMPATIBILITY. MOST COLOR THAT YOU PURCHASE SHOULD ALSO HAVE SOME INFORMATION ON IT'S COEFFICENT OF EXPANSION, WHICH YOU MAY COMPARE TO THAT OF YOUR CLEAR. BUT EVEN EQUAL COEFFICIENTS DON'T NECESSARILY ALWAYS MEAN THAT THEY'LL BE COMPATIBLE! TRIAL AND ERROR OFFERS YET ANOTHER METHOD TO TEST COMPATIBILITY — WHICH WILL OF COURSE YIELD CONCRETE RESULTS, HOWEVER IT IS TIME CONSUMING AND SOMEWHAT EXPENSIVE.

OTHER FACTORS EFFECTING COLOR AND COMPATIBILITY ARE: ANNEALING TIME, HOW "THICK" THE COLOR IS APPLIED, WHERE IT IS APPLIED, WHETHER THE COLOR IS CASED (SANDWICHED BETWEEN LAYERS OF CLEAR) OR NOT, AND IF IT'S COMPATIBLE WITH ANY OTHER COLORS YOU MIGHT BE USING.

Y'KNOW THERE'S NOTHING WORSE THAN SWEATIN' AN' SLAVIN' OVER A PIECE FOR BETTER THAN AN HOUR, ONLY TO HAVE IT EXPLODE IN THE ANNEALER BECAUSE THE COLOR YOU USED DIDN'T 'FIT.'!

MANUFACTURED COLOR COMES IN MANY DIFFERENT FORMS FROM MANY DIFFERENT MANUFACTURERS WORLD-WIDE. IT IS COMMONLY OFFERED IN **ROD**, **FRIT**, AND **POWDERED** FORM. NEARLY EVERY COLOR OF THE RAINBOW IS AVAILABLE. SOME COLORS ARE NATURALLY MORE EXPENSIVE THAN OTHERS, BASED IN LARGE PART TO THE METALS / METALLIC OXIDES USED IN IT'S CREATION.

THE METALS ALSO EFFECT THE MELTING POINT AND **WORKABILITY** OF EACH COLOR. SOME COLORS, SUCH AS WHITE, REFLECT THE HEAT MORE AND CONSEQUENTLY IT BEHAVES MORE STIFF, WHEREAS BLACK TENDS TO **ABSORB** THE HEAT AND STAYS SOFTER, LONGER. AND AGAIN, IT ALL DEPENDS ON HOW YOU USE IT...

using color

IF YOU WANT AN OBJECT TO BE A SPECIFIC COLOR, YOU CAN USE EITHER **ROD**, **FRIT**, OR **POWDER** TO COLOR IT — EACH HAVING THEIR OWN DISTINCT RESULTS OR EFFECTS.

THE VISUAL **DENSITY** OF THE PIECE'S COLOR SCHEME IS DETERMINED BY THE COLOR-TO-CLEAR RATIO, i.e. THE MORE "KUGLER" YOU USE, THE **DARKER** OR MORE **INTENSE** THE RESULTING PIECE WILL BE.

A WORD OF CAUTION:

BLOWING COLORED GLASS, ESPECIALLY OPAQUE ONES, CAN MAKE THE PROCESS DIFFICULT AND FRUSTRATING. IT IS HARD TO TELL EXACTLY WHERE THE BUBBLE IS, AND HOW THIN THE GLASS IS GETTING. YOU HAVE TO RELY ON SUBTLE **CLUES** TO GUIDE YOU, SUCH AS LOOKING FOR A **BULGE** IN THE FORM TO INDICATE THE BUBBLE'S POSITION. IT IS A TECHNIQUE WHICH TAKES SOME TIME AND PRACTICE TO DEVELOP. THE SAD-BUT-TRUE FEELING IS THAT IT IS SUCH A WASTE OF TIME AND EXPENSIVE COLOR.

IT IS FOR THIS REASON THAT MANY INSTRUCTORS PROHIBIT THEIR STUDENTS FROM USING COLOR RIGHT OFF THE BAT. COLOR CAN EASILY COMPLICATE THINGS AND MESS YOU UP. IT'S BEST TO HAVE SOME COMMAND OVER EXECUTING FORMS IN CLEAR GLASS BEFORE EMBARKING INTO THE COLOR REALM, OR SO THE THEORY GOES...

ON THE OTHERHAND, CONTINUALLY BLOWING CLEAR GLASS ALL-THE-TIME CAN SEEM TEDIOUS AND BORING. YOU NEED A LITTLE COLOR TO SPICE THINGS UP A LITTLE. AND Y'KNOW, EVEN THE UGLIEST TURDS YOU MAKE IN COLORED GLASS CAN WIND-UP LOOKING BEAUTIFUL...

COLORED ROD CAN BE USED IN SEVERAL DIFFERENT APPLICATIONS. YOU CAN USE IT TO COLOR YOUR ENTIRE PIECE, OR APPLY THE COLOR AS **TRAILS OR BITS** TO ACCENT CERTAIN PARTS.

IF YOU WANT YOUR WHOLE PIECE TO BE ONE COLOR, PURPLE FOR EXAMPLE, YOU CAN USE A CHUNK OF ROD (PURPLE OF COURSE): PICK IT UP ON A BLOWPIPE, GATHER CLEAR OVER IT AND BLOW IT OUT TO ACHIEVE A UNIFORM DISTRIBUTION OF COLOR.

YOUR FIRST STEP IS TO CUT THE COLOR BAR. WEAR SAFETY GLASSES WHILE DOING THIS, AS FLYING HAZARDS ARE **COMMON**. SET THE ROD ON THE KUGLER CUTTER (IF YOU DON'T HAVE A KUGLER CUTTER - A HAMMER AND CHISEL WORKS THE SAME). LINE UP WHERE YOU WANT THE PIECE TO BREAK OVER THE CHISEL AND SMACK IT FIRM WITH THE CUTTING HAMMER.

IT MAY TAKE AN EXTRA WHACK OR TWO TO GET A CHUNK TO POP-OFF. A 2" - 3" CHUNK SHOULD BE SUFFICIENT.

— CHUNK —

① **CUT THE COLOR BAR**

② **PREHEAT THE COLOR IN A KILN.**

③ **PICK-UP THE COLOR ON A PRE-HEATED BLOWPIPE**

78 YOUR NEXT STEP IS TO PREHEAT THE COLOR IN A KILN. THIS INSURES THE COLOR WILL STICK TO YOUR BLOWPIPE AND IT WON'T BLOW-**UP** INTO LITTLE BITS WHEN YOU GO TO HEAT IT UP.

ASK THE INSTRUCTOR OR SHOP TECHNICIAN FOR A DEMO ON HOW-TO PREHEAT YOUR COLOR BAR, IF YOU ARE UNFAMILIAR ON HOW TO DO SO. IT SEEMS AS THOUGH EVERY STUDIO HAS IT'S OWN SPECIAL WAY OF ACCOMPLISHING THIS...

WHEN YOU'RE SET AN' READY TO BLOW — TAKE A PRE-HEATED BLOWPIPE (BE SURE THAT IT'S GOOD N' GLOWIN' RED HOT) AND GENTLY PRESS DOWN ON YOUR PREHEATED COLOR. IT SHOULD ADHERE WELL TO THE TIP. TAKE IT OVER TO THE GLORY HOLE AS-QUICK-AS-YOU CAN. COLORS COOL-OFF RAPIDLY AND CAN CRACK OR EVEN EXPLODE ON YOU IF YOU DON'T GET THEM TO THE HEAT QUICK ENOUGH.

HEAT THE COLOR THOROUGHLY. YOU NEED TO GET IT AS HOT N' SOUPY AS THE GLASS IN THE FURNACE IN ORDER TO GET YOUR STARTER BUBBLE BLOWN INTO IT EVENLY. AS SOON AS IT GETS GOOD N' HOT, SHAPE UP THE COLOR BY MARVERING THE GLASS ON-CENTER AND POINTING IN UP A BIT.

NEXT, HANG THE PIPE OVER THE BACK EDGE OF THE MARVER AND PUFF YOUR STARTER BUBBLE.

PAY ATTENTION!. WATCH FOR SIGNS OF EXPANSION BY SIGHTING-DOWN THE LENGTH OF THE BLOWPIPE AND WATCHING FOR THE SIDES OF THE COLOR TO INFLATE AS YOU BLOW. SOME COLORS ARE VERY SOFT AND THEY CAN BLOW-OUT IN THE WINK OF AN EYE!

IF YOU BLOW-OUT YOUR COLOR TOO THIN, IT MAY BE IMPOSSIBLE TO **GATHER**-OVER WITHOUT COLLAPSING IT'S **BUBBLE**. SO YOUR BEST BET IS TO KEEP THE STARTER BUBBLE ON THE THICK-SIDE. YOU ONLY NEED A LITTLE BUBBLE IN THE COLOR TO MAKE SURE THAT IT WILL BLOW OUT OKAY AFTER YOU GATHER OVER IT.

ALLOW THE COLOR TO COOL SUFFICIENTLY BEFORE YOU ATTEMPT TO GATHER OVER IT. ALL TRACES OF HEAT (THAT ORANGE COLOR/TINT) SHOULD BE GONE. YOU DON'T WANT TO LOSE ANY OF IT WHILE YOU'RE IN THE FURNACE GATHERING ~ CAUSE YOU RISK **CONTAMINATING** THE WHOLE BATCH WITH YOUR COLOR.

BE SURE TO GATHER COMPLETELY OVER THE COLOR AND UP ON TO THE BLOWPIPE AN INCH OR TWO TO HELP ESTABLISH YOUR MOILE AND INSURE AN EVEN DISTRIBUTION OF GLASS.

FROM THIS POINT ON, IT'S PRETTY MUCH BUSINESS-AS-USUAL. SHAPE, BLOW, GATHER, SHAPE, BLOW, NECK, REHEAT REHEAT REHEAT etc. ONLY YOU NEED TO BE MORE AWARE OF HOW THAT BUBBLE BLOWS-OUT SINCE THE COLOR HAS SUCH TREMENDOUS INFLUENCE ON IT'S ABILITY TO HOLD OR REFLECT THE HEAT.

IN OTHER WORDS➔ **FOCUS** — AND PAY ATTENTION!

USING COLOR BAR CAN GIVE YOU THE MOST EVEN DISTRIBUTION OF COLOR THROUGHOUT A BLOWN PIECE, BUT IT IS NOT THE QUICK-EST METHOD OF APPLICATION. FRITS AND POWDERS TEND TO BE MORE IMMEDIATE, IF NOT SEEMINGLY EASIER TO DEAL WITH. MORE ON THAT IN A MINUTE...

COLOR BAR IS USEFUL FOR APPLYING COLORED BITS, TRAILS AND LIP WRAPS TOO! THE COLORS MAY BE PICKED-UP ON PUNTIES AND ADDED TO YOUR PIECE AT VIRTUALLY ANY STAGE OF THE PROCESS.

IF YOU TAKE A BAR OF COLOR AND CRUSH IT INTO LITTLE BITS YOU END-UP WITH COLORED **FRIT**. IF YOU THEN GRIND THAT FRIT INTO FLOUR, YOU END UP WITH COLORED **POWDER**.

THE FIRST THING YOU NEED TO KNOW ABOUT **FRIT** IS THAT IT'S EASY-TO-USE. THE FIRST THING YOU NEED TO KNOW ABOUT **POWDER** IS THAT IT'S HAZARDOUS TO BREATHE, SO #1 DON'T! AND NUMBER TWO: BE CAREFUL IN HOW YOU HANDLE AND APPLY THE STUFF.

I PERSONALLY LIKE TO USE **FRIT** BECAUSE IT'S EASY TO APPLY, EASY TO CLEAN-UP, AND I LIKE THE WAY IT COLORS MY GLASS. IT MAY NOT APPEAR AS DENSE OR CONCENTRATED AS YOU MIGHT GET WITH POWDERS OR COLOR BAR - BUT AGAIN IT'S DEPENDENT ON HOW YOU USE IT.

FRIT IS AVAILABLE FROM YOUR LOCAL COLOR DISTRIBUTOR IN ALL COLORS AND IN VARIOUS SIZES - FROM TINY, GRANULAR PIECES TO POPCORN-KERNAL-SIZED 'CHUNKS'. YOU CAN, OF COURSE SMASH-UP YOUR OWN COLOR BAR AND CREATE FRIT THAT WAY - BUT IT IS KINDA MESSY, NOISY, AND DIFFICULT TO PRODUCE A CONSISTENT SIZE, IN ANY GREAT QUANTITY.

THE MOST COMMON WAY TO APPLY FRIT IS TO ROLL YOUR HOT GLASS INTO IT. IF YOUR GLASS IS HOT, THE FRIT WILL STICK TO IT. IF YOUR GLASS IS TOO COLD, FRIT WON'T STICK - period. THEREFORE, THE HOTTER THE GLASS IS - THE MORE FRIT WILL STICK TO IT. BASED ON THAT AXIOM, WE CAN ASSUME THAT A GATHER OF GLASS TAKEN DIRECTLY FROM THE FURNACE AND ROLLED INTO SOME FRIT WILL HAVE THE GREATEST ASSURANCE THAT THE COLOR WILL STICK. INDEED, THAT IS THE CASE! - AND IT'S THE BEST AND FASTEST WAY OF COLORING YOUR PIECE WITH FRIT.

SOME GAFFERS WILL LAY THEIR FRIT OUT ON THE MARVER AND ROLL THE HOT GLASS IN IT. YOU KILL TWO BIRDS WITH ONE STONE BY SHAPING N' MARVERING AND PICKING-UP COLOR AT THE SAME TIME! THIS IS ESPECIALLY CON-VENIENT IF YOU WANT TO SELECTIVELY APPLY THE COLOR BY ROLLING SAY JUST THE TOP HALF OR BOTTOM HALF OF THE PIECE IN COLOR AND LEAVING THE REST CLEAR. OR, IF YOU WANT SOME BANDS OF COLOR → YOU COULD LAY-OUT YOUR FRIT IN STRIPS - SIDE-BY-SIDE AND ROLL THEM ON THAT WAY.

PICKING UP FRIT OFF THE MARVER

FRIT IS ALSO CONVENIENT FOR COLORING HANDLES, BITS AND TRAILS TOO! YOU CAN USE ALOT OF FRIT TO FULLY COAT AND COLOR THE BIT, OR ONLY USE A LITTLE TO ACHIEVE A MOTTLED SURFACE.

FRIT CAN OFFER SOME INTERESTING TEXTURE AS WELL. YOU CAN LEAVE IT ROUGH AND BUMBY, OR HEAT IT UP AND MELT IT IN. THE MORE THAT YOU HEAT AND TOOL THE SURFACE, THE LESS PRONOUNCED THE TEXTURE WILL BE.

SOME FASCINATING PATTERNS MAY BE ACHIEVED BY COLORING YOUR BUBBLE WITH FRIT OR POWDER AND BLOWING IT INTO THE OPTIC MOLD. THE MOLD CAUSES THE COLOR TO BE CONCENTRATED IN THE RIBS. WHEN YOU BLOW IT OUT, YOU OBTAIN A VARIAGATED PATTERN. MANY VARIATIONS ON THIS TECHNIQUE ARE POSSIBLE IF YOU TWIST THE OPTIC PATTERN, AND/OR COLOR THE FORM YET ONE MORE TIME, OR STUFF THE MOLD YET ONE MORE TIME, TWIST THE PATTERN AGAIN OR.... WELL, THE SKY'S THE LIMIT!

80 POWDERS CAN BE ROLLED-ON (JUST LIKE FRIT,) RIGHT OFF THE MARVER. OR, SOME GLASSWORKERS PREFER STAINLESS STEEL BOWLS, OR COOKIE SHEETS, OR BREAD TINS AS RECEPTACLES FOR THEIR POWDERS. THAT WAY, THE COLORS ARE EASILY SEPARATED AND TOTALLY ACCESSIBLE, IN ADDITION TO OFFERING A CONVENIENT FORM TO SHAPE YOUR BIT IN.

SOME STUDIOS PROHIBIT THE USE OF POWDERS ON THE MARVER, FOR FEAR OF CONTAMINATION, AND THE FACT THAT IT'S MESSY, NOT-TOO-MENTION UNHEALTHY TO WORK WITH, (WITHOUT TAKING CERTAIN PRECAUTIONS.) A SEPARATE SPACE IS OFTEN DEDICATED SPECIFICALLY FOR THIS PURPOSE.

POWDERS SHOULD BE APPLIED IN A WELL, VENTILATED AREA. UNDER THE HOOD, (FOR EXAMPLE) THERE OUGHT TO BE ENOUGH SUCTION TO DRAW AWAY ANY NASTIES YOU MIGHT ENCOUNTER BY ROLLING-IN POWDERS. YOU CERTAINLY DON'T WANT TO BE TAKING ANY BIG WHIFFS OF COLOR AS ITS BEING MELTED ONTO THE SURFACE! ☠ YUCK! NASTY!

SPECIAL **POWDERING BOOTHS** - WHICH FILTER AWAY AIRBORN ☠ PARTICULATES AND FUMES ARE DESIREABLE IN SITUATIONS WHERE THERE'S EXTENSIVE USE OF COLORED POWDERS.

ANOTHER WAY TO APPLY POWDERS IS TO DUST THEM ONTO THE SURFACE OF THE GLASS. IT'S EASIEST WHEN YOU WORK WITH AN ASSISTANT. WHOEVER DOES THE DUSTING SHOULD WEAR A DUST MASK, OR BETTER STILL, AN APPROVED RESPIRATOR (FOR PROTECTION.).

YOU CAN SIFT COLORS ON WITH KITCHEN STRAINERS. SIMPLY LOAD 'EM UP WITH THE DESIRED COLOR AND WAIT.

AFTER THE GAFFER TAKES A SOLID REHEAT, THEY POSITION THEIR PIECE IN THE POWDERING ZONE (MAKE SURE THE VENT FAN IS "ON"). A YOKE CAN HELP STABILIZE THE PIPE WHILE DUSTING. THE PIECE SHOULD BE POSITIONED OVER A CATCH-PAN AND UNDERNEATH THE STRAINER.

THE ASSISTANT SHAKES OR TAPS THE STRAINER TO RELEASE THE POWDER AND VOILA - YOU'RE COLORING THE PIECE! YOU CAN GET PRETTY ACCURATE WITH THE PLACEMENT OF YOUR POWDERS BY CHANGING ANGLES AND POSITIONS, AND/OR BY USING SMALLER STRAINERS. AGAIN, THE HOTTER THE GLASS IS, THE MORE THAT'LL STICK TO IT.

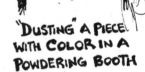

"DUSTING" A PIECE WITH COLOR IN A POWDERING BOOTH

FOR PRACTICE:

MIX N' MATCH VARIOUS COLOR TECHNIQUES. TRY SOME COLOR TESTS. KEEP THE PIECES SIMPLE IN TERMS OF SHAPE AND FORM. THAT WAY YOU CAN EXPLORE MANY MORE COMBINATIONS WITHOUT SACRIFICING TIME ON COMPLICATED FORMS. SEE WHAT TRANSPARENT COLORS DO COMPARED TO OPAQUE ONES. TAKE NOTES AS WHAT DOES WHAT.

PRACTICE MAKING A BASIC VESSEL WITH A CHUNK OF COLOR BAR. REMAKE THE SAME VESSEL, ONLY THIS TIME TRY DOING IT WITH FRIT. THEN SEE WHAT EFFECT USING POWDER HAS, REMAKING THE VESSEL A THIRD TIME. COMPARE AND CONTRAST THE RESULTS AND BECOME A BETTER GLASSBLOWER FOR IT!

ALSO, CHECK OUT A **CHIHULY** BOOK FROM THE LIBRARY. IN IT YOU'LL FIND SOME WINNING COMBINATIONS OF COLOR. WRITE THEM DOWN. THEY'RE EASY TO DECIPHER - YOU ONLY NEED TO READ THE TITLE OF THE PIECE, USUALLY! NEVERTHELESS, THEY'RE BEAUTIFUL!

SOME OF THE BEST EXAMPLES OF POWDERED GLASS HANDLING MAY BE SEEN IN THE WORKS OF **WILLIAM MORRIS** AND TEAM (IN ADDITION TO SOME OF THE BEST HOT GLASS SCULPTING AROUND!) CHECK THEM OUT TOO!

The Lip Wrap

A TRIED-AND-TRUE METHOD FOR COMPLETING YOUR VESSEL WITH A TOUCH OF COLOR — THE "WRIP WRAP" CAN BE A TRICKY BUGGER BECAUSE OF THE NUMBER OF VARIABLES INVOLVED IN IT'S SUCCESSFUL EXECUTION.

FIRST AND FOREMOST IS PROPER PREPARATION OF THE VESSEL'S LIP. AFTER THE PIECE IS TRANSFERRED, THE LIP IS HEATED AND PADDLED SMOOTH. YOU MAY USE THE JACKS TO OPEN THE MOUTH SLIGHTLY, BUT MORE IMPORTANTLY YOU NEED TO CONCENTRATE ON EVENING-OUT THE LIP INSIDE AND OUT. **DO NOT OPEN THE VESSEL ANY MORE THAN YOU HAVE TO AT THIS POINT.** IF NECESSARY, YOU MAY WANT TO TRIM THE LIP OF THE PIECE PRIOR TO APPLYING THE LIP WRAP. IT'S A GAFFER'S CHOICE.

YOUR ASSISTANT SHOULD HAVE THE COLOR HEATED AND MARVERED TO A TAPERED POINT ON A PUNTY.

HE/SHE BRINGS IT TO YOU FROM BEHIND THE BENCH AND YOU GRIP THE PUNTY-CLOSE TO THE COLOR WITH YOUR SHEARS.

WHILE ROTATING THE PIECE (AWAY FROM YOU) WITH YOUR LEFT HAND, TOUCH UP THE COLORED BIT -GENTLY!- TO THE LIP OF THE VESSEL ~ SIMULTANEOUSLY TRAVELING WITH THE PIECE ⇒ MAINTAING YOUR DISTANCE (ca 2"-3") ⇒ ALLOWING THE ROLLING MOTION TO P U L L THE COLOR OFF THE PUNTY AND THREAD RIGHT ONTO THE LIP.

TRY AND GET THE COLOR TO GO ON AS EVEN AS POSSIBLE. SOMETIMES YOU HAVE TO ROLL THE PIPE FASTER OR SLOWER, OR BRING THE COLOR/PUNTY CLOSER OR FARTHER AWAY TO COMPENSATE FOR IRREGULLARITIES WHICH MIGHT OCCUR. THAT'S WHY PROPER HEATING IN THE BIT IS SO CRUCIAL TO A SUCCESSFUL LIP WRAP. YOU DON'T WANT THE COLOR TO COME-OFF IN AN UNSIGHTLY BLOB (DUE TO INCOMPLETE HEATING OF THE COLOR)!

NEARING COMPLETION OF THE ENTIRE LIP, YOU CAN QUICKLY ROLL THE VESSEL AND PULL BACK→DOWN AND OFF WITH THE PUNTY TO FINISH THE TRAIL AND BREAK IT FREE. OR SOME GAFFERS PREFER TO JUST SNIP THE TRAIL/COLOR CLOSE TO THE LIP WITH THE SHEARS.

LIPWRAPS TAKE PRACTICE! THE COLOR MUST BE HEATED AND SHAPED JUST RIGHT. YOUR VESSEL SHOULD BE WARM, NOT TOO HOT, NOT TOO COLD. YOU MUST ALSO CONCENTRATE ON HOW THAT COLOR IS COMING OFF AND JUST HOW FAST TO TURN THE PIECE TO MAKE IT EVEN, AND KNOWING WHEN TO STOP!

ONCE YOU MANAGE TO WRAP-THE-LIP WITH COLOR, YOU CAN REHEAT IT, (MELTING THE COLOR IN,) AND PROCEED TO OPEN AND PADDLE THE LIP SMOOTH.

TURN

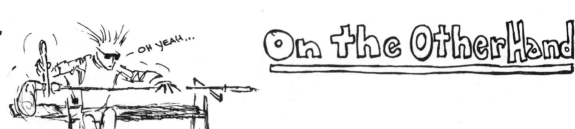

— OH YEAH...

On the Other Hand

ALL OF THE TECHNIQUES THAT HAVE BEEN ADDRESSED UP UNTIL THIS POINT HAVE CONCENTRATED ON WHAT'S HAPPENING ON THE END OF THE "STICK." LET'S NOT OVER-LOOK THE VITALLY IMPORTANT ROLE THAT THE LEFT HAND IS PLAYING IN THE CREATION OF PHENOMENAL GLASS.

SOMETIMES THIS MOLTEN MANIPULATION CAN FEEL ALOT LIKE RUBBING YOUR BELLY, PATTING YOUR HEAD, READING THE LATEST JOURNAL ON FUNDAMENTAL PHYSICS, DISCUSSING GLOBAL WARMING AND THINKING ABOUT YOUR HOT DATE TONIGHT — ALL AT THE SAME TIME! IT'S NOT THAT EASY! AND, OF COURSE, IT TAKES PRACTICE TO DO IT WELL.

TRAINING YOUR LEFT HAND TO ROLL THE PIPE SMOOTH N' **FLUIDLY** IS A VITAL STEP TO SUCCESSFUL GLASSMAKING. LIKE LEARNING TO WALK, IT TAKES AN INITIATION PERIOD TO LEARN: TIMING, BALANCE, AND MOVEMENT BEFORE IT SEEMS 'NATURAL' — AND YOU DON'T HAVE TO THINK ABOUT IT.

Tip: WATCH OTHER ADVANCED GLASSWORKERS WHENEVER YOU CAN. PAY PARTICULAR ATTENTION TO THEIR HANDS. IT CAN PROVIDE YOU WITH MORE VISUAL CLUES AS TO HOW TO GO ABOUT TURNING THE PIPE, CORRECTLY HOLDING TOOLS AND SUBTLE THINGS WHICH MAKE LIFE EASIER.

TRY THE OPEN-PALM APPROACH TO ROLL THE PIPE ON THE BENCH. SOME PEOPLE WILL ROLL FROM THEIR FINGERTIPS TO THEIR ELBOWS! BUT MOST WILL JUST USE THE OPEN FACE OF THEIR HAND TO CONTROL THE PIPE BACK-AND-FORTH. ONCE YOU DEVELOP THE SKILL AND THE WORKING RHYTHM, YOU'LL BE ABLE TO ROLL THE PIPE FAIRLY CONSISTENTLY, WITHOUT MUCH EFFORT.

WHEN MORE FINESSE IS NEEDED TRY THE CRAWL OR WALK METHOD, WHERE YOUR FINGERS ALTERNATE THE FUNCTION OF TURNING AND ACTING AS A GUIDE IN STABILIZ-ING THE ROTATION OF THE PIPE. YOUR THUMB BALANCES OUT THE PUSHING AND PULLING ACTION THAT THE FINGERTIPS INITIATE. IN SOME INSTANCES, THE THUMB IS ENTIRELY RESPONSIBLE FOR TURNING THE PIPE AND THE FINGERTIPS HELP GUIDE IT ALONG.

FOR PRACTICE:

BESIDES WATCHING OTHER GLASS-BLOWERS AT WORK, THE BEST WAY TO LEARN HOW-TO ROLL THE PIPE IS BY ACTUALLY DOING IT! (YOU DON'T EVEN NEED HOT GLASS FOR THIS!) AT AN OPEN BENCH, PRACTICE ROLLING A PIPE WITH YOUR LEFT HAND.

TRY BOTH TECHNIQUES — GET A FEEL FOR IT! DO IT WITH YOUR EYES CLOSED!

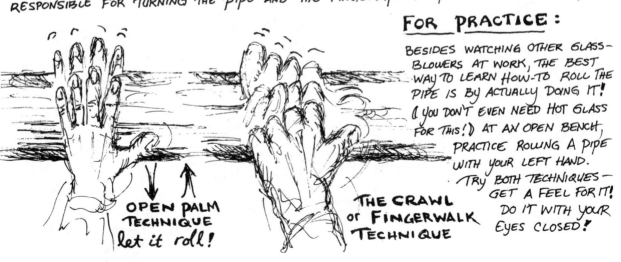

OPEN PALM TECHNIQUE
let it roll!

THE CRAWL or FINGERWALK TECHNIQUE

Troubleshooting

"TAKE THIS SUCKER"

UGLY

As comprehensive as I've tried to write this manual, there are always a few things which seem to selectively slip-off the conscious train-of-thought. Hopefully, they will reappear somewhere within this section.

This glassblowing activity involves a plethora of skills and techniques. Unfortunately most people can't practice every day. Because of the constraints of limited bench time - you're forced to concentrate and try to remember everything you have learned all at once. Sometimes it's a bit too much for a young devoloping glass mind to handle ↝ **MISTAKES HAPPEN,** and fortunately you can learn from them.

Nevertheless, notwithstanding, henceforth this section exists primarily for those people who seem to have recurring nightmares with a particular technique or **dilemma.** For example, upon close examination of the "stuff" that comes out of the annealer, with a touch of disdain, you may discover "the bottoms broke out!" or "the lips are too thick", or "why does this piece have annealer face?"...

There are answers and solutions to nearly every problem that you will encounter. Don't hesitate in seeking-out the advice of more-skilled glassworkers as well. Quite often they've had to overcome the same hurdles as you, and more-often-than-not, they'll offer-up a quick cure for whatever ails you, or that which you seek. Granted, it may take you weeks or even years to perfect, but at least you'll know what to do.

So, in the following pages are some symtoms and solutions for some of the more common problems facing glassworkers during their formative days, weeks, months... years... etc. Read through them for advice on how to avoid certain calamities, or how to cure those recurring afflictions.

Last, but not least — **you**, yourself may have to don a 'thinking-cap' and brainstorm your way to the correct solution ↝ should you not find it here. Oftentimes, it feels more rewarding when you come up with the right answer all on your lonesome ↝ especially if it works! and... believe it or not, that's how many techniques were learned or improved upon — by people like yourself saying **"what if..."**? or **"how come..."**? Who knows.... maybe by asking the right question - you may uncover a whole 'nother realm of glassmaking that nobody's even thought of...

"MY BUBBLE WON'T STAY CENTERED",

or

"MY BUBBLE NEVER BLOWS-OUT STRAIGHT."

and the instructor made it look so easy!

FIRST, CHECK YOUR BLOWPIPE. IS IT STRAIGHT? ALWAYS ROLL IT ON THE BENCH PRIOR TO YOUR FIRST GATHER. IF IT'S BENT, YOU WILL HAVE A DIFFICULT TIME GETTING THINGS ON-CENTER.

SECOND, IF YOUR STARTER BUBBLE (OR FIRST GATHER) IS UNEVEN IN EITHER MASS OR TEMPERATURE, IT WILL BLOW OUT FUNKY. ADDITIONAL GATHERS ON TOP OF AN UNEVEN BUBBLE ONLY ADD TO OR COMPOUND THE DILEMMA - NOT CURE IT! PLEASE REFER TO PAGES 20-21 FOR MORE INFO.

THIRD, KEEP YOUR EYE ON THE GLASS AT ALL TIMES! IF IT'S FALLING OFF-CENTER, STOP IT FOR A SECOND ON THE HIGH-SPOT AND ALLOW IT TO FALL BACK TO THE AXIS. PLUS, USE HEAT-NOT FORCE-TO CORRECT THE PROBLEM.

"I SMELL BURNING HAIR EVERY TIME I PUT SOMETHING IN THE ANNEALER".

NUMBER ONE: STOP INSERTING YOUR HEAD IN THE ANNEALER WHEN LOADING IT! MAKE SURE YOUR ARMS ARE COVERED AND YOUR HAIR IS TIED BACK, OR PROTECTED WITH A BANDANA OR SOMETHING.

WITHOUT PROTECTION, YOU CAN GET A FREE (BUT POORLY EXECUTED) HAIRCUT THAT SMELLS REALLY BAD- AND LOOKS EVEN WORSE!

SOME PEOPLE ALSO WEAR FULL-FACE SHIELDS WHEN BOXING PIECES — A GOOD IDEA ESPECIALLY IF YOU HAVE FACIAL HAIR WHICH YOU WOULD LIKE TO KEEP.

"MY ASSISTANT ALWAYS SCREWS THINGS UP!"

Butthead

"Now look what you made me do!"

CONGRATULATIONS! YOU'VE DISCOVERED THE FIRST POSTULATE OF TEAMWORK:

"IT'S ALWAYS THE ASSISTANT'S FAULT" (WHEN THINGS DON'T GO RIGHT...).

IN ALL ACTUALITY IT'S REALLY THE GAFFER WHO'S TO BLAME WHEN THINGS DON'T GO EXACTLY AS "PLANNED". IT IS THEIR RESPONSIBILITY TO TRAIN THE TEAM RIGHT IN THE FIRST PLACE.

THERE'S NO TIME TO READ MINDS WHILE BLOWING GLASS. GET A CLUE -

GIVE A CLUE

SKETCH IT OUT!

SYMPTOM

"MY BUBBLE WON'T BLOW OUT AT ALL — NO MATTER HOW HARD I TRY."

SOLUTION

FIRST, DID YOU CHECK THE PIPE (BY BLOWING THROUGH IT) BEFORE YOUR FIRST GATHER? IF THE PIPE WAS CLOGGED, IT WOULD EASILY PREVENT YOU FROM BLOWING ANY KIND OF BUBBLE IN IT. SEE PAGES **10-11** FOR INFORMATION ON HOW-TO UNCLOG YOUR PIPES.

SECOND, IT IS POSSIBLE THAT YOU ARE NOT GETTING THE GLASS HOT ENOUGH TO BLOW INTO IT, OR MORE-THAN-LIKELY YOU ARE CHILLING THE GLASS TOO MUCH RIGHT OFF THE BAT. REMEMBER:

HOT GOOD — COLD BAD.

SOMETIMES JUST A BIT OF EXTRA HEAT IS ALL YOU NEED TO BLOW EASIER, OR TRY THE BLOW AND CAP METHOD:

"BLOW AND CAP" OR "CAP AND BLOW"

WHATEVER YOU CALL IT — IT MAY MAKE YOUR LIFE ALOT EASIER WHEN IT COMES TO STARTING YOUR BEGINNING BUBBLE. IT TAKES SOME PEOPLE A WHILE TO GET THE KNACK OF THIS TECHNIQUE, SO DON'T BE DISCOURAGED IF IT DOESN'T WORK FOR YOU RIGHT FROM THE START.

#1. GET YOUR GATHER OF GLASS. **#2.** SHAPE THE GLASS QUICKLY, AIR MARVERING AS MUCH AS YOU CAN, SO YOU DON'T ROB YOUR GLASS OF IT'S ORIGINAL HEAT. **#3.** ONCE YOU OBTAIN THE CORRECT SHAPE — STICK YOUR THUMB AND BLOWPIPE IN YOUR MOUTH.
#4. PUFF HARD INTO THE PIPE AND IMMEDIATELY SLIP YOUR THUMB OVER THE PIPE'S MOUTH-PIECE TO CAP (OR TRAP) THE AIR <u>IN</u> THE BLOWPIPE.

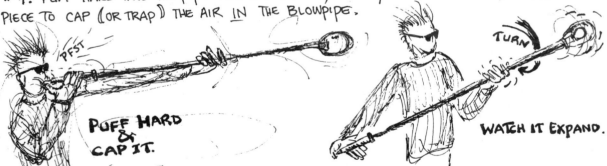

PFST

PUFF HARD & CAP IT.

TURN

WATCH IT EXPAND.

#5 KEEP YOUR THUMB ON THE END OF THE PIPE TO MAINTAIN A PERFECT SEAL. THE "COMPRESSED AIR" (YOUR PUFF) WILL CAUSE THE GLASS TO EXPAND — LIKE MAGIC — IF AND ONLY IF THE GLASS IS HOT ENOUGH AND IF YOU MANAGED TO GET A GOOD PUFF TRAPPED IN THE PIPE. **#6.** KEEP YOUR EYES ON THE GLASS AND <u>WAIT</u> FOR SIGNS OF EXPANSION. IT MAY TAKE SEVERAL SECONDS TO TAKE EFFECT. AS SOON AS THE BUBBLE BLOWS OUT TO A SIZE YOU CAN DEAL WITH — TAKE YOUR THUMB OFF THE END OF THE BLOWPIPE TO HALT ANY FURTHER EXPANSION! IT CAN EASILY OVERINFLATE YOUR BUBBLE, FORCING YOU TO DO IT ALL OVER AGAIN. **#7.** YOU MAY NEED TO RESHAPE AND BLOW YOUR BUBBLE A LITTLE MORE JUST TO GET EVERYTHING "LOOKING RIGHT."

WATCH OTHER (EXPERIENCED) GLASSBLOWERS PERFORM THIS TRICK FOR ADDITIONAL CLUES, AND **PRACTICE, PRACTICE, PRACTICE** UNTIL YOU GET THE HANG OF IT!

SYMPTOM   SOLUTION

"MY GATHERS COME OUT UNEVEN"
OR
"MY GATHERS ARE ALL LUMPY"

UNEVEN AND LUMPY GATHERS USUALLY ARE THE RESULT OF INCOMPLETE ROTATIONS OF THE PIPE WHILE IN THE MOLTEN GLASS. QUITE OFTEN IT STEMS FROM A PERSON BEING INTIMIDATED BY THE FEROCIOUS HEAT OF THE FURNACE AND THE DESIRE TO ESCAPE FROM IT'S INFERNAL BREATH AS QUICKLY AS POSSIBLE!   THERE A 3 BASIC WAYS TO INSURE THAT YOU MAKE COMPLETE REVOLUTIONS IN THE GLASS WHILE GATHERING:

1. LEARN WHERE TO STAND WHILE GATHERING, SO THAT YOU DON'T GET FRIED (OR JUST ENDURE THE PAIN.).

2. SEEK OUT A HEAT SHIELD OR CLOSE DOWN THE FURNACE DOOR (IF POSSIBLE) WHILE GATHERING

3. HAVE AN ASSITANT DO THE GATHERS FOR YOU.

" MY GATHERS COME OUT SO SMALL "
OR
" I CAN'T SEEM TO GET ENOUGH GLASS "

SEVERAL THINGS MIGHT BE TO BLAME HERE. THE ANGLE AT WHICH YOU EXIT THE FURNACE AT, HAS TREMENDOUS IMPACT ON HOW MUCH GLASS YOU WILL END-UP WITH ON THE END OF YOUR BLOWPIPE, AFTER GATHERING. IF YOU TILT THE PIPE DOWN — THE GLASS WILL TRAIL-OFF - BACK INTO THE FURNACE → REDUCING THE AMOUNT OF THE GATHER.

IF YOU WANT MORE GLASS, DRIVE FORWARD DURING THE GATHER AND FINISH IN A HORIZONTAL FASHION, OR TILT THE HEAD OF THE PIPE UP SOMEWHAT AS YOU EXIT THE FURNACE.

ALSO, IF FOR WHATEVER REASON YOU STOP ROTATING THE PIPE DURING THE GATHER — YOU'LL WINDUP WITH A SMALLER GATHER. YOU MUST KEEP THE PIPE TURNING AT ALL TIMES.

FINALLY, THE FURNACE MAY TURNED-UP SO HIGH N' HOT THAT IT'S IMPOSSIBLE FOR ANYONE TO MAKE LARGE GATHERS. GRIMACE AND BEAR IT, DIP A FEW MORE TIMES...

"WHEN I GO HOME AT NIGHT, I STINK REALLY BAD, I HAVE CALLOUSES ON MY PALMS AND DIRTY BLACK STUFF IN MY FINGERS AND CLOTHES. WHAT DO I DO?"

STOP WHINING.
THESE ARE JUST A FEW SIGNS THAT YOU HAVE BITTEN BY THE GLASS BUG. WEAR IT, ENDURE IT AND SMILE WITH PRIDE.
YOU'RE A GLASSBLOWER!

"MY GLASS IS UGLY"

TWO POSSIBLE PROBLEMS HERE:
BLAME THE DESIGNER, OR
BLAME THE GAFFER!!

O.K. I KNOW... SOMETIMES IT TAKES A
BIT OF A STRETCH OF THE IMAGINATION, BUT TRY
TO SEEK OUT THE BEAUTY IN ALL THAT YOU MAKE.
IF THAT DOESN'T WORK, YOU CAN EITHER CHANGE
OR ENHANCE THE DESIGN - AND TRY BETTER NEXT
TIME, OR JUST DEAL WITH WHAT YOU'VE GOT.
BELIEVE ME, COLDWORKING CAN DO WONDERS!

'COURSE, IF IT'S REALLY BUTT-UGLY YOU CAN AL-
WAYS ONLOAD IT ON GRANDMA.... SHE'S BOUND TO
STILL HAVE SOME WINDOW-SILL SPACE SOMEWHERE...

"MY PIECES ARE ALL TOO THICK,"
(FLINTSTONE-WARE SYNDROME).

THINGS COULD BE WORSE...
ANYWAYS, NOBODY EXPECTS YOU TO MAKE
WAFER-THIN VENETIAN-STYLE GLASS YOUR FIRST
TIME OUT BLOWING GLASS.

IN ACTUALITY, THICK PIECES OFFER YOU MORE
CONTROL AND STABILITY, AND THEY'RE NOT QUITE
AS THERMALLY TEMPERMENTAL AS THINLY-BLOWN
WARES. IN TIME AND WITH PRACTICE
YOU'LL START WORKING HOTTER AND FASTER,
YOU'LL BE MORE AGGRESSIVE AND HAVE A BETTER
UNDERSTANDING WHAT DOES WHAT.

SOMETIMES IT JUST TAKES A LITTLE MORE
GUTS TO BLOW THINNER AND WALK THAT LINE
BETWEEN TOTAL COLLAPSE AND LIGHTER GLASS!

"MY PIECES HAVE DEVELOPED THIS BAD HABIT OF JUMPING OFF MY PUNTIES"

REMEMBER: YOUR PUNTY IS ONE SENSI-
TIVE PUPPY WHICH REQUIRES SPECIAL CARE
AND CONSTANT ATTENTION.

THINKABOUTITFORASEC—
YOU DEMAND ALOT FROM YOUR PUNTY.
IT'S BRITTLE GRIP IS LIMITED TO A
SPACE NOT MUCH LARGER THAN A DIME,
AND IT'S HOLDING ONTO SOMETHING MUCH
LARGER, THAT'S GETTING TORQUED-ON, AND
WORKED ON. THE SLIGHTEST JARRING
OF THE PUNTY CAN CAUSE YOUR PIECE TO JUMP-OFF,
SO AVOID ANY UNNECESSARY BUMPS OR TAPS - AND
TAKE CARE SETTING IT DOWN ON THE YOKE OR BENCH.

YOU MUST KEEP YOUR PUNTY WARM - ALWAYS.
ALWAYS FLASH THE PUNTY - BEFORE AND AFTER
REHEATING, AND FREQUENTLY DURING WORKING.
FINALLY, PRACTICE OTHER STYLES OF PUNTIES
IF THE ONE YOU'RE USING DOESN'T WORK FOR YOU.

"MY PARENTS FREAKED WHEN I TOLD THEM I WANTED TO STUDY GLASSBLOWING"

you wanna what? — — oh my lord...

COMMON AMONGST MANY GLASSBLOWERS IS THE ONSET OF "PARENTAL PANIC" WHEN YOU DECIDE FOR YOURSELF THAT 'WORKING WITH THIS 'ART FORM' IS WHAT YOU WANNA DO WITH YOUR LIFE.

OFTEN (AND INCORRECTLY) ASSOCIATED WITH BASKETWEAVING, BLOWING GLASS IS RARELY CONSIDERED A PROFITABLE AND REWARDING CAREER BY THOSE RESPONSIBLE FOR YOUR UP-BRINGING.

PHRASES SUCH AS " WHERE DID WE GO WRONG?" OR " YOU'LL NEVER MAKE A LIVING AT IT", OR "I HOPE THIS IS JUST ANOTHER ONE OF THOSE PHASES YOU'RE GOING THROUGH"... - SEEM TO DRIFT IN AND OUT OF THOSE HEARTFELT CONVERSATIONS. FOR THE MOST PART THEY ARE RIGHT — BUT DON'T LET THAT BOTHER YOU. AFTER A YEAR OR SO OF YOU BLOWING, THEY'LL START TO GET REALLY NICE BIRTHDAY AND CHRISTMAS PRESENTS AND YOU'LL BE ONE BIG HAPPY FAMILY AGAIN. BUT BEWARE! IT CAN BACKFIRE TOO! ESPECIALLY IF YOU ARE ABLE TO SELL SOME OF YOUR WORK ~ YOUR PARENTS MAY BECOME REALLY INTERESTED! AND WHO KNOWS... MAYBE THEY'LL WANNA START BLOWING GLASS THEMSELVES.

"I FEEL DIZZY WHEN BLOWING GLASS."

THE FIRST THING THAT COMES TO MIND IS THAT YOU'RE SUFFERING FROM OXYGEN-DE-PRIVATION FROM TRYING TO START A BUBBLE INTO SOMETHING MORE SOLID THAN THE ROCK OF GIBRALTAR. **HOT GOOD — COLD BAD.**

ANOTHER POSSIBILITY IS THAT YOU ARE EXPERIENCING ONE PHENOMENAL ART REVELATION OR DIVINE INTERVENTION. OR YOU FIND GLASSBLOWING SO TITILLATING THAT YOU'RE BEGINNING TO LOSE IT.

MORE-THAN-LIKELY, HOWEVER, YOU MAY BE SUFFERING FROM HEAT EXHAUSTION OR HEAT FATIGUE. IF YOU FEEL DIZZY: PUT THE PIPE AWAY AND GO COOL-OFF!

SERIOUS INJURY TO YOURSELF OR SOMEONE ELSE MAY HAPPEN IF YOU WERE TO PASS-OUT. REMEMBER TO DRINK PLENTY OF WATER WHILE BLOWING GLASS.

THE FINAL POSSIBILITY MIGHT BE THAT THE ALCOHOL OR DRUGS YOU IMBIBED-IN HAVE TAKEN EFFECT ~ COMPOUNDED BY THE HEAT OF THE FURNACE, YOUR COORDINATION BECOMES IMPAIRED AND YOU BASICALLY DO NO ONE GOOD. THERE'S A TIME AND A PLACE FOR EVERYTHING. GLASSBLOWING IS HARD ENOUGH AS IT IS, AND REQUIRES GREAT CONCENTRATION AND SHARP REFLEXES.

DON'T BLOW IT! Enough said.

"THE LIPS ON MY VESSELS ARE TOO THICK."

TRY BLOWING THE PIECE OUT MORE WHILE IT'S STILL ON THE PIPE, ESPECIALLY UP AT THE SHOULDERS PRIOR TO THE NECKING PROCESS.

WORK THE PIECE HOTTER. IF YOU ALLOW THE PIECE TO STRETCH OUT A BIT, IT WILL ALSO HELP THIN-OUT THE LIPS.

TRY NECKING FURTHER OFF THE PIPE, AND MORE ON THE BUBBLE. IF YOU HAVE AN ASSISTANT HELP YOU TURN THE PIPE WHILE YOU NECK THE PIECE, YOU CAN GET A PRETTY CRISP NECKLINE EXACTLY WHERE YOU WANT IT.

TRIMMING THE VESSEL AFTER IT'S TRANSFERRED IS ANOTHER OPTION TO THINNING THE LIPS, SEE PAGES 68-71.

FINALLY, IF POSSIBLE, LEARN BY WATCHING THE BEST GLASSBLOWERS YOU CAN FIND. PAY ATTENTION TO THEIR HANDS. THE MOVES ARE SUBTLE, BUT THEY'RE THERE.

"I CAN'T SEE THE LEVEL OF GLASS IN THE FURNACE WHILE I'M GATHERING."

FIRST, ARE YOU WEARING YOUR SAFETY GLASSES? SOMETIMES A FURNACE CAN PRODUCE SO MUCH LIGHT THAT IT'S BLINDING YOU. PROPER SAFETY GLASSES (DESIGNED FOR BLOWING GLASS) SHOULD FILTER-OUT MOST OF THE HARMFUL WAVELENGTHS OF LIGHT AND ALLOW YOU TO CLEARLY SEE WHAT YOU'RE DOING.

SECOND, ARE YOU TALL ENOUGH TO ACTUALLY SEE THE SURFACE OF THE GLASS TO BEGIN WITH? IF NOT, FIND A CINDER BLOCK OR RISER OF SORTS, TO CORRECT THE SITUATION. YOU SHOULD BE ABLE TO READ A REFLECTION OF YOUR BLOW-PIPE ON THE SURFACE OF THE GLASS AS YOU ENTER THE FURNACE TO GATHER.

"I HAD A 'HAPPY ACCIDENT' MY FIRST YEAR WORKING IN GLASS. I MADE A NICELY DECORATED PERFUME BOTTLE (OR WAS IT A PAPERWEIGHT?) - SOLD IT, AND THEN ANOTHER, AND ANOTHER, AND NOW, TEN YEARS LATER - I'M STILL MAKING THEM!

MY PROBLEM IS... I WANNA MAKE STUFF THAT'S FUN, THAT SAYS SOMETHING - BUT THE MONEY'S TOO GOOD, AND I HAVEN'T THE TIME.

WHAT DO I DO?..."

FIRST, IT'S HOPELESS. SECOND, YOU'RE DOOMED.

SORRY...

SYMPTOM

"MY PIECES COME OUT OF THE ANNEALER AND THEY'VE GOT THIS WEIRD TEXTURE ON THEM. WHAT'S UP WITH THAT?"

SOLUTION

"IT'S HARD TELLIN', NOT KNOWIN'," OR WITHOUT BEING ACTUALLY ABLE TO SEE THE TYPE OF TEXTURE.

IT COULD BE CHILL MARKS - FROM MARVERING THE GLASS TOO COLD, ESPECIALLY IF THE TEXTURE LOOKS LIKE ORANGE PEEL SKIN.

IF ON THE OTHERHAND, YOUR PIECE HAS BOTH TEXTURE AND CHUNKS OF BRICK OR FIBREFRAX (FUNNY WHITE STUFF) FUSED TO THE SURFACE — YOU HAVE A CLASSIC EXAMPLE OF "ANNEALER FACE". THERE ARE TWO LIKELY POSSIBILITIES IF THAT'S THE CASE: EITHER YOU PUT THE PIECE AWAY TOO HOT AND IT SLUMPED AND FUSED ITSELF TO THE BOTTOM OF YOUR ANNEALER OR YOUR ANNEALER IS (OR WAS) SET TOO-HIGH AND THE GLASS SLUMPED SOMEWHAT DURING THE "ANNEAL". SHOW IT (YOUR PIECE) TO THE INSTRUCTOR OR SHOP TECHNICIAN FOR A SECOND DIAGNOSIS.

"THE BOTTOMS KEEP BREAKING OUT OF MY PIECES WHEN I TRY TO PUT THEM AWAY [IN THE ANNEALER]."

NUMBER ONE, STOP BLOWING THE BOTTOMS-OUT SO THIN. LEAVE A LITTLE MORE GLASS DOWN THERE FOR STRUCTURAL SUPPORT.

NUMBER TWO, TRY A DIFFERENT STYLE OF PUNTY, OR SIMPLY DON'T APPLY THEM SO HOT! IF THEY GET STUCK ON TOO HOT, YOU'LL HAVE NO CHOICE BUT TAKE OUT A BIG CHUNCK OF THE BOTTOM.

FINALLY, YOU MAY NEED TO CHANGE THE METHOD YOU USE TO TAKE THE PIECE OFF OF THE PUNTY. PERHAPS USE A DROP OR TWO MORE OF WATER TO GET IT TO RELEASE.

GREAT. NOW I'VE GOT ANOTHER FLOWER POT!

"I HAD ONE INSTRUCTOR SAY, "DO IT THIS WAY" AND NOW I'VE GOT THIS NEW TEACHER TELLIN' ME "NO, DO IT THIS WAY!"
WHO DO I BELIEVE?
I'M GETTING SOO..... CONFUSED!"

EITHER BELIEVE BOTH OF THEM OR NEITHER OF THEM.
TRUST YOUR INSTINCTS.

THE WISE GLASSBLOWER WILL TRY TO MAKE USE OF ALL INFORMATION AVAILABLE TO THEM.

TRY EVERYTHING, AND USE WHICHEVER METHOD WORKS BEST FOR YOU.

APPENDIX A
SOME FAMOUS & INFAMOUS FORMS OF PUNTIES

THE ITALIAN-STYLE GOBLET PUNTY → A WELL-MADE GOBLET PUNTY MAY BE USED FOR SEVERAL PIECES, IF NOT ALL DAY LONG, IF KEPT AT A STABLE TEMPERATURE IN THE PIPE WARMER. THESE TYPES OF PUNTIES ARE MOST SUITED FOR DELICATE WORK — WHERE JUST A SLIGHT TAP CAUSES THE PIECE TO RELEASE, LEAVING A PUNTY SCAR SMALLER THAN THE HEAD OF A PENCIL ERASER.

VERY LITTLE GLASS ON TOP

COMPACT FORM MARVERED TIGHTLY NO EXCESS GLASS.

GOBLET-STYLE PUNTY

TO MAKE ONE: VERSION A GATHER A ONE INCH BLOB O' GLASS ON A LIGHTWEIGHT PUNTY, IMMEDIATELY HOLDING IT UP TOWARDS THE CEILING - ALLOWING GRAVITY TO PULL THE GLASS DOWN ONTO THE PUNTY. THIS MOVE PRACTICALLY MAKES A PERFECT PUNTY FOR YOU!

GATHER THEN HOLD IT STRAIGHT UP.

① ② ③ ④ ⑤

TIGHTEN-UP THE FORM BY MARVERING THE GLASS ↑ FIRST IN A PERPENDICULAR FASHION TO SQUEEZE-OFF ANY EXCESS GLASS ON THE TIP. NEXT, MARVER WITH A SLIGHT ANGLE TO POINT-UP WHAT REMAINING GLASS THERE IS ON THE TIP. (②)
THEN QUICKLY DRIVE FORWARD LOWERING YOUR HANDS TO A HORIZONTAL LEVEL TO SHAPE THE SIDEWALLS OF THE PUNTY AND TO SQUEEZE ANY EXCESS FURTHER TOWARDS THE BACK OF THE PUNTY. (③ & ④)
FINALLY, TIGHTEN-UP THE BACK-END OF THE PUNTY BY MARVERING THE GLASS ON THE EDGE OF THE MARVER. (⑤)
A BRIEF REHEAT MAY BE WARRANTED, AND THEN PUNTY-UP IN THE USUAL FASHION.
THIS TYPE OF PUNTY CAN BE MADE IN A JIFFY AND OFFERS GOOD HOLDING POWER.
IF, FOR WHATEVER REASON, YOU DON'T LIKE THAT STYLE AND/OR WANT LESS GLASS YOU CAN TRY **VERSION B.**

VERSION B
GATHER A ONE INCH BLOB OF GLASS, ON A LIGHT-WEIGHT PUNTY. USE THE BACK OF YOUR JACKS → AS A MINI-MARVER, AND 'MARVER' THE GLASS OFF THE END OF THE PUNTY.
USE YOUR DIAMOND SHEARS AND CUT-OFF ALL THE EXCESS GLASS.
AGAIN, USE THE BACK OF YOUR JACKS TO MARVER SMOOTH THE TIP AND SIDES.
REHEAT THE PUNTY BRIEFLY BEFORE STICKING IT UP IN THE USUAL FASHION.

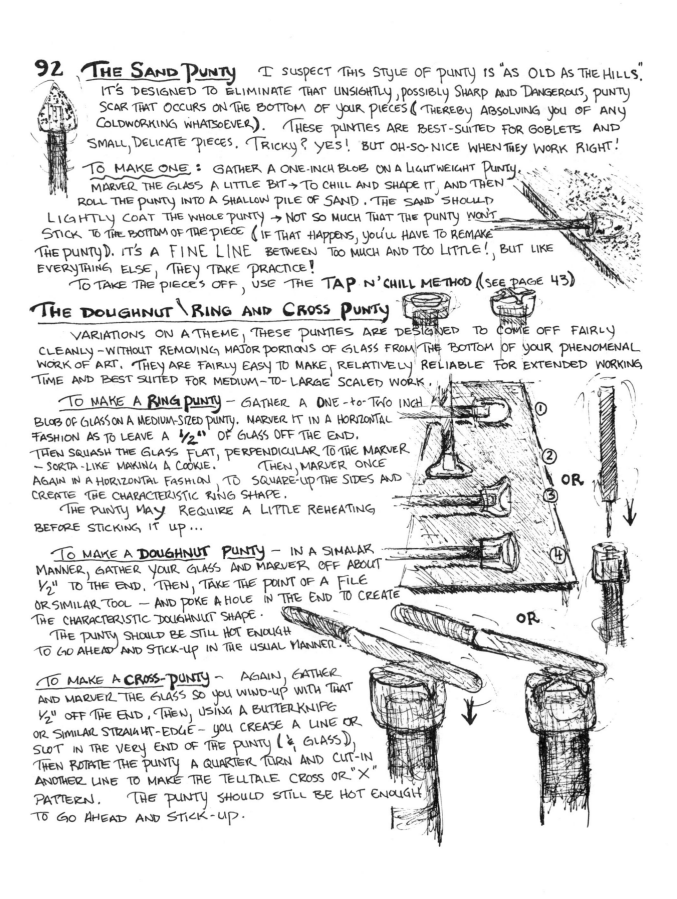

92 The Sand Punty

I suspect this style of punty is "as old as the hills." It's designed to eliminate that unsightly, possibly sharp and dangerous, punty scar that occurs on the bottom of your pieces (thereby absolving you of any coldworking whatsoever). These punties are best-suited for goblets and small, delicate pieces. Tricky? Yes! But oh-so-nice when they work right!

To make one : Gather a one-inch blob on a lightweight punty. Marver the glass a little bit → to chill and shape it, and then roll the punty into a shallow pile of sand. The sand should lightly coat the whole punty → not so much that the punty won't stick to the bottom of the piece (if that happens, you'll have to remake the punty). It's a FINE LINE between too much and too little!, but like everything else, they take practice!

To take the pieces off, use the TAP N' CHILL METHOD (see page 43)

The Doughnut \ Ring and Cross Punty

Variations on a theme, these punties are designed to come off fairly cleanly — without removing major portions of glass from the bottom of your phenomenal work of art. They are fairly easy to make, relatively reliable for extended working time and best suited for medium-to-large scaled work.

To make a RING PUNTY — gather a one-to-two inch blob of glass on a medium-sized punty. Marver it in a horizontal fashion as to leave a 1/2" of glass off the end. Then squash the glass flat, perpendicular to the marver — sorta-like making a cookie. Then, marver once again in a horizontal fashion, to square-up the sides and create the characteristic ring shape.

The punty may require a little reheating before sticking it up...

To make a DOUGHNUT PUNTY — in a similar manner, gather your glass and marver off about 1/2" to the end. Then, take the point of a file or similar tool — and poke a hole in the end to create the characteristic doughnut shape.

The punty should be still hot enough to go ahead and stick-up in the usual manner.

To make a CROSS-PUNTY — again, gather and marver the glass so you wind-up with that 1/2" off the end. Then, using a butter knife or similar straight-edge — you crease a line or slot in the very end of the punty (& glass), then rotate the punty a quarter turn and cut-in another line to make the telltale cross or "X" pattern. The punty should still be hot enough to go ahead and stick-up.

NOT ALL THAT DISSIMILAR FROM THE PREVIOUS PUNTIES, THE CHEATER OR SCULPTURE PUNTY IS APPROPRIATE FOR LARGER WORK AND IS CONVENIENT FOR SOLO BLOWING. IT DIFFERS IN THAT YOU'LL LEAVE A SMALL KNOB OR "BUTTON" ON THE BOTTOM OF THE PIECE WHEN YOU CRACK IT OFF UPON COMPLETION. THIS BUTTON CAN BE IGNORED OR COLDWORKED WITH SPECIAL PUNTY GRINDING WHEELS AT A LATER DATE.

TO MAKE ONE: GATHER A TWO INCH BLOB OF GLASS ON A HEAVYWEIGHT PUNTY, MARVER THE SIDES HORIZONTALLY ⇒ DELIBERATELY LEAVING ½" OR SO OF GLASS OFF THE END. CHILL AND SHAPE IT WITH CONTINUED ROTATIONS ON THE MARVER. DO NOT MARVER THE TIP!

STICK IT UP ONCE THE GLASS APPEARS 'SET-UP'. CENTER THE PUNTY AS BEST YOU CAN, AND THEN NECK A LINE IN THE PUNTY WITH THE JACKS. THE JACKLINE SHOULD BE JUST OFF THE EDGE OF THE PUNTY.

DO NOT NECK IT TOO TIGHT! YOU CAN JEOPARDIZE THE STRENGTH AND INTEGRITY OF THE PUNTY. THE NECKLINE IS WHERE THE PIECE WILL EVENTUALLY BREAK-OFF, BUT YOU DON'T WANT THAT HAPPENING ANY SOONER THAN YOU NEED IT TO!

BE SURE TO LET THE GLASS / PUNTY SET-UP A LITTLE MORE BEFORE THE TRANSFER, OR YOU'LL HAVE ONE HELLUVA FLOPPY PIECE ON YOUR HANDS. SOMETIMES YOU CAN BLOW ON THE PUNTY WITH A SOFFIETTA TO CHILL IT OUT QUICKER.

THE CROWN PUNTY

THIS **KING-DADDY** OF ALL PUNTIES IS USED PRIMARILY FOR VERY LARGE PIECES. IF MADE CORRECTLY, IT LEAVES VERY LITTLE GLASS ON THE FINISHED PIECE, SAVE A BOTTLE-CAP LOOKING DOUGHNUT.

LET ME WALK YOU THROUGH THE STEPS TO MAKE ONE:

TAKE YOUR FIRST GATHER — SOMEWHAT DEEP — AND MARVER IT ALL BACK ON THE PUNTY

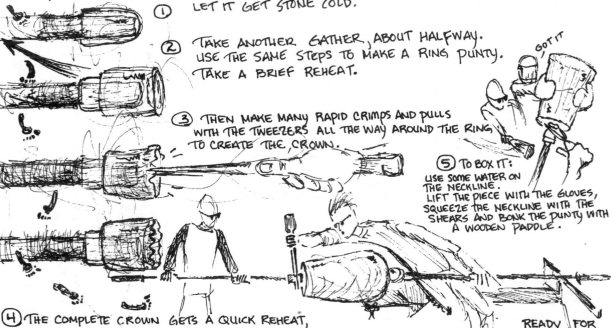

① LET IT GET STONE COLD.

② TAKE ANOTHER GATHER, ABOUT HALFWAY. USE THE SAME STEPS TO MAKE A RING PUNTY. TAKE A BRIEF REHEAT.

③ THEN MAKE MANY RAPID CRIMPS AND PULLS WITH THE TWEEZERS ALL THE WAY AROUND THE RING, TO CREATE THE CROWN.

GOT IT

⑤ TO BOX IT: USE SOME WATER ON THE NECKLINE. LIFT THE PIECE WITH THE GLOVES, SQUEEZE THE NECKLINE WITH THE SHEARS AND BONK THE PUNTY WITH A WOODEN PADDLE.

④ THE COMPLETE CROWN GETS A QUICK REHEAT, AND IS PRESENTED TO THE GAFFER. THE GAFFER CUTS A NECKLINE IN WITH THE JACKS. **READY FOR TRANSFER!**

APPENDIX B
COOKING WITH GLASS

GLASSBLOWING CAN BE SOMEWHAT PHYSICALLY DEMANDING. YOU BURN A LOT OF CALORIES WHILE BLOWING — YOU GET THIRSTY AND SOMETIMES HUNGRY. LEAVE THE STUDIO, JUST TO TAKE A BREAK? FOR SOME OF YOU — THAT IS SIMPLY NOT AN OPTION. THEREFORE, THIS SECTION EXISTS — FOR THOSE PEOPLE WHO WISH TO COMBINE TWO HOPELESS ADDICTIONS — (NAMELY EATING AND GLASSBLOWING) INTO ONE, AND KILL THE PROVERBIAL TWO BIRDS WITH ONE STONE.

HERE ARE FEW WAYS TO MAKE USE OF THE EXCESS HEAT AND EXPENSIVE GLASS EQUIPMENT TO YOUR ADVANTAGE:

AUTHOR'S NOTE ⇒ AS EATING WITH DIRTY HANDS IS AN UNHEALTHY PRACTICE, SO IS BLOWING GLASS. ESPECIALLY IF YOUR FINGERS ARE GREASY — YOU'LL FIND IT NEXT-TO-IMPOSSIBLE TO GRIP THE PIPE PROPERLY. ALWAYS WASH YOUR HANDS BEFORE BLOWING GLASS (AND YOU MIGHT WANNA WASH THEM AFTERWARDS TOO!).

THE SEVEN SECOND HOT DOG
JUST TAKE YOUR FAVORITE BRAND OF WEENIE, INSERT IT ON A GOBLET-PUNTY, GIVE IT A QUICK FLASH IN THE GLORY HOLE AND PRESTO — BON APPETITE!

— YUM!

GOOD PLACE TO BREW THAT CUP OF EARLY MORNING ESPRESSO. 'COURSE, IF YOUR FURNACE IS NOT BUILT AS SUCH, YOU CAN ALWAYS DROP A HOT COOKIE OF GLASS ON THE MARVER AND SLAP YOUR COFFEE POT ON TOP. IT COOKS IN SECONDS!

DRIP-OFF BUCKET

HEY! THAT DRIP-OFF BUCKET WORKS GREAT FOR BOILING STUFF. NEED BREAKFAST? HOW 'BOUT A COUPLE OF EGGS? AFTER DRIPPING SOME HOT GLASS IN THE WATER, WHY NOT DROP SOME EGGS IN FOR A COUPLE OF MINUTES IN SOME RETRIEVABLE FORM OF BASKET (don't use your hands!). YOU MIGHT TRY THROWING SOME BAY LEAVES, GARLIC, AND MISCELLANEOUS SPICES TO MAKE A CRAB OR LOBSTER BOIL. OR WHY NOT UTILIZE SOME OF THAT PREVAILING STEAM AND DO-UP SOME VEGGIES?

GOOD EATS AT ANNEALER JOE'S
TAKE-OUT ONLY

BIG OPEN HOUSE SOON?
IS THE 25th BATTALION COMING OVER FOR SUPPER? THAT BIG ANNEALER DOES GREAT ON TURKEYS, SPUDS, PIZZAS — YOU NAME IT! (IT IS AFTERALL JUST A LARGE EXPENSIVE OVEN!). TURN IT UP TO 350°F — LOAD IT WHEN IT'S PREHEATED — (BLOW GLASS FOR A WHILE) LET IT BAKE & CHOW!

COLD COFFEE?
MARVER-UP A BLOB ON A PUNTY AND IMMERSE IT FOR A FEW SECONDS IN YOUR CUP TO RE-JUVENATE YOUR FAVORITE BEVERAGE.

JAVA

HEY! — WE'D LOVE TO INCLUDE YOUR FAVORITE HOT-SHOP RECIPES. JUST JOT THEM DOWN ON A POSTCARD & MAIL IT TO US AT GLASS MOUNTAIN. (ADDRESS IN THE FRONT OF THIS BOOK).

APPENDIX C
SURVIVAL TIPS

WILL BLOW GLASS FOR FOOD

NOW, IF/THAT YOU'VE BEEN BITTEN BY THE GLASS BUG, HOW DO YOU CONTINUE? IT SHOULD BE PAINFULLY EVIDENT BY NOW THAT THIS GLASSBLOWING ACTIVITY IS MOST COSTLY. NO LIE.

HOT GLASS IS ONE OF THE MOST EXPENSIVE ART FORMS TO WORK WITH, AND ONE OF THE MOST CHALLENGING TO 'MASTER'.

SELLING GLASS THAT YOU'VE MADE IS ONE AVENUE THAT IS BOTH SATISFYING AND REWARDING (i.e. IF PEOPLE ARE LIKING AND BUYING IT). THE THING MOST ART SCHOOLS OFTEN OVERLOOK WHEN INSTRUCTING THEIR STUDENTS IS PRACTICAL INFORMATION ON THE BUSINESS OF THIS ART-MAKING BUSINESS. HELL, I WENT INTO **THE ARTS** TO AVOID **THE BUSINESS WORLD** AS MUCH AS POSSIBLE — BUT THAT PIPEDREAM WENT UP IN SMOKE AS SOON AS I REALIZED I NEEDED TO MARKET MY WARES/SKILLS TO LIVE. FOR EXAMPLE, I HAVE YET TO FIND A FORMULA OR PHILOSOPHY THAT MAKES SENSE REGARDING 'HOW-TO' PRICE YOUR PIECES. SOME FOLKS SAY: "AS MUCH AS THE MARKET WILL BEAR" (OR WHATEVER EVERYONE ELSE CHARGES FOR SIMILAR WORKS). OTHER PEOPLE SAY " DOUBLE WHAT IT COSTS YOU TO MAKE ANOTHER", OR "WHAT DO YOU THINK IT'S WORTH?" THE CORRECT ANSWER TO THAT DILEMMA MAY REMAIN AS VAGUE AS THE DAY IS LONG. IN ANY CASE, HERE'S A FEW THINGS TO REMEMBER TO HELP YOU GET BY:

OUTLETS FOR YOUR GLASSWORK ARE EVERYWHERE. ART GALLERIES AND CRAFT STORES ARE JUST PART OF 'THE SCENE'. THEY CAN BE EXCELLENT VEHICLES THROUGH WHICH TO MOVE YOUR WORK AND RECEIVE "FREE" EXPOSURE. DEALING WITH CONSIGNMENTS, CONTRACTS, COMMISSIONS AND THE **FIFTY-FIFTY** SPLIT CAN BE DISHEARTENING OR DISENCHANTING → BUT IT'S PART OF THE GAME.

NOW, IF SITTING OUTSIDE IN THE SUN (OR RAIN, OR COLD, OR HIGH WINDS) IS YOUR 'BAG', AND TALKING TO HUNDREDS OF PEOPLE ABOUT GLASS AS THEY FONDLE PRECIOUS OBJECTS YOU'VE MADE ON THE DISPLAY AREA IN FRONT OF YOU, THEN MAYBE THE CRAFT FAIR IS THE TRIP FOR YOU.

CRAFT FAIRS CAN BE EXCELLENT OPPORTUNITIES TO SELL LOTS OF WORK VERY FAST AND A CHANCE TO RECEIVE UNSOLICITED, HONEST FEEDBACK (IF NOT SOMETIMES, ILL-INFORMED), ABOUT WHAT YOU MAKE. **NOTE:** QUALITY PRESENTATION IS THE NAME OF THE GAME. YOU MUST TAKE THE EXTRA EFFORT AND EXPENSE TO DISPLAY YOUR WARES AS BEST AS POSSIBLE IF YOU HOPE TO MAKE A SUCCESS OF THIS TYPE OF VENTURE.

MY ADVICE IS TO VISIT A CRAFT SHOW AND REALLY LOOK AT WHAT'S INVOLVED (TAKE NOTES!). PAY ATTENTION TO HOW THINGS ARE LAID-OUT, WHICH BOOTHS/ TABLES ARE SELLING, WHICH ONES AREN'T AND THE PROFESSIONAL NATURE OF THOSE MOST-SUCCESSFUL. CRAFT FAIRS/SHOWS ARE UNQUESTIONABLY ALOT OF WORK TO DO, BUT THEY CAN BE VERY WORTHWHILE (IF PEOPLE ARE BUYING) AND SOMEWHAT ENLIGHTENING.

96

"HOLY MOL'EH! So, That's what it looks Like on a big screen!"

IT'S A GOOD IDEA TO DOCUMENT, IN SOME FASHION, THE WORK THAT YOU MAKE. **SLIDES** ARE PRETTY MUCH THE MOST POPULAR METHOD USED BY ARTISTS. SLIDES CAN BE ALMOST MORE IMPORTANT THAN THE WORK ITSELF! **SLIDES ARE ALSO THE BIGGEST LIARS IN THE ART WORLD!** ACCEPTING THAT AS TRUE , WHY NOT MAKE IT WORK FOR YOU?

SEEING HOW SLIDES ARE RESPONSIBLE FOR GETTING YOU INTO GALLERIES, JURYING FOR COMPETITIONS, COMMISIONS, GRANTS, CRAFT FAIRS AND NATIONAL / INTERNATIONAL EXPOSURE → IT'S IMPORTANT THAT YOU GET THE BEST IMAGES MADE POSSIBLE. REMEMBER, A GREAT SLIDE OF BAD WORK IS ALMOST ALWAYS BETTER THAT A POOR SLIDE OF REALLY GREAT WORK.

MANY GLASS ARTISTS SEEK-OUT THE ASSISTANCE OF PROFESSIONAL PHOTO- GRAPHERS - FAMILIAR WITH STUDIO LIGHTING AND SHOOTING GLASS OBJECTS. UNFORTUNATELY YOU MAY HAVE TO PAY-THROUGH-THE-NOSE FOR A HANDFUL OF QUALITY IMAGES. OR, IF YOU'RE LUCKY, YOU MIGHT TRY BARTERING WITH THE PHOTOGRAPHER. OR, IF YOU'RE SKILL- ED WITH YOUR OWN CAMERA AND HAVE ACCESS TO STUDIO-LIGHTING SET-UP (SORRY, THE BLACK VELVET CURTAIN JUST DOESN'T CUT IT ANYMORE FOR BACKDROPS), AND HAVE THE TIME AND PATIENCE → GO FOR IT! FOR ME, WHEN I'M SHOOTING SLIDES, IT'S THE ONE TIME THAT I REALLY GET TO L O O K AT MY WORK AND SEE IT IN A DIFFERENT LIGHT.

THE OTHER REASON TO DOCUMENT YOUR WORK IS TO HAVE AT LEAST ONE OTHER RECORD OF THE WORK WHICH YOU PRODUCE. YOU NEVER KNOW WHAT MIGHT HAPPEN TO IT (THE PIECE). PLUS, IT'S NICE TO HAVE A RECORD OF PAST ACCOMPLISHMENTS FOR FUTURE REFERENCE.

ANOTHER AVENUE TO CONSIDER, ESPECIALLY IF YOU'RE JUST STARTING-OUT AN' WANNA BLOW GLASS EACH N' EVERY DAY IS TO GET HOOKED-UP WITH A PRIVATE STUDIO AND WORK ON A TEAM. IT CAN BE A MIXED-BLESSING. YOU WILL GET OUT OF IT WHAT YOU WHAT YOU PUT INTO IT. YOU MAY SUFFER THE AGONY OF REPETITIOUS ACTIVITY OFTEN ASSOCIATED WITH PRODUCTION. SEE THE NEXT THREE PAGES FOR VALUABLE TIPS ON HOW TO BE A GOOD ASSISTANT. IT MAY BE WHAT GETS YOUR "FOOT-IN-THE-DOOR."

IF, ON THE OTHER HAND, MAKING UNIQUE 'ONE-OF-A-KIND' SCULPTURES OR EN- VIORNMENTAL INSTALLATIONS IS MORE YOUR CUP-OF-TEA ~ B E W A R E ~ IT'S A HARD ROAD A-HOAD. ARM YOURSELF WITH KNOWLEDGE (GO TO ART SCHOOL) - COUPLE IT WITH EXPERIENCE (SEE THE WORLD) AND SURF MORE THAN JUST THE INTERNET.

WHEN YOU PUT YOUR HEART AND MIND INTO YOUR WORK ~ IT SHOULD EXUDE YOUR SOUL ~ AND WORK WHICH EXHIBITS THAT - THAT SAYS "I AM" or "I WAS" IN SOME WAY, WILL LIVE FOREVER.

DARE TO BE DIFFERENT ~ ENDEAVOR TO HAVE A VOICE, AND SPEAK YOUR MIND.

WHICH ONE DO YOU LIKE?

I DUNNO... THEY'RE ALL SO... "DIFFERENT"

GLASSBLOWER "AT WORK"

APPENDIX D
ASSISTING THE GAFFER

ONE OF THE FASTEST WAYS TO LEARN THE ART OF GLASSBLOWING IS TO PARTICIPATE ON A TEAM AND ASSIST THE GAFFER. EVEN IF YOU HAVE LITTLE OR NO SKILL IN GLASSWORKING, YOU CAN STILL PERFORM SOME HELPFUL TASKS WHICH WILL BENEFIT YOU AND THE GAFFER. THERE ARE, HOWEVER, A FEW THINGS YOU SHOULD BE AWARE OF THAT CAN MAKE THE DIFFERENCE BETWEEN WHETHER YOU ARE A HELP OR A HINDRANCE TO THE TEAM.

#1. ASK FIRST. NEVER ASSUME THAT SOMEONE WANTS HELP IN THE FIRST PLACE. SOME GAFFERS PREFER TO DO MOST EVERYTHING THEMSELVES AND MAY FREAK-OUT IF YOU START DOING STUFF FOR THEM.

#2. PAY ATTENTION. WATCH WHAT THE GAFFER IS DOING, AND NOT WHAT OTHER GLASSBLOWERS IN THE SHOP ARE DOING. THE SUREST WAY OF GETTING BOOTED-OFF A TEAM IS TO 'FALL-ASLEEP-AT-THE-WHEEL'!

#3. SHOW UP ON-TIME. BE SURE TO ARRIVE FOR THE BLOW-SLOT ON-TIME (OR YOU MAY BE LEFT OUT). ALMOST AS IMPORTANT, OR MORE SO, IS THAT YOU STAY FOR THE WHOLE THING. IT'S ONE THING TO WORK WITH NO ASSISTANTS AND EXPECT NOTHING, AND ANOTHER THING TO BE PLANNING ON HAVING ASSISTANTS ONLY TO HAVE THEM NOT SHOW UP OR BAIL HALFWAY THROUGH THE SLOT!

#4. ANTICIPATE THE GAFFERS MOVES. TRY YOUR BEST TO STAY ON TOP OF EVERYTHING. ARRANGE TOOLS, OFFER PROTECTION, OR HELP "TURN POLE", IF AND ONLY IF YOU HAVE BEEN INSTRUCTED ON 'HOW THEY LIKE IT'. IN TIME, WITH PRACTICE, VALUABLE SECONDS WON'T BE WASTED IF EVERYONE'S AWARE OF THEIR DUTIES AND WHAT THE NEXT STEP IS.

#5. SMILE ONCE IN A WHILE.
BESIDES BEING VERY CONTAGIOUS, A SMILE CAN DO WONDERS. NOBODY LIKES A SOURPUSS ESPECIALLY AS AN ASSISTANT. IF YOUR HEART ISN'T INTO IT, YOU MAY BECOME MORE OF A HINDRANCE THAN HELP. THEN IT MAY BE TIME TO FIND SOMETHING ELSE TO DO.

WHEN "DOING DOORS" WATCH THE GAFFERS FACE, ESPECIALLY CONCENTRATE ON THEIR EYES AND MOUTH, DON'T STARE AT THE PIECE - WHAT'S GOING ON THERE DOESN'T REALLY CONCERN YOU. THEIR FIRST INDICATION THAT THEY'LL NEED A DOOR OPENED WILL BE EITHER WITH A NOD OF THE HEAD OR AN ORAL CLUE SUCH AS "OPEN PLEASE".

THERE ARE TIMES WHEN THE GAFFER WILL WANT THE DOORS OPEN FOR REHEATING, AND OTHER TIMES WHEN THEY'LL NEED THE PIECE "BOXED-IN" (THE DOORS CLOSED-IN ON THE PIECE TO GET THE HIGHEST CONCENTRATION OF HEAT). LISTEN AND PAY ATTENTION! IT IS NOT THE TIME TO 'SPACE-OUT' OR BECOME MESMERIZED BY WHAT'S ROTATING ON THE END OF THE STICK.

98 EVERY STUDIO HAS THEIR OWN STYLE OF GLORY HOLE, AND SYSTEM FOR DOOR OPENING. SOME ARE EVEN PNEUMATICALLY-OPERATED AND REQUIRE NO ASSISTANCE. LIKEWISE, EVERY GAFFER HAS THEIR OWN TOLERANCE FOR PAIN OR MANNER IN WHICH THEY WISH THE DOORS TO BE OPEN DURING REHEATING. DO YOUR BEST TO COMPLY.

WHEN **BENCHBLOWING**, IT'S THE SAME → KEEP YOUR EYES ON THE GAFFER'S FACE - NOT SO MUCH THE PIECE. TRY TO 'TRACK' WITH THE ROLL OF THE BLOWPIPE. IT'S EASIER TO DO IF YOU HAVE A ROLLER STOOL OR CINDERBLOCK OR SOMETHING TO SIT ON.

WHEN INDICATED TO BLOW – **BLOW SOFTLY AT FIRST.** YOU NEVER KNOW HOW HOT THE GLASS IS, AND THE GAFFER CAN ALWAYS TELL YOU TO "BLOW HARDER". SOMETIMES, THE CLUE TO BLOW WILL SIMPLY BE A NOD OF THEIR HEAD. WATCH FOR IT! THE GAFFER WILL LET YOU KNOW THAT YOU SHOULD STOP BLOWING BY EITHER PULLING THE PIPE AWAY FROM YOUR MOUTH, OR MERELY SAY "STOP BLOWING" (AVOID SAYING WHOA! IT SOUNDS ALOT LIKE "BLOW" - AND THAT MAY BE THE LAST THING YOU NEED!)

BENCHBLOWING

SOMETIMES THE PIECES CAN GET QUITE BIG & HEAVY, AND HARD TO TURN ON THE BLOWPIPE. IT HELPS TO HAVE SOMEONE '**TURN POLE**" FOR THE GAFFER. THIS IS BEST DONE FROM INSIDE OF THE BENCH, OPPOSITE THE GAFFER). YOU CAN KEEP YOUR EYES ON THE PIECE AND ANTICIPATE THE ↓ GAFFER'S MOTIONS.

ALLOW THE GAFFER TO INITIATE THE SHIFTS IN ROTATION, AND TRY TO FOLLOW-THROUGH WITH THE SAME SPEED.

OVERHEAD VIEW
ASSISTING THE GAFFER

OTHERTIMES WHILE TURNING POLE YOU MAY BE ASKED TO TILT THE PIPE OR TAKE COMPLETE CONTROL OF IT WHILE THE GAFFER CONCENTRATES ON SHAPING OR NECKING THE PIECE WITH BOTH HANDS. SO, PAY ATTENTION AND STAY ON YOUR TOES!

OFFERING "PROTECTION"
SHIELDING THE GAFFER

PERHAPS ONE OF THE MOST VALUABLE FUNCTIONS YOU'LL PERFORM AS AN ASSISTANT IS **PROTECTING THE GAFFER** FROM GETTING BURNED BY THEIR OWN WORK. THESE SIMPLE PROCEDURES SHOULD GUARD THE GAFFER FROM THE RADIANT HEAT OF THE PIECE YET ALLOW FULL VISUAL ACCESS WHILE WORKING.

SITUATE YOURSELF BEHIND THE GAFFER TO BE WITHIN AN ARM'S REACH AT ALL TIMES. ALWAYS MOVE WITH THE GAFFER AND AVOID TOUCHING THEIR TOOLS OR INTERFERRING WITH THEIR MOVEMENTS / VISION.

WHILE BLOCKING OR PAPERING, YOUR LARGE PADDLE MAY HOWEVER REST LIGHTLY ON THE GAFFER'S BLOCK OR NEWSPAPER, PROTECTING THEIR ENTIRE ARM FROM THE HEAT.

During the necking procedure, the underside of the gaffer's hand can get pretty **HOT**. Try to slip a paddle up underneath the gaffer's hand to shield them from the heat.

The paddles used for shielding the gaffer should be **LIGHTWEIGHT** enough so that they are quick to move and control. Many paddles are made of cherry wood so that they can double as flattening tools.

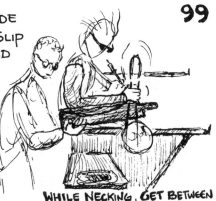

WHILE NECKING, GET BETWEEN THE PIECE AND THE GAFFER'S HAND.

Once again, while shielding, think about how the glass is RADIATING heat. Recognize that larger pieces will produce more heat than smaller ones and therefore more protection is necessary while working on larger pieces.

Proximity to the glass is also critical. For example, trimming or cutting with the shears can be quite punishing without protection. The thumb (because of it's proximity) is especially vulnerable, so try to shield that part while the gaffer is trimming or applying bits. Watch-out for trailings or trimmings! They should be guided away from the piece (never pull on them as that can distort the gaffer's work). Be ready to move at a moment's notice. You have to anticipate the gaffer's movements and do your best not to obstruct them.

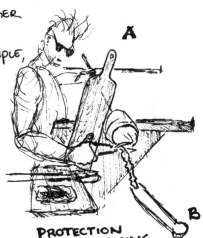

PROTECTION WHILE TRIMMING.
- SHIELD @ POSITION A.
- GUIDE @ POSITION B.

If the shielding technique or protection you are are offering is not effective, (and the gaffer is grimacing in pain) you may have to reposition your paddles or reposition yourself (in front of the bench, for example) in order to approach it from a different angle.

Remember: being 'flexible' and responsive to the gaffer's needs is **90%** of what being a good assistant is.

When opening vessels, the inside of the gaffer's arm and biceps are vulnerable to the radiant heat emanating from the piece. Try to slip in there with a paddle to offer some protection.

Some gaffers, however, will wear an old sock (with a hole cut in it for their hand to go through) or a special protective sleeve slipped over their arm to shield them from the heat. If that's the case your job as "protector-in-chief" may be alot easier!

WHEN OPENING VESSELS, PROTECT THE INSIDE OF THE GAFFER'S ARM. COME IN FROM UNDERNEATH WITH THE PADDLE.

STAY!

APPENDIX E
SOLO BLOWING

HANGING YOKE

TEAMWORK, AS WE HAVE LEARNED, IS BY-FAR THE EASIEST AND MOST PREFERRED METHOD OF GLASSBLOWING FOR MANY PEOPLE. UNFORTUNATELY, IT'S NOT ALWAYS FEASIBLE WITH EVERYONE'S BUSY, HECTIC AND PATHETICALLY-COMPLEXED SCHEDULES. FINDING A PARTNER TO WORK WITH CAN SOMETIMES BE MORE OF A CHORE THAN THE ACTUAL GLASSBLOWING ITSELF. SO, IN THE EVENT THAT YOU HAVE TO BLOW SOLO, HERE'S A FEW THINGS THAT MIGHT HELP YOU OUT.

WORKING BY YOURSELF IS A CHALLENGE. FIRST, YOU HAVE NO ONE TO BLAME FOR YOUR MISTAKES EXCEPT YOU! SECOND, YOU'RE FORCED TO WORK HOTTER AND FASTER (WHICH IS ACTUALLY GOOD PRACTICE). THIRD, YOU BECOME MORE FAMILIAR WITH EVERY STEP OF THE PROCESS OUT OF NECESSITY AND DEVELOP SKILLS AT PIPE AND PUNTY JUGGLING (AND, WELL...THAT'S GOOD FOR YOU TOO!).

THE KEY TO SOLO BLOWING IS TO GET SET-UP CORRECTLY TO BEGIN WITH. THIS MEANS PHYSICALLY PREPARING THE WORKSPACE AND MENTALLY PREPARING YOURSELF FOR THE TASK AT HAND. FOR EXAMPLE, ALWAYS MAKE SURE YOU HAVE AN AMPLE SUPPLY OF PIPES AND PUNTIES PREHEATED AND READY-TO-GO. STATION A PIPE BUCKET (FOR 'SPENT' PIPES) WITHIN AN ARM'S REACH OF THE BENCH OR GLORY HOLE. THAT WAY, YOU CAN TRASH A PIPE WITHOUT HAVING TO GO TOO FAR AND CAN CONCENTRATE ON THE BUSINESS AT HAND.

SOME SOLO BLOWERS WILL POSITION THEIR BENCH CLOSER TO THE GLORY HOLE TO REDUCE THE AMOUNT OF STEPS TAKEN DURING REHEATS, GOING BACK AND FORTH TO THE BENCH. REMEMBER, TIMING IS EVERYTHING IN SOLO BLOWING. ANY SECONDS YOU CAN SAVE DURING THE PROCESS MAY BENEFIT YOU IN THE LONG RUN.

YOU CAN **BENCHBLOW** YOUR PIECES WITH AN OPTIONAL DEVICE CALLED A BLOWHOSE. THEY ARE COMMONLY USED BY SCIENTIFIC GLASSWORKERS AND NEON TUBE BENDERS. ESSENTIALLY IT'S JUST A RUBBER HOSE WITH A SWIVEL MOUNTED ON THE FITTING WHICH SLIPS ONTO THE BLOWPIPE'S MOUTHPIECE AND ALLOWS YOU TO BLOW AND TURN THE PIPE WITHOUT BUNCHING-UP THE HOSE INTO A HORRIBLE KNOT. IT TAKES A BIT OF PRACTICE TO GET USED-TO WORKING WITH BLOWHOSES, AND KEEP THEM OUT OF THE WAY OF YOUR HOT BLOWPIPE, NOT-TO-MENTION PUTTING THEM ON AND TAKING THEM OFF — BUT THE REWARDS ARE WORTH IT. YOU CAN FULLY CONTROL THE EXACT AMOUNT OF AIR YOU BLOW INTO THE PIECE WHILE SIMULTANEOUSLY SHAPING IT WITH YOUR TOOLS.

SOLO BENCHBLOWING

THE SOLO TRANSFER MAY BE ACCOMPLISHED IN TWO DIFFERENT WAYS. ONE WAY IS TO JUST PARK YOUR PIPE SOMEWHERE AND RUN N' GATHER-UP A PUNTY. A HANGING YOKE IS A HANDY TOOL, IN THAT IF YOUR PIECE SAGS OR STRETCHES IN THE TIME IT TAKES YOU TO MAKE YOUR PUNTY — AT LEAST IT WILL STAY ON-CENTER. PLEASE NOTE THAT MOTHER EARTH'S GRAVITATIONAL PULL REALLY LIKES TO ATTRACT YOUR PHENOMENAL WORK OF ART HER WAY, ESPECIALLY IF THE GLASS IS STILL A BIT HOT SOMEWHERE. MAKE SURE THAT WHEN YOU HANG IT UP THAT IT'S NOT MOVING, AND RELATIVELY STONE COLD.

THE OTHER WAY IS TO GATHER UP YOUR PUNTY WITH ONE HAND WHILE TURNING YOUR PIECE WITH THE OTHER HAND. THIS WILL ELIMINATE ANY UNWANTED ELONGATION OR OFF-CENTERNESS. IT IS HOWEVER SOMEWHAT A CHALLENGE TO MAKE THE PERFECT PUNTY. YOU HAVE TO FIND THE BALANCING POINT ON BOTH RODS AND MAINTAIN CONSISTENT, EVEN ROTATIONS.

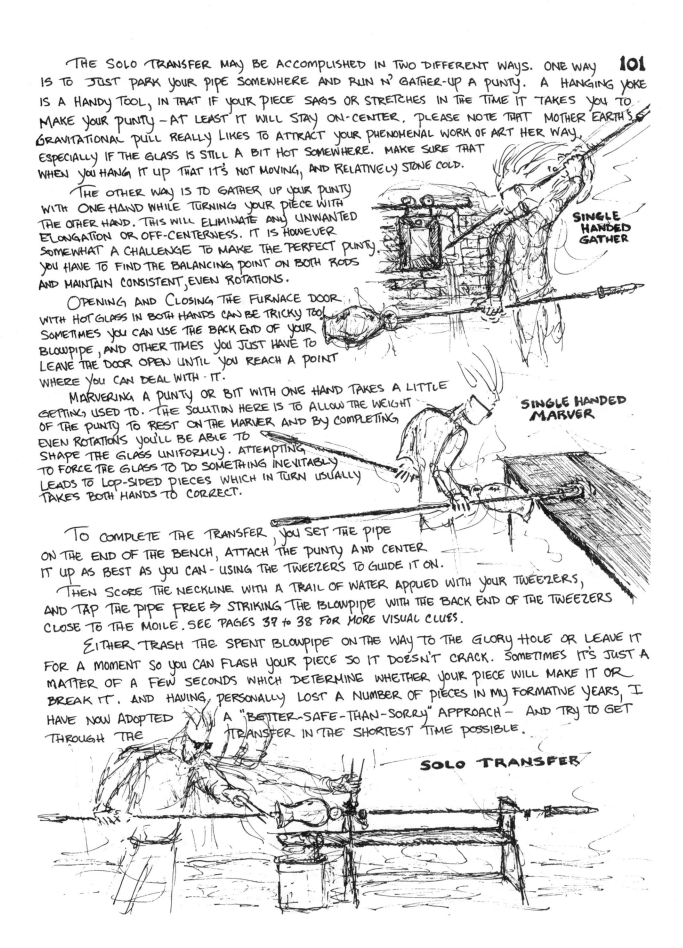

SINGLE HANDED GATHER

OPENING AND CLOSING THE FURNACE DOOR WITH HOT GLASS IN BOTH HANDS CAN BE TRICKY TOO! SOMETIMES YOU CAN USE THE BACK END OF YOUR BLOWPIPE, AND OTHER TIMES YOU JUST HAVE TO LEAVE THE DOOR OPEN UNTIL YOU REACH A POINT WHERE YOU CAN DEAL WITH IT.

MARVERING A PUNTY OR BIT WITH ONE HAND TAKES A LITTLE GETTING USED TO. THE SOLUTION HERE IS TO ALLOW THE WEIGHT OF THE PUNTY TO REST ON THE MARVER AND BY COMPLETING EVEN ROTATIONS YOU'LL BE ABLE TO SHAPE THE GLASS UNIFORMLY. ATTEMPTING TO FORCE THE GLASS TO DO SOMETHING INEVITABLY LEADS TO LOP-SIDED PIECES WHICH IN TURN USUALLY TAKES BOTH HANDS TO CORRECT.

SINGLE HANDED MARVER

TO COMPLETE THE TRANSFER, YOU SET THE PIPE ON THE END OF THE BENCH, ATTACH THE PUNTY AND CENTER IT UP AS BEST AS YOU CAN - USING THE TWEEZERS TO GUIDE IT ON.

THEN SCORE THE NECKLINE WITH A TRAIL OF WATER APPLIED WITH YOUR TWEEZERS, AND TAP THE PIPE FREE ⇒ STRIKING THE BLOWPIPE WITH THE BACK END OF THE TWEEZERS CLOSE TO THE MOILE. SEE PAGES 37 to 38 FOR MORE VISUAL CLUES.

EITHER TRASH THE SPENT BLOWPIPE ON THE WAY TO THE GLORY HOLE OR LEAVE IT FOR A MOMENT SO YOU CAN FLASH YOUR PIECE SO IT DOESN'T CRACK. SOMETIMES IT'S JUST A MATTER OF A FEW SECONDS WHICH DETERMINE WHETHER YOUR PIECE WILL MAKE IT OR BREAK IT. AND HAVING PERSONALLY LOST A NUMBER OF PIECES IN MY FORMATIVE YEARS, I HAVE NOW ADOPTED A "BETTER-SAFE-THAN-SORRY" APPROACH — AND TRY TO GET THROUGH THE TRANSFER IN THE SHORTEST TIME POSSIBLE.

SOLO TRANSFER

After you complete the transfer, it's pretty much business-as-usual. You can heat, trim and finish-up your vessel as you see fit. If you'd like to puff-out the shoulders on your piece, you can use a steamstick (as described on page 69), or if one's available — you can use a special curved soffietta designed for solo glassblowers. First, you must prepare the piece in order for it to work effectively.

You need to heat the shoulders well, and smooth the lip of the vessel flat and round (with the jacks) so that you create a uniform mating surface between the lip and puffer unit (or steamstick).

Then, merely insert the tool - making full contact with the entire lip and puff to inflate the piece. Do your best not to push the lip in so much. Just try to maintain a consistent seal and allow the pressure to puff the piece as much as you desire. You can then finish the vessel in whichever manner that you prefer.

You can thread or add trails to your piece in solo blowing, too. It requires impeccable timing and some finesse. First, give the piece a good flash, gather up a fresh bit, or heat-up a premade color bit. Next, run back to the bench, sit down with the pipe close to you and hold the punty as close to the bit as you dare (to get a better feel and greater accuracy in handling) - touch-up the bit and roll the work away from you to trail the bit on.

It helps to have a pipe bucket behind the bench to trash your punty in after you're done with it.

Then, reheat your piece to melt the threads or trails in so that they don't pop-off on you later.

Finally when it's time to box your work give the piece one good long flash. At a break-off tray, chill the punty and/or add a drop of water and bonk the piece off. Set the punty aside (where it won't burn you or anything else), put on the gloves and quickly load the piece in the kiln.

Or if you can set the piece in on it's lip (and you're going-in to a top-loader), you may opt to tap the work off directly into the annealer - eliminating the need to don the gloves.

Back when I was my age (and had incredible amounts of energy) I remember executing colored triple-bubble compotes/bowls all by myself! It was nuts!, or, maybe I was... needless to say, the kill ratio was pretty high, and not many pieces survived. But, at least I did!

The point of this amusing anecdote is to encourage you to design and blow within your ability. It can be extremely frustrating to continually lose pieces just because you lack help or one small thing or another.

APPENDIX F
HEALTH & SAFETY

THERE IS SOME INHERENT DANGER WORKING WITH A MATERIAL SUCH AS GLASS. IN BOTH THE HOT AND COLD STATE, GLASS HAS THE POTENTIAL TO INJURE YOU IN A VARIETY OF WAYS. THE KEY TO AVOIDING INJURY IS TO BECOME AWARE OF THE RISKS FIRST. KNOWING ALSO WHAT TO DO JUST IN CASE A SITUATION ARISES IS YOUR SECOND BEST DEFENSE.

OUTLINED BELOW ARE SOME OF THE FACTORS AND RISKS YOU MAY ENCOUNTER WHILE IN A GLASS SHOP, AND HOW TO DEAL WITH THEM ACCORDINGLY. THIS INFORMATION SHOULD BE AS FAMILIAR TO YOU AS BLOCKING, MARVERING, AND BLOWING.

RULE NUMERO UNO: SAFETY FIRST!

EVERY CLASS YOU TAKE IN GLASSBLOWING SHOULD BEGIN WITH A HEALTH AND SAFETY DISCUSSION. YOU SHOULD KNOW EXACTLY WHERE THE FIRST AID KIT IS AND THAT IS STOCKED WITH ADEQUATE SUPPLIES. YOU SHOULD ALSO KNOW WHERE THE CLOSEST PHONE IS ⇒ DIALING 9·1·1 IN AN EMERGENCY SITUATION MAY BE YOUR BEST AND WISEST MOVE. YOU SHOULD USE COMMON SENSE WHILE WORKING IN A GLASS STUDIO. DON'T PANIC! AVOID THOSE SITUATIONS WHICH PUT YOU AND/OR YOUR STUDIO MATES AT RISK. NEVER PERFORM FIRST-AID UNLESS YOU HAVE BEEN INSTRUCTED TO DO SO.

CUTS, PUNCTURES AND ABRASIONS

WHERE THE SURFACE OF THE SKIN IS BROKEN WILL REQUIRE DIRECT PRESSURE TO STOP THE BLEEDING. USE A FRESH STERILE GUAZE OR BANDAGE AND APPLY PRESSURE TO THE WOUND. IF IT IS DEEP, LONG OR CONTINUES BLEEDING AFTER SEVERAL MINUTES → SEEK PROFESSIONAL MEDICAL ATTENTION. NOTIFY THE INSTRUCTOR OR SHOP SUPERVISOR AND MAKE THEM AWARE OF THE SITUATION. WOUNDS NEED TO BE WASHED WELL, WITH DISINFECTANT SOAP TO PREVENT THE RISK OF INFECTION. KEEPING THE WOUND CLEAN AND DRY WILL AID IN THE HEALING PROCESS. SOMETIMES A STITCH OR TWO CAN SAVE YOU WEEKS IN HEALING TIME.

BURNS

RESULT (USUALLY) FROM EXPOSURE TO HEAT, ELECTRICITY, RADIATION OR CAUSTIC CHEMICALS. MOST FREQUENTLY IT'LL HAPPEN TO YOU IN THE HOT SHOP (OR IN MY CASE, MY KITCHEN!).

FIRST DEGREE BURNS APPEAR AS REDDENING OF THE SKIN.
SECOND DEGREE BURNS APPEARS AS THE FORMATION OF BLISTERS - USUALLY FROM CLOSE OR DIRECT CONTACT WITH HEAT. DO NOT "POP" BLISTERS - THEY'RE YOUR BODY'S NATURAL HEALING PROCESS AT WORK AND OFFER YOU PROTECTION AGAINST INFECTION. IF YOU NOTICE THESE TYPES OF BURNS - SEEK MEDICAL ATTENTION.
THIRD DEGREE BURNS DESTROY BOTH UPPER AND LOWER LAYERS OF YOUR SKIN AND ARE THE MOST SERIOUS OF BURNS. YOU MUST SEEK MEDICAL ATTENTION TO REDUCE PAIN, SHOCK AND INFECTION.

TREATMENT: IF YOU GET BURNED WHILE BLOWING, PUT THE GLASS PIECE DOWN AND DEAL WITH IT IMMEDIATELY! THERE IS A RUMOR GOING AROUND THAT IF YOU GET YOUR BURN ON ICE WITHIN TEN SECONDS IT WILL SIGNIFICANTLY REDUCE THE BURN AND PAIN AND SUFFERING. I TRIED IT ONCE AND IT SEEMED TO WORK! IN ANY CASE, DO YOUR BEST TO IMMERSE THE INJURED AREA IN A 'BATH' OF CLEAN ICE WATER. THIS WILL PREVENT OXYGEN FROM "FEEDING THE FIRE". YOUR SKIN CONTINUES TO BURN UP TO 20 MINUTES AFTER EXPOSURE - GIVEN THE OXYGEN TO DO SO.

THE PAIN FROM BURNS CAN BE EXCRUCIATING. A COUPLE OF ASPIRIN OR IBUPROFEN MAY BE TAKEN FOR TEMPORARY RELIEF UNTIL YOU SEE A DOCTOR. SILVADENE, A PRESCRIBED OINTMENT MAY BE APPLIED TO THE BURN TO RELIEVE THE PAIN AND CONTAINS MEDICATION TO AID IN HEALING. ALOE VERA AND VITAMIN E CAN WORK WONDERS AS WELL.

HEAT EXPOSURE \ HEAT STRESS

IMAGINE IF YOU WILL... YOU'RE BLOWING IN THE HOT AND HUMID SUMMER... AFTER A PERIOD OF TIME YOU START FEELING: A LITTLE LIGHT-HEADED, SWEATING PUDDLES, AND BECOMING TIRED AND WEAK. THESE ARE SOME OF THE SYMPTOMS OF HEAT STRESS/EXPOSURE.

IT'S VERY EASY TO BECOME DIZZY AND PASS-OUT FROM TOO MUCH HEAT. YOUR BODY SHUTS DOWN WHEN IT CAN NO LONGER COPE WITH PROLONGED EXPOSURE TO HEAT. ITS NATURAL COOLING SYSTEM ⇒ SWEATING - IS INEFFECTIVE AND YOUR BODY BEGINS TO FREAK-OUT.

104 "IF YOU CAN'T STAND THE HEAT—THEN STAY OUT OF THE KITCHEN!" SO THE OL' CLICHE GOES. AS WITH MANY OF OUR COLORFUL IDIOMS SUCH AS THIS, THERE IS A RING OF TRUTH TO THEM. IF YOU'RE FEELING DIZZY, GET AWAY FROM THE HEAT SOURCE.

SOME STUDIOS ARE SIMPLY HOTTER TO WORK IN THAN OTHERS, MERELY BY THE WAY THEY ARE LAID-OUT AND BY THE TYPE OF VENTILATION SYSTEM THEY'VE INSTALLED.

SOME DAYS ARE HOTTER THAN OTHERS. YOU MAY HAVE TO RESCHEDULE YOUR BLOWSLOT TO THE EVENING HOURS—WHEN IT'S COOLER, OR SIMPLY LIMIT THE AMOUNT OF TIME IN WHICH YOU ARE EXPOSED TO THE HEAT.

IT TAKES TIME TO ACCLIMATE YOURSELF TO WORKING IN FRONT OF A FURNACE AND GLORY HOLE. SOMETIMES IT TAKES LONGER FOR SOME PEOPLE TO GET USED TO IT. AND SOME PEOPLE SIMPLY NEVER WILL. BELOW ARE SOME OF THE MOST FAMILIAR WARNING SIGNS OF HEAT ILLNESS AND METHODS TO TREAT IT.

HEAT FATIGUE IS RECOGNIZED BY LOSS IN MOTOR SKILLS, IMPAIRED
PERFORMANCE—MENTAL OR PHYSICAL—WHEN EXPOSED TO HEAT. OFTENTIMES IT'S FROM A LACK OF ACCLIMATIZATION, COMPOUNDED BY THE FACT THAT YOU'RE TIRED.

INSTEAD OF WORKING STRAIGHT THROUGH YOUR BLOWSLOT, BREAK IT UP A BIT. TRADE OFF WITH YOUR PARTNER, ALLOW THEM TO GAFF A PIECE WHILE YOU KICK-BACK FOR A BIT. TAKE A BREAK ONCE IN A WHILE. GET FRESH AIR, BE SURE TO HAVE SOME FOOD IN YOUR SYSTEM AND DRINK PLENTY OF FLUIDS.

HEAT RASH A.K.A. PRICKLY HEAT COMES FROM SWEATING
CONTINUOSLY IN HUMID HEAT. YOUR SWEAT GLANDS GET PLUGGED AND TURN RED. MILD DRYING LOTIONS AND CLEANING YOUR SKIN SHOULD HELP, AS WELL AS RELAXING IN COOLER AREAS.

HEAT CRAMPS ARE PAINFUL MUSCLE SPASMS WHICH CAN OCCUR FROM WORKING LONG AND HARD IN
THE HEAT—SWEATING ALOT AND ONLY DRINKING WATER. THIS IN TURN DEPLETES YOUR BODY OF SALT. IT'S IMPORTANT TO CONSUME SOME SALT IN YOUR DIET IF YOU ANTICIPATE WORKING AND SWEATING IN HOT ENVIORNMENTS. OR MAKE A POINT OF DRINKING THOSE THIRST QUENCHERS POPULAR WITH ATHELETES.

HEAT EXHAUSTION MAY BE FELT AS NAUSEA, FATIGUE OR HEADACHE. YOUR SKIN MAY BE CLAMMY
AND MOIST, PALE, AND POSSIBLY FLUSH COMPLEXION. OFTEN IT'S FROM WORKING TOO LONG IN FRONT OF THE HEAT, NOT BEING USED TO IT, AND MOST LIKELY A RESULT OF DEHYDRATION. USUALLY, TOO, YOUR URINE VOLUME IS SMALL AND HIGHLY CONCENTRATED. TREATMENT: MOVE TO A COOLER ENVIORNMENT ⇒ OUTSIDE, DOWNSTAIRS TO A BASEMENT, SEATTLE OR ICELAND, LIE DOWN AND CHILL-OUT! DRINK PLENTY OF FLUIDS TO MAINTAIN AN EQUILIBRIUM AND TAKE IT EASY!

"I DON'T FEEL SO GOOD"

HEAT STROKE IS RECOGNIZABLE BY HOT DRY RED SKIN, CONFUSION, AND LOSS OF CONSCIOUSNESS.
CONTRIBUTING FACTORS INCLUDE: SUSTAINED EXERTION IN HEAT, LACK OF PHYSICAL FITNESS AND OBESITY, RECENT ALCOHOL INTAKE, DEHYDRATION, INDIVIDUAL SUSCEPTIBILITY AND CHRONIC CARDIOVASCULAR DISEASE. IT'S BEST TREATED BY RAPID COOLING → IMMERSION IN CHILLED WATER OR WRAPPING UP IN A WET SHEET, AND FANNING WITH COOL DRY AIR, AND TREATING FOR SHOCK IF NECESSARY.

PREVENTION IS THE KEY TO AVOIDING THESE SITUATIONS. PEOPLE TYPICALLY DON'T RECOGNIZE
HEAT STRESS FOR WHAT IT IS. THEY'RE TOO ENGAGED IN CONCENTRATING ON KEEPING THEIR BUBBLE ON-CENTER AND THE COMPLETION OF THEIR MASTERPIECE TO WORRY ABOUT BEING TOO 'HOT'.

REMEMBER TO TAKE BREAKS, DRINK PLENTY OF FLUIDS AND MINIMIZE YOUR EXPOSURE TO THE HEAT, i.e. STAND BACK FROM THE FURNACES AND GLORY HOLES, USE HEAT SHIELDS AND HAVE YOUR ASSISTANTS PROTECT YOU FROM THE HEAT AS MUCH AS POSSIBLE. ALSO TRY TO HAVE SOME FRESH AIR ALWAYS FLOWING THROUGH THE STUDIO.

NOISE IS OFTEN OVERLOOKED AS A POTENTIAL HEALTH RISK, YET PROLONGED EXPOSURE WILL
CONTRIBUTE TO REDUCED HEARING OR EVEN DEAFNESS. INDUSTRIAL HYGENISTS WILL TELL YOU THAT THIS IS A SERIOUS HAZARD AND STEPS SHOULD BE TAKEN TO REDUCE THE LEVEL OF EXPOSURE IN THE WORKPLACE — EITHER DIRECTLY OR LOCALLY.

USE OF SOUND SHIELDS/BARRIERS AROUND NOISY EQUIPMENT: BLOWERS, BURNERS, GRINDERS ETC. WILL HELP CONTAIN THE SOUND FROM REACHING YOU. YOU MAY OPT TO WEAR EARPHONES OR EAR-PLUGS SHOULD THERE BE NO WAY—PHYSICALLY OR FINANCIALLY—TO DEAL WITH THE SITUATION. THESE SIMPLE DEVICES CAN DRASTICALLY REDUCE THE DECIBEL LEVEL AND STILL ALLOW YOU TO HEAR DIRECTIONS OR PEOPLE TALK.

CRANKING UP THE STEREO IS NOT A SOLUTION! IT ONLY COMPOUNDS YOUR LEVEL OF NOISE EXPOSURE. PERSONAL STEREOS (WALKMANS AND THE LIKE) CAN MAKE YOU DEAF TO THE WORLD AND THEREBY POTENTIALLY HAZARDOUS AS WELL.

AIR QUALITY

AIR QUALITY IN THE GLASS STUDIO IS VITALLY IMPORTANT. THERE ARE A NUMBER OF FACTORS, AGENTS AND SITUATIONS WHICH DIRECTLY EFFECT THE AIR YOU BREATHE. THERE ARE ALSO A NUMBER OF STEPS WHICH MAY BE TAKEN TO INSURE THAT IT IS THE CLEANEST AND FRESHEST AVAILABLE.

FIRST, IF YOU SMOKE - QUIT!! THIS CAN GREATLY REDUCE NUMEROUS HEALTH RISKS. THE SMOKER HAS LITTLE IN THE WAY OF PROTECTIVE TISSUES WHICH THE BODY PROVIDES AS NATURAL FILTRATION SYSTEMS. IN ADDITION, THE TAR AND RESIN FROM THE THINGS YOU SMOKE ACT AS GLUE FOR NASTIES TO STICK TO YOUR LUNGS, THUS INCREASING YOUR SUSCEPTIBILITY TO RESPIRTORY HAZARDS AND ILLNESS.

ALSO, IT STINKS!

LIKE NOISE, AIR POLLUTION CAN BE DEALT WITH DIRECTLY OR LOCALLY. VENTILATION IS THE KEY TO CLEARING AND CLEANING UP THE OVERALL PICTURE IN ANY SHOP. THE EXHAUST OF BURNING GASES FROM FURNACES AND GLORY HOLES CONTAINS CARBON MONOXIDE. OVEREXPOSURE TO CARBON MONOXIDE CAN CAUSE HEADACHES, NAUSEA, WEAKNESS, DIZZINESS, CONFUSION HALLUCINATIONS AND FAINTING. SMOKERS ARE EVEN MORE SUSCEPTIBLE TO IT'S EFFECTS.

A **VENTILATION HOOD** OVER THE FURNACE AND GLORY HOLES ARE STRONGLY RECOMMENDED FOR ANY HOT SHOP. AN ADEQUATE SUPPLY OF FRESH AIR SHOULD BE AVAILABLE AS WELL. THOSE PIECES OF EQUIPMENT WHICH COMBUST GASES ARE COMPETING FOR THE SAME AIR THAT YOU BREATHE. AN OPEN WINDOW, DOOR, OR VENT SHOULD ALLOW AIR TO GET IN.

NUISANCES SUCH AS DUST, AIRBORNS, PARTICULATES, AND OFF-GASES MUST ALSO BE ADDRESSED. SOME OF THESE MAY NEVER HAVE AN ODOR, SUCH AS ASBESTOS OR SILICA DUST, WHILE OTHERS MAY BRING TEARS TO YOUR EYES (Y'KNOW THAT COOL FLOURINE SMELL YOU GET FROM WHITE POWDERED GLASS THAT REEL·Y CLEANS OUT THE OL' SINUSES?). PREVENTION, ONCE AGAIN, IS THE BEST DETERENT IN COMBATING THIS PROBLEM.

V IS FOR **VENTILATION** — IF YOU'RE USING POWDERED GLASS TO COLOR YOUR PIECES, DO IT IN A POWDERING BOOTH OR AT LEAST UNDER THE HOOD. WEAR AN APPROVED RESPIRATOR OR AT LEAST A DUST MASK. A 'NECKERCHIEF DON'T CUT IT PAL! THE CHEMICALS IN THOSE PRETTY GLASS POWDERS ARE VERY EASY AND VERY BAD TO BREATHE! THE VAPORS GIVEN OFF WHEN THEY MAKE CONTACT WITH HOT GLASS ARE TOXIC AS WELL, SO DO YOUR BEST TO KEEP AWAY FROM THEM DURING APPLICATION.

SILICA, THE MAIN INGREDIENT IN GLASS, IS AKIN TO ASBESTOS. IT IS A HOOK-SHAPED PARTICLE WHICH ENTERS THE LUNGS AND ATTACHES TO THE CILIA THERE **PERMANENTLY**. AFTER PROLONGED EXPOSURE, ENOUGH OF THESE PARTICLES BUNCH-UP AND FORM NODULES, CONTRIBUTING TO THEIR OWN FORM OF LUNG CANCER KNOWN AS SILICOSIS. AGAIN, PREVENTION IS THE KEY IN LIMITING YOUR EXPOSURE TO THIS NASTY, BUT NECESSARY ELEMENT.

POWDERED GLASS CONTAINS A LARGE PERCENTAGE OF FREE (UNMELTED) SILICA. BATCHED GLASS, POWDERED OR PELLETIZED, CONTAINS SILICA AND MUST BE HANDLED WITH CARE. A SEPARATE ROOM, WELL-VENTILATED AND DRY IS RECOMMENDED FOR MIXING AND STORING, AND BAGGING BATCH THAT IS TO BE CHARGED. ALL SURFACES AND FLOORS SHOULD GO THROUGH PERIODIC CLEANING TO CUT DOWN ON HAZARDOUS DUSTS WHICH TEND TO ACCUMULATE WITH TIME. USE FLOOR SWEEPING COMPOUNDS OR WET CLEAN-UP METHODS TO KEEP THOSE DUSTS DOWN, AND WEAR A RESPIRATOR.

A WORD OR TWO ON **RESPIRATORS**: IT'S IMPORTANT TO USE THE CORRECT RESPIRATOR FOR THE TYPE OF TASK WHICH YOU ARE PERFORMING. MANY DUST MASKS WILL PROTECT AGAINST DUSTS, MISTS AND WELDING FUMES; BUT NOT AGAINST GASES AND VAPORS. FOR GAS AND VAPOR, A CARTRIDGE RESPIRATOR MAY BE REQUIRED. FOR A PROPER FIT — A USER CANNOT HAVE FACIAL GROWTH (BEARDS) — ANY BREAK IN THE SEAL OF THE MASK NEGATES THE EFFECTIVENESS OF THE RESPIRATOR. TIGHTEN THE STRAPS AND BLOW OUT TO SEE IF THE MASK PUSHES AWAY FROM THE FACE, THEN SUCK IN TO SEE IF THE MASK GETS TIGHTER ON THE FACE. A CHANGE IN SIZE MAY BE NECESSARY TO ACHIEVE A COMPLETE SEAL.

STORE YOUR RESPIRATOR IN A SEALED PLASTIC BAG WHEN NOT IN USE; THIS WILL PREVENT CONTAMINATION. ALSO, CHANGE THE FILTERS AS NEEDED ← THIS DEPENDS ON HOW OFTEN YOU USE IT. CLOGGED CARTRIDGES CAN, IN SOME CASES, BE MORE HARMFUL THAN HELPFUL, GIVING YOU FALSE CONFIDENCE IN SOMETHING WHICH DOESN'T WORK.

CHARGING GLASS EXPOSES YOU TO A DOUBLE-DOSE OF HEALTH HAZARDS: HEAT AND PARTICULATES. A FACE SHIELD, PROTECTIVE SAFETY GLASSES, GLOVES (KEVLAR ARE RECOMMENDED) PROPER CLOTHING AND A RESPIRATOR SHOULD CUT DOWN ON MOST OF THE PROBLEMS YOU MAY ENCOUNTER.

"GET IN & GET OUT AS QUICK AS YOU CAN" IS MY MOTTO, ESPECIALLY WITH POWDERED / SANDY BATCH — ALOT OF AIRBORN MATERIAL IS KICKED-UP DURING THE CHARGING PROCESS. SIMPLY MOVING THE BATCH FROM THE BARREL

OR MIXING RECEPTACLE TO THE CHARGING SCOOP / SHOVEL - TO THE FURNACE PRODUCES A FAIR AMOUNT OF AIRBORNS. AND THAT'S JUST CLEAR GLASS! COLORED GLASS BATCH HAS A WHOLE HOST OF NASTIES IN IT THAT SHOULD AVOIDED AT ALL COSTS. IT'S A FUNNY TRICK OF NATURE AND CHEMISTRY THAT THE PRETTIEST COLORS ARE ALSO THE MOST TOXIC!

BAGGING YOUR BATCH IS A SIMPLE AND EFFECTIVE METHOD FOR CUTTING DOWN ON SUPERFLUOUS DUSTS COMMON TO THE CHARGING PROCESS. BATCH MAY BE TRANSFERRED TO PAPER LUNCH BAGS, SEALED AND CHUCKED-IN TO THE AWAITING HUNGRY FURNACE. THE BAGS BURN UP WITHOUT A TRACE SO YOU CAN BREATHE EASY.

KEEP THE SCENE CLEAN. PACK IT IN, PACK IT OUT! CLEANLINESS IS NEXT TO GODLINESS. WHICHEVER SLOGAN YOU MAY SUBSCRIBE TO, KEEPING YOUR STUDIO CLEAN IS IMPORTANT FOR MANY REASONS. FIRST, IT'S EASIER TO FIND THINGS. SECOND, IT LOOKS BETTER. THIRD, IT'S HEALTHIER FOR ALL OF THE PEOPLE USING THE FACILITIES.

MOST STUDIOS THAT I'VE WORKED IN REQUIRE THAT YOU CLEAN-UP YOUR MESS WHEN YOU'RE DONE WORKING. THIS INCLUDES THE AREA AROUND YOUR BENCH, THE GLORY HOLE AND FURNACE, AND ANY OTHER EQUIPMENT YOU'VE BEEN USING. USE FLOOR-SWEEPING COMPOUNDS TO KEEP THE HAZARDOUS DUSTS DOWN, AND IF POSSIBLE, HOSE AND SQUEEGEE THE FLOOR AFTERWORDS. AVOID LEAVING STANDING WATER / PUDDLES IN THE BLOWING AREA WHERE IT MAY BE SLIPPERY AND DANGEROUS FOR BLOWERS WORKING AFTER YOU.

BE CAREFUL WHEN SWEEPING AND DISPOSING OF **FLOOR MODELS**. THEY ARE MOST LIKELY SHARP AND HOT, NOT ONLY WILL IT BURN YOUR BROOM (OR SKIN - SO DON'T TOUCH!), IT MAY IGNITE YOUR TRASH BARREL ON FIRE! PLACE ALL POTENTIALLY HOT TRASH IN A METAL WASTE BARREL DEDICATED TO THIS SPECIFIC PURPOSE.

AS VISUAL ARTISTS YOUR **EYES** MAY BE YOUR MOST COVETED ORGANS. THEY TOO, ARE SUSCEPTIBLE TO THEIR OWN SET OF HAZARDS WHILE BLOWING GLASS.

HEAT FIRST AND FOREMOST, WILL EFFECT YOUR EYES. ANY PAIR OF GLASSES WILL PROTECT YOU FROM EXCESSIVE HEAT RADIATION, AND FROM THEM DRYING OUT (YOUR EYES).

INFRARED AND ULTRA-VIOLET RADIATION ARE TWO OTHER BY-PRODUCTS OF GLASS MELTING CHAMBERS (AND MOST TORCHES AS WELL). DIDYMIUM GLASSES, POPULAR WITH MOST LAMPWORKERS ARE NOT COMPLETELY SUFFICIENT IN FILTERING ALL HARMFUL WAVELENGTHS OF **U/V** AND **IR** EXPERIENCED IN FURNACE-STYLE GLASSBLOWING. WELDERS LENSES WITH A 2.3 RATING OR BETTER CAN HELP FILTER MOST OF THE HARMFUL RADIATION YOU'LL ENCOUNTER.

THERE ARE NOW SUPPLIERS OF SAFETY GLASSES WHICH SPECIALIZE IN MAKING LENSES SPECIFICALLY DESIGNED FOR FURNACE GLASSBLOWERS (TO YOUR PRESCRIPTION TOO!). THEY CLAIM THEIR PRODUCT WILL FILTER OUT ALL OF THE HARMFUL WAVELENGTHS OF **U/V** AND INFRARED WITHOUT LEAVING YOU IN THE DARK LIKE SOME WELDING GLASSES CAN. I WOULD RECOMMEND THE INVESTMENT IF YOU'RE CONSIDERING BLOWING GLASS WITH ANY GREAT REGULARITY.

THE OTHER BENEFIT TO WEARING PROPER EYE PROTECTION IS THE SAFETY THEY PROVIDE IN SHIELDING YOUR EYES FROM FLYING OBJECTS. FREQUENTLY, GLASS POPS OFF THE END OF COOLING PIPES, OR FROM ONES BEING PREHEATED. GLASS BREAKS. FLYING HAZARDS OCCUR. AN UNNECESSARY ACCIDENT MAY ONLY TAKE A SPLIT-SECOND AND NO AMOUNT OF "I SHOULD DA..." OR "IF ONLY I'D...!" WILL REVERSE POTENTIALLY PERMANENT DAMAGE. AGAIN, SAFETY GLASSES WITH SIDE-SHIELDS ARE YOUR BEST FORM OF PROTECTION. AND THEY ONLY WORK IF THEY'RE ON YOUR FACE, NOT JUST HANGING AROUND YOUR NECK!

ERGONOMICS IS ANOTHER MATTER TO BE AWARE OF. GLASSBLOWING IS, AS YOU'RE PROBABLY AWARE OF, A VERY PHYSICALLY DEMANDING PROCESS. IT IS EASY TO OVERDO IT! PROBLEMS SUCH AS TENDONITIS, CARPUL TUNNEL SYNDROME AND BACK STRAIN ARE COMMON AILMENTS EXPERIENCED BY GLASSBLOWERS WHO OVEREXTEND AND REPEAT THE SAME MOTIONS FREQUENTLY. THIS OFTEN SEEN IN PRODUCTION STYLE SITUATIONS WHICH REQUIRE CONSTANT REPETITION THE KEY TO AVOIDING THESE FORMS OF OVEREXERTION IS TO RECOGNIZE THEM BEFOREHAND AND ADAPT. THIS MAY MEAN ADJUSTING YOUR BODY ENGLISH (LANGUAGE), i.e. HOW YOU SIT OR STAND, HOW YOU TURN THE PIPE AND WORK AND HOLD YOUR TOOLS. CHANGING YOUR POSITION SLIGHTLY MAY MAKE A DRAMATIC DIFFERENCE ON THE NEGATIVE IMPACTS OF THE PROCESS. IF YOU PERFORM REPETITIOUS TASKS - BREAK THEM UP BY PERFORMING OTHER JOBS WHICH USE OTHER MUSCLE GROUPS.

ANTI-FATIGUE MATS, ALTHOUGH PRETTY SMELLY WHEN YOU DROP HOT GLASS ON THEM, CAN REDUCE BACK STRAIN AND FOOT INJURY. THEY'LL MAKE YOUR DAY GO BETTER, ESPECIALLY IF YOU HAVE TO BE STANDING ON YOUR FEET ON CONCRETE FLOORS, TURNING POLE. A BACKREST AT THE BENCH MAY OFFER SOME RELIEF AS WELL. GOOD SHOES, WITH ANKLE SUPPORT, CAN HELP QUITE A BIT TOO!

IF YOUR GLORY HOLE AND FURNACE GATHERING PORTS ARE HIGH, YOU MAY RISK OVEREXERTING YOUR BACK, SHOULDER AND ARMS BY CONSTANTLY LIFTING UP YOUR GLASS PIECES, PARTICULARLY WITH THICK OR LARGE OBJECTS. TRY LOWERING, IF POSSIBLE, THE GLORY HOLE TO A HEIGHT CLOSER TO YOUR WAIST. THE LESS UP AND DOWN LIFTING/LOWERING OF YOUR BLOWPIPE YOU HAVE TO DO, THE BETTER!

THE DIAMETER OF THE BLOWPIPE OR PUNTY YOU ARE USING ALSO PLAYS AN IMPORTANT ROLE IN THE ERGONOMIC OUTLOOK. IT IS NOT ADVISED TO USE GOBLET PIPES TO BLOW LARGE BOWLS OR PLATTERS. YOU ARE SIMPLY FORCED TO TURN THESE SMALL DIAMETER PIPES MORE FREQUENTLY AND SUBSEQUENTLY OVER-WORK YOUR WRISTS. USE THE LARGEST DIAMETER PIPE YOU CAN - APPROPRIATE FOR THE PIECE AT HAND - TO REDUCE OVER-EXERTION ON YOUR WRISTS.

MANY GLASSBLOWERS HAVE ADOPTED WEARING WRISTBANDS WHEN WORKING ON LARGE AND HEAVY PIECES TO LIMIT OVEREXTENSION WHILE TURNING AND LIFTING THE PIPE.

A PIPE COOLER CAN MAKE YOUR LIFE EASIER AS WELL. BEING ABLE TO GRIP AND TURN THE PIPE CLOSER TO THE PIECE WILL MAKE BETTER USE OF YOUR ENERGY, GIVE YOU BETTER BALANCE, MORE CONTROL, AND MAKE YOU CLOSER FRIENDS WITH YOUR ARTWORK.

IF YOU'RE WORKING WITH ASSISTANTS, ALLOW THEM TO TURN POLE, TAKE REHEATS AND GATHERS FOR YOU. THAT WAY YOU DON'T FRY YOURSELF OUT TRYING TO TAKE CARE OF EVERYTHING.

GET HELP WHEN LIFTING HEAVY OBJECTS. DON'T ALLOW THE PIPE BUCKETS TO BECOME TOO FULL BEFORE YOU HAVE TO EMPTY THEM. MAKE A PRACTICE OF DUMPING THEM SAFELY EVERY DAY, OR BEFORE THEY'RE ONE-THIRD FULL. BE CAREFUL OF HOT GLASS, SHARP GLASS AND GLASS DUST WITHIN! WEAR GLOVES, PROTECTIVE EYE-GLASSES, A DUST MASK, AND LIFT WITH YOUR LEGS, NOT YOUR BACK!

FIRE! BACK IN THE GOOD OL' DAYS GLASS STUDIOS USED TO BE BUILT WITH WOOD AND FUELED WITH WOOD (OR COAL). THEY BECAME NOTORIOUS FOR BURNING TO THE GROUND (ONCE IN WHILE,) AND THE THREAT OF FIRE WAS VERY REAL.

IT'S ALOT MORE RARE THESE DAYS FOR GLASS STUDIOS TO BURN DOWN. MOST FURNACES ARE RUN OFF GAS OR ELECTRICITY. THE "FIRE" IS CONTAINED BY WELL-DESIGNED, HEAVILY INSULATED, AND FINELY-CRAFTED FURNACES. THAT DOES NOT MEAN, HOWEVER, THAT YOU SHOULD BE CARELESS ABOUT HOW YOU WORK WITH THIS **FIRE-ART-FORM.**

KEEP YOUR WORKSPACE CLEAN. REMOVE FLAMMABLE OBJECTS AND WATCH OUT FOR THINGS WHICH ARE POTENTIAL FIRE HAZARDS. ALSO BE AWARE OF CUT-OFFS AND CHUNKS OF EXCESS GLASS THAT ARE TRIMMED OFF WORKS IN PROGRESS. THEY MAY END UP TOUCHING SOMETHING FLAMMABLE AND CREATE A TIMED-DELAY FIRE.

PAY ATTENTION TO WHAT GOES INTO YOUR **TRASH** BUCKET AND WHAT TRASH GOES INTO YOUR **PIPE** BUCKET. YOU DON'T WANT ANY UNEXPECTED FLARE-UPS HAPPENING AS A RESULT OF SOMEONE'S CARELESSNESS IN SEPARATING THEIR TRASH! (AUTHORS NOTE: TRUST ME! THIS ONE'S HAPPENED ONE-TOO-MANY-A-TIME NOT TO BE TAKEN **SERIOUSLY**).

MOST HOT GLASS CLASSES THAT YOU TAKE WILL BEGIN WITH A WORD OR TWO ON HEALTH, SAFETY AND FIRE ISSUES - AND WHAT TO DO IN THE EVENT OF AN EMERGENCY. NEVERTHELESS - TAKE SOME TIME OUT TO NOTE WHERE THE FIRE EXTINGUISHERS ARE, THE CLOSEST EXITS, AND THE LOCATION OF THE NEAREST TELEPHONE.

IT WOULD BE WISE ALSO TO ENROLL IN A FIRST-AID CLASS AND/OR TAKE SOME TIME OUT TO FAMILIARIZE YOURSELF WITH THE TECHNIQUES OF FIGHTING FIRES. LOCAL FIRE DEPARTMENTS OFTEN SPONSER SUCH CLASSES FROM TIME-TO-TIME - SO CHECK THEM OUT. IT MAY BE WHAT SAVES THE HOT SHOP WHERE YOU'RE WORKING, YOUR LIFE, OR SOMEONE ELSES.

IN MOST CASES, IF YOU DISCOVER A SMALL 'CONTAINED' FIRE, YOU MAY DEAL WITH IT: BY YANKING THE EXTINGUISHER OFF THE WALL, PULL THE SAFETY PIN/RING, AND SQUEEZE THE TRIGGER UNIT WHILE AIMING AT THE BASE OF THE FIRE (NOT JUST THE FLAMES) - UNTIL IT'S EXTINGUISHED.

IF THE FIRE IS MORE THAN YOU CAN HANDLE AND GETTING OUT-OF-CONTROL, → ALERT ALL

OF THE PEOPLE IN THE BUILDING TO GET OUT (PULL A FIRE A ARM, IF IT'S AVAILABLE) AND GET TO SAFETY YOURSELF. AS IN ANY EMERGENCY SITUATION OR FIRST AID CRISIS, CALL **911** AND GET HELP. STAY ON THE PHONE TO BE SURE TO PROVIDE THE DISPATCHER WITH ALL OF THE NECESSARY INFORMATION.

THAT'S IT FOR THE HEALTH & SAFETY SECTION FOR THIS BOOK. NOW, TO LEAVE YOU ON A MORE HUMOROUS NOTE, HERE'S A REFERENCE CHART FOR YOU, IN CASE YOU RUN OUT OF IDEAS OF WHAT TO MAKE.

101 THINGS YOU CAN DO TO A HOT GLASS BUBBLE

GLOSSARY

A.K.A. ALSO·KNOW·AS...

AIR MARVER SHAPING HOT GLASS ON A PUNTY OR PIPE USING ONLY GRAVITY AND ROTATION.

ANNEAL THE PROCESS OF SLOWLY COOLING GLASS IN ORDER RELIEVE INTERNAL STRESS AND THERMAL INBALANCES

ANNEALER A.K.A. "THE BOX" INSULATED CHAMBER DESIGNED TO ANNEAL GLASS. OFTEN HEATED BY ELECTRICAL ELEMENTS, AND CONTROLLED BY COMPUTERS OR MANUALLY. OLD-STYLE ANNEALERS WERE GAS-FIRED OR RUN OFF WASTE HEAT FROM THE FURNACE.

ANNEALER FACE DIRECT IMPRESSION OF A BRICK OR THE BOTTOM OF THE ANNEALER ON THE SURFACE OF YOUR GLASS. IT'S USUALLY A SIGN THAT THE PIECE WAS PUT AWAY TOO HOT, OR THAT THE ANNEALER WAS TURNED UP TOO HIGH.

B-TEAM NOT OF THE "A"-TEAM. BUNCH OF CRAZY ARTISTS DETERMINED TO EXPOSE THE WORLD TO THE PHENOMENA OF GLASS BLOWING THROUGH PERFORMANCES (HIGHLY ENTERTAINING!) & EXHIBITIONS.

BATCH TERM FOR THE RAW CHEMICALS WHICH MAKE UP THE GLASS FORMULA. WHEN HEATED TO IT'S MELTING POINT, IT TURNS INTO GLASS.

BENCHBLOW THE PROCESS OF BLOWING INTO THE PIPE. DONE BY AN ASSISTANT WHILE THE **GAFFER** WORKS THE GLASS – SEATED AT THE BENCH.

BIG GUNS TOP O' THE HEAP. THOSE PEOPLE MOST SUCCESSFUL AT SELLING GLASS, HAVING SOLO SHOWS AND MAKING US 'SMALL PISTOLS' JEALOUS.

BIT A BLOB OF GLASS, QUITE OFTEN GATHERED ON A PUNTY AND USED TO DECORATE GLASSWORK AND OR AS AN ATTACHMENT OF SORTS.

BLOCK – CUP-SHAPED WOODEN TOOL USED TO SHAPE GLASS OR THE ACTIVITY OF SHAPING THE GLASS WITH THE TOOL.

BONK – TO STRIKE A PIPE OR PUNTY INTENTIONALLY IN ORDER TO RELEASE THE OBJECT ON IT'S END

BONKER A LENGTH OF DENSE WOOD USED TO 'BONK' WITH.

BOX 1. ANNEALER. 2. THE PROCESS OF PUTTING A PIECE INTO AN ANNEALER

CANE GLASS WHICH HAS BEEN DRAWN OUT INTO A ROD. CAN BE COLORED OR CLEAR.

CAP THE PROCESS OF SEALING THE END OF THE BLOWPIPE – WITH THE THUMB, FINGER OR PALM – SO THAT THE BLOWN FORM (ON THE HOT END) DOESN'T COLLAPSE.

CHARGE PROCESS OF SHOVELING BATCH OR CULLET INTO A FURNACE TO MELT GLASS. NOTE: IF CHARGING BATCH – WEAR A RESPIRATOR. ALWAYS USE PROPER SAFETY GEAR AS WELL, E.G. SAFETY GLASSES / FACE SHIELD, GLOVES, PROTECTIVE CLOTHING

CHARGER THE PERSON RESPONSIBLE FOR CHARGING.

CHECK 1. TERM FOR A VISIBLE CRACKLINE IN GLASS DUE TO STRESS AND IMPROPER ANNEALING OR HANDLING. 2. THAT WHICH YOU HOPE IS "IN THE MAIL".

CHIHULY, DALE A FOUNDER OF THE PILCHUCK GLASS SCHOOL AND A VERY **BIG GUN**. THANK HIM WHEN YOU SEE HIM, HE'S DONE ALOT FOR US.

CHILL MARKS VISIBLE INDENTATIONS IN THE SURFACE OF YOUR GLASS CAUSED BY COLD TOOLS, OR GLOVES (WHEN BOXING PIECES) OR POSSIBLY FROM DROPS OF WATER HITTING THE PIECE PRIOR TO ANNEALING.

COLD SHOP A PLACE WHERE YOU COLDWORK.

COLD WORK PROCESS OF MANIPULATING GLASS WHEN IT'S IN A SOLID STATE E.G. GRINDING, CUTTING, POLISHING, ENGRAVING ETC.

COLOR A.K.A. ROD, FRIT, POWDER, KUGLER REFERS TO GLASS WHICH IS 'FLAVORED' WITH METALLIC OXIDES TO A WHOLE PALETTE OF HUES. IT MAY BE TRANSPARENT OR OPAQUE, COMPATIBLE OR NOT.

COMPATIBLE A.K.A. "FIT" (EACH OTHER) DESCRIBES TWO DIFFERENT GLASSES WITH RELATIVELY THE SAME THERMAL COEFFICIENT OF EXPANSION, I.E. THEY WILL EXPAND AND CONTRACT AT NEARLY THE SAME RATES WHEN HEATED AND COOLED. INCOMPATIBLE GLASSES, HOWEVER, WILL SHOW SIGNS OF STRESS WHEN VIEWED UNDER A POLARISCOPE, OR SHOW-UP AS CRACKS IN YOUR COLORED GLASS' MASTERPIECES.

110 CONTINUOUS
A TYPE OF GLASS MELTING FURNACE WHICH CONSTANTLY MELTS THE MATERIAL BY CHARGING IN ONE END AND PULLING GLASS OUT OF THE OTHER END. MORE COMMONLY FOUND IN LARGE STUDIOS, SCHOOLS OR FACTORIES WHERE GLASS CONSUMPTION IS EXCESSIVE.

COOKIE
A SMALL-TO-LARGE GATHER OF GLASS WHICH IS ALLOWED TO PUDDLE ON THE MARVER TO FORM THE CHARACTERISTIC SHAPE. IT MAY BE USED AS THE FOOT FOR A GOBLET OR AS A BASE FOR MOST ANY TYPE OF PIECE.

CORDS
VISIBLE STRIATIONS IN MOLTEN GLASS OBJECTS DUE IN LARGE PART TO INCONSISTENT BATCHING AND/OR MELTING PRACTICES. OFTEN THEY ARE FOUND CLOSER TO THE BOTTOM OF THE FURNACE'S TANK OR CRUCIBLE - WHERE THE 'STALE' GLASS HANGS OUT.

CRACKLE
A SURFACE TECHNIQUE WHERE YOU PLUNGE YOUR HOT GLASS INTO A BUCKET OF WATER TO CRACK THE SURFACE OF YOUR GLASS. THE INTERIOR OF THE PIECE REMAINS HOT AND INTACT (IF IT'S THICK ENOUGH) AND THE OUTSIDE GETS A B'ZILLION CRACKS ALL OVER THE SURFACE.

CRIMPS
A FORM OF TWEEZERS A.K.A. LEAF TOOLS USED TO SQUEEZE HOT GLASS BITS - THEY COME IN GROOVED AND SMOOTH STYLES.

CRUCIBLE A.K.A. POT
A SPECIALLY FORMULATED CERAMIC BOWL WHICH IS DESIGNED TO WITHSTAND THE RIGORS OF MOLTEN GLASS. THEY RANGE IN A VARIETY OF SIZES AND MAY LAST A YEAR OR MORE BEFORE THEY NEED TO BE REPLACED.

CRYSTAL
1. CLEAR GLASS 2. LEAD CRYSTAL - A SPECIFIC BATCH FORMULATED WITH A PERCENTAGE OF LEAD WHICH INCREASES IT'S OPTIC CLEARITY AND CUTTING BRILLANCE. IT IS ALSO MORE EXPENSIVE TO MELT THAN THE STANDARD SODA-LIME GLASS MIXTURE COMMONLY FOUND IN NORTH AMERICAN STUDIOS.

CULLET
SOLID GLASS WHICH HAS BEEN PREVIOUSLY MELTED ~ OFTEN BROKEN UP INTO SMALLER PIECES OR CHUNKS. THIS GETS CHARGED INTO A FURNACE, AND IS EASIER TO MELT, LESS CORROSIVE, AND LESS TOXIC THAN **BATCH.**

DAY TANK
A TYPE OF FURNACE WHERE GLASS IS CHARGED, MELTED AND USED - IDEALLY WITHIN A 24 HOUR PERIOD. USUALLY LARGER IN SIZE THAN MOST **POT** FURNACES, THE DAY TANK MAY TOLERATE MORE ABUSE AND COST MORE TO BUILD AND OPERATE - BUT OFFER SO MUCH MORE GLASS IN RETURN!

DIAMOND SHEARS A.K.A. COMBINATION SHEARS
JAW LIKE SCISSORS DESIGNED TO CUT HOT GLASS OR GRIP BLOWPIPES, PUNTIES OR OTHER HOT OBJECTS.

DIDYMIUM
A SPECIAL GLASS MANUFACTURED TO FILTER OUT MUCH OF THE HARMFUL INFRA RED AND ULTRA-VIOLET RADIATION CREATED BY THE FURNACE AND GLORY HOLES / TORCHES. OFTEN USED FOR LENSES IN SAFETY GLASSES FOR GLASSWORKERS.

DIP
ANOTHER TERM FOR **GATHER.**

DUCKBILL SHEARS

SPECIAL "SCISSORS" - THEY USUALLY HAVE SHORT BLADES WITH CURVED-BLUNT TIPS. USED PRIMARILY FOR TRIMMING THE LIPS OF VESSELS.

ED
1. FIRST NAME OF THE AUTHOR OF THIS BOOK. 2. SHORT FOR EDITOR. IN THIS CASE, IT'S THE SAME PERSON.

ELEMENTS
ELECTRICAL WIRING FOUND IN ANNEALERS WHICH GENERATE THE HEAT NECESSARY FOR THEM TO GET HOT AND HOLD AT ANNEALING TEMPERATURE.
AVOID TOUCHING PIPES/PUNTIES OR OTHER METAL OBJECTS AGAINST THEM! THEY MAY BE "LIVE" AND YOU RISK ELECTROCUTION.

FEATHERING
DECORATIVE TECHNIQUE OF PULLING/COMBING A THREADED PATTERN ON HOT GLASS - RESULTING IN A FEATHER-LIKE DESIGN.
FROM ANCIENT CORE-FORMED VESSELS TO TIFFANY AND THE ART NOUVEAU DESIGNERS/CRAFTSMEN TO PRESENT DAY ARTISTS ~THIS TECHNIQUE IS A TIMELESS BEST-SELLER MOVE.

FIBER-FRAX A.K.A. FRAX
SPECIALLY FORMULATED INSULATION MATERIAL OFTEN FOUND AROUND HOT SHOPS. RESEMBLES A FLUFFY WHITE BLANKET, BUT STINGS LIKE A MILLION MICROSCOPIC ANTS IF YOUR SKIN COMES IN CONTACT WITH IT. HAZARDOUS TO BREATHE & HANDLE - BE SURE TO WEAR PROPER SAFETY EQUIPMENT WHENEVER YOU'RE WORKING WITH IT.

FILIGRANA
A TYPE OF CANE - USUALLY A COLOR THAT IS CASED BY CLEAR - AND ONE WHICH MAY BE USED IN A VARIETY OF HOT GLASS TECHNIQUES.

FINE
PROCESS OF ALLOWING MELTING GLASS AMPLE TIME TO SIT AND LET AIR BUBBLES (TRAPPED FROM THE CHARGING PROCESS) FLOAT TO THE SURFACE AND DISAPPEAR (BURST). THE LONGER THE FINING PERIOD - THE LESS SEEDS THERE ARE, AND THE CLEANER THE GLASS APPEARS.

FLAMEWORKING
SEE **LAMPWORKING**

FLASH
TO EXPOSE A PIECE OF (HOT) GLASS TO HEAT FOR A VERY SHORT TIME (ca. 5 sec.) EITHER IN A GLORY HOLE OR THE FURNACE. THE PURPOSE OF THE FLASH IS TO MAINTAIN A PIECE'S TEMPERATURE AND TO PREVENT IT FROM CRACKING OR BREAKING PREMATURELY.

FLOOR MODEL THE UNWANTED RESULT OF THE LEARNING PROCESS IN ACTION. USUALLY GRAVITY AND THE CONCRETE FLOOR WIN, AND YOU BECOME BETTER EDUCATED IN "WHAT NOT TO DO" IN THE FUTURE.

FRAX SEE FIBERFRAX PREVIOUS PAGE

FRIGGER A.K.A. **END-OF-THE-DAY PIECE** HISTORICALLY, A FUN ITEM OR NOVELTY CREATED BY FACTORY GLASSMAKERS DURING THEIR LUNCH BREAKS AND AFTER WORK — THESE 'KNOCK-OFFS' INCLUDED PAPERWEIGHTS, WALKING CANES, MUSICAL INSTRUMENTS AND FIGURINES MADE PRIMARILY AS GIFTS AND NOT TO BE SOLD.

FRIT CRUSHED GLASS, OFTEN COLORED. IT MAY BE SIFTED INTO SPECIFIC MESH SIZES & RESEMBLES FISH TANK GRAVEL. IT MAY BE INCORPORATED IN MANY WAYS TO COLOR HOT GLASS.

FRONT LOADER A TYPE OF ANNEALER → ONE WHICH HAS IT'S DOORS HINGED IN THE FRONT (LIKE A REFRIGERATOR) VERSUS ON TOP.

FURNACE GLASS — TERM FOR GLASSBLOWING OUT OF A FURNACE VERSUS OVER A TORCH, AS IN LAMPWORKING.

GABBERT — "O.J." → DISTRIBUTOR OF GLASS CULLET IN WEST VIRGINIA.

GAFFER THE HEAD HONCHO OF A GLASSBLOWING TEAM. THE PERSON WHO DIRECTS THE ASSISTANTS AND MAKES PHENOMENAL GLASS OCCUR.

GARAGE A HEATED INSULATED SPACE (SORTA-LIKE AN ANNEALING OVEN) WHERE GLASS PIECES MAY BE "PARKED" AT ANNEALING TEMP. AND USED/INCORPORATED AT A LATER TIME. OFTEN USED IN MORE ADVANCED STYLES OF GLASSWORKING.

G.A.S. ACRONYMN FOR THE GLASS ART SOCIETY

GATHER A.K.A. A **DIP** THE METHOD OF REMOVING MOLTEN GLASS FROM THE FURNACE BY DIPPING A PIPE OR PUNTY IN IT AND TURNING. THE GLASS MAY BE ACCUMULATED WITH SUCCESSIVE LAYERS OR GATHERS TO OBTAIN A DESIRED SIZE OR VOLUME.

GLASS 1. AN AMORPHOUS SOLID. 2. A SEDUCTIVE MISTRESS WHO WILL CORRUPT YOUR WORLD VIEW AND CAUSE YOU TO FOCUS ALL OF YOUR ENERGY AND BEING INTO HER LITTLE WORLD.

GLASS BUG ONCE BITTEN, THIS EVIL PARASITE INVADES THE BODY AND FORCES THE HOST TO WANT TO DO NOTHING BUT MAKE MORE GLASS, LIVING, BREATHING AND EATING IT FOR BREAKFAST, LUNCH, AND DINNER.

THOUGHT TO BE INTRODUCED BY DIRECT CONTACT (LIKE HANDLING HANDBLOWN GLASS FOR EXAMPLE) WE NOW KNOW THAT THE MERE SIGHT OF THE GLASSBLOWING PROCESS IN ACTION IS ENOUGH FOR A PERSON TO BECOME "BITTEN", (& INFECTED.) CURRENTLY THERE EXISTS NO KNOWN CURE.

GLORY HOLE INSULATED DRUM FIRED WITH A GIANT TORCH (A BURNER USING GAS AND FORCED AIR) USED BY GLASSBLOWERS TO MAKE COLD GLASS HOT (AND THUS "GOOD"). GLORY HOLES RANGE IN SIZES AND DESIGNS.

GOBLET

GENERALLY A **3**-PART DRINKING VESSEL CONSISTING OF A BOWL, STEM, AND A FOOT.
PERHAPS ONE OF THE MOST CHALLENGING FORMS FOR GLASSBLOWERS TO MASTER, GOBLETS ARE NEARLY INFINITE IN THEIR STYLES AND POSSIBILITIES.

GRAVITY IF YOU UNDERSTAND IT'S NATURAL ATTRACTION—SHE CAN BE YOUR **FRIEND**. IF YOU FAIL TO GRASP IT'S INFLUENCE, IT COULD DEVELOP INTO YOUR SWORN **ENEMY**.

HEAT SHIELDS DEVICES DESIGNED TO PROTECT YOU FROM EXCESSIVE HEAT EMINATING FROM HOT SHOP EQUIPMENT

HOT SHOP A PLACE WHERE PEOPLE BLOW GLASS AND/OR USE MOLTEN GLASS IN ONE FORM OR ANOTHER.

INCLUSION AN ELEMENT OF GLASS (OR SOME OTHER MATERIAL) WITHIN THE SURFACE OF THE GLASS OBJECT ENCASED BY ONE MEANS OR ANOTHER.

JACKS

SPECIAL TONG-LIKE TOOLS MADE OF METAL, USED BY GLASSBLOWERS TO NECK AND SHADE MOLTEN GLASS. THEY COME IN VARIOUS SIZES AND SHAPES. THE ONES WITH WOODEN DOWELS FOR BLADES ARE CALLED "PACIOFFI'S."

KEVLAR SUPER-FANTASTIC FABRIC USED TO MAKE BULLET-PROOF CLOTHING AND FIRE-PROOF GLOVES & PROTECTIVE WEAR.

KILN — SEE **ANNEALER, BOX**

KUGLER ANOTHER TERM FOR COLOR, THE BRAND NAME OF COLOR BAR IMPORTED IN FROM GERMANY FOR USE IN HOT GLASS PROCESSES.

KUGLER OVEN A SMALL OVEN DESIGNED TO PREHEAT PIECES OF GLASS ESP. KUGLER AND SUCH.

LAMPWORKING THE TECHNIQUE OF USING A TORCH TO HEAT UP YOUR GLASS. OFTEN INCORPORATING THE USE OF RODS AND TUBING TO CREATE WORKS OF "ART." OFTEN (ALTHOUGH NOT LIMITED TO) WORKING IN SMALL-ER-SCALED PIECES OF INCREDIBLE DETAIL AND COM-PLEXITY — LAMPWORKING IS WHAT MOST OF THE GENERAL PUBLIC THINKS OF WHEN YOU MENTION "GLASSBLOWING".

LATTICINO FICTICIOUS TERM FOR FANCY CANE. DON'T USE THIS TERM - IT DRIVES THE ITALIAN GLASS-BLOWERS NUTS! THE PROPER TERM - DEPENDING ON THE STYLE OF THE CANE IS **ZANFIRICO**.

LINO - SEE **TAGLIAPIETRA**.

LIP 1. UNWANTED ADVICE FROM A SMART ASS. 2. TOP OF A VESSEL A.K.A. **RIM**

LIP WRAP A THREAD OF GLASS APPLIED TO THE MOUTH OF A VESSEL, OFTEN COLORED, JUST BEFORE IT'S FULLY OPENED.

MAESTRO ITALIAN TERM FOR MASTER ONLY THE BEST OF THE BEST GLASSBLOWERS <u>EARN</u> THIS DISTINCTION ~ USUALLY FROM DECADES OF HARD WORK AND DEVOLOPING TREMENDOUS SKILL. HE / SHE USUALLY HEADS THE GLASS TEAM / PRODUCTION.

MARVER
FROM THE FRENCH TERM FOR "MARBLE" LARGE FLAT SURFACE ON WHICH HOT GLASS MAY BE MANI-PULATED. USUALLY YOU'LL SEE STEEL VERSIONS OF THESE BUT ORIGINALLY THEY WERE MADE OF STONE.

MOILE
REFERS TO THE GLASS WHICH IS GATHERED <u>ON</u> THE BLOWPIPE (OR PUNTY). IT PROVIDES STRUCTURAL SUPPORT FOR THE GLASS OFF THE END. USUALLY, IT'S THAT BLOB RIGHT ABOVE THE NECKLINE.

MOLD A CAVITY WHICH IS DESIGNED TO BE FILLED WITH ANOTHER MATERIAL (SUCH AS GLASS) TO CREATE AN OBJECT WITH A PREDETERMINED SHAPE. IT CAN BE CAST OR BLOWN INTO AND MAY BE MADE OF A VARIETY OF MATERIALS.

MURANO, ITALY. A SMALL ISLAND ACCROSS THE LAGOON FROM VENICE, WHICH HAS A VERY LONG STANDING TRADITION OF EXCELLENCE IN GLASSMAKING.

NECK 1. THE CONSTRICTED AREA ON A VESSEL CLOSEST TO THE LIP. 2. THE PROCESS OF CUTTING-IN A TRANSFER POINT ~ TRANSFER LINE BY ROTATING HOT GLASS ON A PIPE AND GENTLY SQUEEZING THE **JACKS** AT THE DESIRED POINT, USUALLY CLOSE TO, BUT BELOW THE **MOILE.**

NECK WRAP A.K.A. MOILE WRAP. A METHOD OF MAINTAINING HEAT ON THE NECK / MOILE AREA WITHOUT THE NEED OF DEEP REHEATS IN THE GLORY HOLE. ESSENTIALLY IT'S JUST A HOT GATHER OF GLASS APPLIED TO THE MOILE WHEN IT SHOWS SIGNS OF STRESS OR CRACKING (DUE TO INSUFICIENT HEAT ON THAT AREA).

OPTIC (MOLD) AN INVERTED CONE-SHAPED UNIT WITH SYMMETRICAL RIBS ON IT'S INTERIOR, USUALLY MADE OF CAST METAL e.g. ALUMINUM OR BRONZE OR BRASS. THEY COME IN COUNTLESS SIZES AND CONFIGURATIONS AND CAN BE USED TO SIMULATE "CUT CRYSTAL" OPTICAL PATTERNS IN BLOWN GLASS.

OVERLAY THE TECHNIQUE OF PLACING ONE COLOR OVER ANOTHER.

PACIOFFI's WOODEN TIPPED JACKS USED TO OPEN LARGE VESSELS WITHOUT LEAVING THE MARKS THAT STEEL JACKS CAN.

PAD THE ARENA OR AREA WHERE GLASSBLOWING TAKES PLACE.

PADDLE A WOODEN BOARD USED TO FLATTEN / SMOOTH HOT GLASS. CAN BE USED DRY OR SOAKED IN WATER. MAY ALSO BE USED TO SHIELD THE GAFFER FROM EXCESSIVE HEAT.

PAPER A FLEXIBLE **BLOCK** OF SORTS MADE ENTIRELY OF WET NEWSPAPER. CAN BE USED TO SHAPE HOT GLASS AND OFFERS YOU THE BEST FEEL FOR THE MATERIAL WITHOUT GETTING BURNED.

PARISON THE MASS OF GLASS ON THE END OF THE BLOWPIPE - USUALLY ROUND-ISH IN SHAPE, & ESSENTIALLY A FANCY NAME FOR A BUBBLE.

PENLAND CRAFT SCHOOL IN PENLAND, NORTH CAROLINA. YOU CAN STUDY GLASSWORKING AMONGST OTHER ART DISCIPLINES THERE. PRIMARILY A SUMMER SCHOOL, THEY DO OFFER LIMITED RESIDENCIES AND INTENSIVES ALL YEAR LONG.

PILCHUCK - GLASS SCHOOL IN STANWOOD, WASHINGTON IS A PLACE (PRIMARILY A SUMMER SCHOOL) WHERE YOU MAY STUDY GLASSMAKING WITH A 'MASTER' FOR A $2\frac{1}{2}$ WEEK SESSION. IT COSTS PILES OF MONEY TO ATTEND, BUT IS USUALLY WORTH THE EXPERIENCE, FOR THOSE OF US WHO ARE SERIOUSLY AFFLICTED (WITH THE **GLASS BUG**).

PIPE SPECIALLY DESIGNED AND FABRICATED STEEL / STAINLESS STEEL TUBES ON WHICH HOT GLASS MAY BE BLOWN. MANY DIFFERENT STYLES AND SIZES ARE AVAILABLE.

PIPE COOLER A MANUAL OR AUTOMATIC TOOL USED TO CHILL HOT PIPES / PUNTIES THAT BECOME TOO-HOT-TO-HANDLE (USUALLY AFTER GATHERING). IT COOLS THE PIPE BY RUNNING COLD WATER OVER THE SURFACE OF THE PIPE.

PIPE WARMER AN OPEN-FACED CHAMBER (HEATED W/ GAS) WHERE YOU PLACE YOUR PIPES / PUNTIES TO PREHEAT THEM BEFORE GATHERING.

PONTIL C'MON, NOBODY CALLS IT THAT ANYMORE! IT'S A **PUNTY**!

POLE TURNER ONE WHO "TURNS POLE", OR IN OTHER WORDS, AN INVALUABLE ASSISTANT WHO CAN BE TRUSTED TO TURN THE PIPE FOR YOU (AMONGST MANY OTHER THINGS), IN ORDER TO MAKE YOUR LIFE EASIER.

POT ANOTHER NAME FOR A **CRUCIBLE**

POT FURNACE A FREE STANDING OR INVESTED CRUCIBLE IN A FURNACE USED FOR MELTING GLASS. MOST PRIVATE STUDIOS HAVE THIS TYPE OF FURNACE FOR IT'S LOW COST OF CONSTRUCTION AND EASE OF OPERATION.

POWDER COLORED GLASS WHICH HAS BE PUL-VERIZED INTO A FLOUR-LIKE CONSISTENCY. IT MAY BE DUSTED-ON OR ROLLED-INTO HOT GLASS IN ORDER TO COLOR THE OBJECT BEING MADE.

POWDER BOOTH / BOX A DEVICE DESIGNED TO SAFELY FILTER AND CARRY AWAY THE ILL-EF-FECTS OF POWDERING HOT GLASS.

PROTECTION PROVIDING A HEAT SHIELD FOR SOMEONE BEING EXPOSED TO HOT GLASS RADIATION.

PRUNT A DECORATIVE **BIT** APPLIED TO BLOWN GLASS. A POPULAR MOTIF FOR WALDGLAS GLASSBLOWERS IN BOHEMIA DURING THE DARK AGES—THE PRUNT KEPT THE GLASSWARE FROM SLIPPING OUT THE DRINKERS GREASY MUTTON-ENCRUSTED FINGERS.

Prunts

PUFFER SEE **SOFFIETTA** →

PUNTY A METAL ROD OR TUBE USED TO GATHER GLASS AND TRANSFER ONE PIECE OF HOT GLASS TO ANOTHER.

PUNTY WRAP SAME AS A **MOILE** OR **NECKWRAP** BUT DONE ON A PUNTY. IT WILL HOPEFULLY PREVENT FLOOR MODELS FROM HAPPENING WHEN THE PUNTY EXHIBITS SIGNS OF FATIGUE OR CRACKING.

PYREX A BRAND-NAME OF BOROSILICATE GLASS USED PRIMARILY FOR **LAMPWORKING** (AND ALSO FOR KITCHEN WARE) HIGHLY RESISTENT TO THERMAL SHOCK.

PYROMETER SPECIAL THERMOMETER USED TO GAUGE HIGH TEMPERATURES COMMONLY FOUND IN THE FIRE ARTS (e.g. GLASSBLOWING), ESPECIALLY FOR READING FURNACE AND ANNEALER TEMPERATURES.

QUENCH TO STICK SOMETHING HOT INTO COLD WATER IN ORDER TO CRACK OR CHILL THE SURFACE RAPIDLY. IT MAY BE DONE TO PIPES AND PUNTIES TO ACCELERATE THE "CLEANING PROCESS" (TO POP THE MOILES OFF AFTER YOU'RE DONE USING 'EM) ALTHOUGH THE PRACTICE IS TOOL UNFRIENDLY—AND SHORTENS THE LIFESPAN OF THE METAL. SEE ALSO **CRACKLE**.

REHEAT THE PROCESS OF EXPOSING GLASS TO HEAT IN THE FURNACE OR GLORY HOLE TO REGAIN PLASTICITY AND THUS MAKE IT EASIER TO BLOW OR MANIPULATE THE GLASS.

RESPIRATOR A FANCY DUST MASK DESIGNED TO ALLOW THE WEARER TO BREATHE EASY; AND EFFECTIVELY FILTER OUT HARMFUL DUST MISTS AND/OR OTHER NUISANCES.

SEED A SMALL AIR BUBBLE FOUND IN MOLTEN GLASS. MOST FREQUENTLY DUE TO SHORT FINING PERIODS DURING THE CHARGING/MELTING PROCESS.

SHARDS PIECES OF BROKEN GLASS → OFTEN COLORED WHICH MAY BE PICKED-UP AND USED FOR DECORATIONS OR **INCLUSIONS**.

SHIELD TO OFFER PROTECTION FOR ANOTHER GLASSBLOWER, USUALLY DONE WITH A **PADDLE**.

SLUMP TO HEAT A PIECE OF GLASS ABOVE IT'S ANNEALING POINT SO THAT IT BEGINS TO SOFTEN AND MOVE. MAY BE DONE INTENTIONALLY OR MIGHT OCCUR ACCIDENTLY (ESPECIALLY IF THE ANNEALER IS SET TOO HIGH OR GOES HAYWIRE).

SOFFIETTA A.K.A. PUFFER

A HOLLOW METAL TUBE WITH A CONE-SHAPED UNIT ON IT'S END – THROUGH WHICH ITEMS MAY BE BLOWN OR 'PUFFED ON'. USED FREQUENTLY IN GOBLET MAKING.

SPRUCE PINE A BRAND NAME OF BATCH (FROM SPRUCE PINE, NORTH CAROLINA) POPULAR WITH MANY PRIVATE AND PUBLIC STUDIOS.

STEAMSTICK A WET, WOODEN CONE-SHAPED UNIT WHICH IS DESIGNED TO PUFF-OUT PIECES (WHEN THEY ARE ON THE PUNTY). IT GETS INSERTED INTO THE LIP OF A VESSEL (WHEN THE GLASS IS HOT) – THE WATER IN THE WOOD VAPORIZES INTO STEAM, AND THE EXPANDING GAS CAUSES THE HOT GLASS FORM TO EXPAND OR "PUFF-OUT".

STEINERT A MANUFACTURER OF BLOWPIPES AND TOOLS FOR GLASSBLOWERS. LOCATED IN KENT, OHIO.

STONE COLD THE TEMPERATURE OF A HOT GLASS PIECE WHERE LITTLE-TO-NO MOVEMENT IS OBSERVED WHEN THE PIPE ROTATION IS HALTED.

STONES SMALL, ROCK-LIKE LOOKING PARTICLES WHICH CONTAMINATE MOLTEN GLASS. THEY MAY BE BY-PRODUCTS OF THE CHARGING PROCESS, OR A SIGN THAT YOUR CRUCIBLE OR TANK (IN THE FURNACE) HAS CORRODED, AND IT'S TIME TO BE REPLACED.

TAGLIAPIETRA, LINO
A MAESTRO FROM MURANO WHO HAS GRACIOUSLY UNVEILED COUNTLESS VENETIAN GLASSBLOWING TECHNIQUES FOR HUNDREDS OF GLASSTHIRSTY AMERICANS (AND GLASSBLOWERS WORLD WIDE). THE FLUIDITY HE EXHIBITS WHILE WORKING, AS WELL AS PHENOMENAL SKILL IS A JOY TO WATCH. THANK HIM WHEN YOU SEE HIM, HE'S DONE ALOT FOR US.

THERMAL SHOCK A TEMPERATURE DIFFERENTIATION WITHIN A PIECE OF GLASS WHICH CAUSES IT TO CHECK, CRACK OR POSSIBLY EXPLODE. IT USUALLY OCCURS WHEN THE EXTERIOR OF A PIECE IS COOLED MORE RAPIDLY THAN IT'S INTERIOR.

THREAD

THE TECHNIQUE OF APPLYING A HOT BIT OF GLASS TO A ROTATING PARISON TO CREATE A LINEAR PATTERN, OR FORM OF SURFACE DECORATION. IT MAY DONE WITH CLEAR OR COLORED GLASS.

114 TOP LOADER
A TYPE OF ANNEALER; ONE WHICH IS HINGED ON THE TOP VERSUS THE SIDE, AND PIECES ARE LOADED DOWN INTO IT.

TRANSFER TO PUNTY UP. IT USUALLY MEANS ADHERING ONE PIECE OF HOT GLASS TO ANOTHER PUNTY AND BREAKING IT FREE FROM IT'S ORIGINAL PIPE OR PUNTY.

TUMBLER A SIMPLE STRAIGHT WALLED VESSEL OF INDETERMINATE SIZES AND THICKNESSES.

TURN POLE SEE POLE TURNER

TWEEZERS A.K.A. PINCERS A POINTED TONG-LIKE TOOL USED TO GRAB OR MANIPULATE HOT GLASS OR OTHER HOT TOOLS OR OBJECTS

VENETIAN-STYLE INACCURATE GEOGRAPHICAL REFERENCE TO GLASS WORK AND TECHNIQUES LIKELY ORIGINATING FROM MURANO. IT'S TYPIFIED BY THINLY BLOWN OR EXPERTLY-CRAFTED GLASS.

VENETIAN-VIRUS A SUB-GENUS OF THE GLASS BUG. IT CAUSES THE HOST TO WANT FOR NOTHING OTHER THAN TO MAKE PERFECT VENETIAN-STYLE GLASSWARE DAY-IN & DAY-OUT. THOUGHT TO BE TERMINAL,... THERE CURRENTLY EXISTS NO KNOWN CURE.

WAX BEESWAX IS USED TO LUBRICATE THE BLADES OF HOT JACKS. IT PREVENTS THE METAL FROM SCRATCHING, SQUEELING, OR MARRING THE SURFACE OF THE HOT GLASS WHILE NECKING OR SHAPING WITH THE TOOL.

WRAP THE PROCESS OF ADDING A HOT BLOB OF GLASS AROUND ANOTHER PIECE OF GLASS. IT CAN BE ORNAMENTAL — SUCH AS IN THE CASE OF THREADING, OR AS A PRECAUTIONARY METHOD SUCH AS IN MOILE OR NECK WRAPS.

YOKE A PLACE TO SET YOUR PIPE OR PUNTY DURING REHEATS AT THE GLORY HOLE. OFTEN CONSTRUCTED OF A SET OF BALL BEARINGS (WHICH ALLOW YOU TO ROTATE THE PIPE WITHOUT MUCH RESISTENCE), WHICH ARE MOUNTED ON SOME SORT OF FIXED STAND OR MOBILIZED UNIT.

ZANFIRICO FANCY CANE, SOMETIMES EXHIBITING SPIRAL PATTERNS OR LACEY QUALITIES INSIDE.

ZIMMERMANN MANUFACTURER OF COLORED GLASS - LOCATED IN GERMANY.

About the Author

OKAY, NOW FOR A LITTLE BIT MORE INFORMATION ABOUT THE GUY THAT WROTE THIS BOOK. QUITE OFTEN, PEOPLE ASK ME HOW I FIRST FOUND OUT ABOUT GLASSBLOWING. WELL, FOR ME, IT HAPPENED BY ACCIDENT. IT WAS DURING ONE OF THOSE FAMILY VACATIONS IN THE EARLY 1970's THAT MY PARENTS TOOK US ON; FIVE SCREAMING BRATS IN A STATION WAGON PACKED-TO-THE-HILT EN ROUTE TO WASHINGTON D.C.. WE MADE A SIDE TRIP TO "HISTORIC JAMESTOWN, VIRGINIA" (SITE OF AMERICA'S FIRST INDUSTRY - GLASSBLOWING) - TO SEE HOW THE FIRST SETTLERS LIVED. IT WAS THERE THAT I GOT TO OBSERVE GLASSMAKING IN A RECREATED BEE-HIVE FURNACE. THERE WERE A BUNCH OF GUYS IN FUNNY COSTUMES WHIPPING THIS GOOEY, HOT, MOLTEN STUFF AROUND. TRANSFIXED BY ALL OF THAT ACTIVITY, I BECAME HOOKED (& KNEW RIGHT THERE AND THEN THAT THAT'S WHAT I WANTED TO DO FOR THE REST OF MY LIFE!). MY PARENTS HAD TO LITERALLY DRAG ME AWAY...

IT WASN'T UNTIL THE SPRING OF 1984 THAT I CAME IN CONTACT WITH HOT GLASS AGAIN. I SPOTTED "INTRODUCTION TO MOLTEN GLASSBLOWING" IN OUR COURSE CATALOG AT THE U of I WHILE LOOKING FOR AN ART ELECTIVE TO TAKE. LUCKILY, THE PROFESSOR, Bill Carlson, LET ME INTO THE CLASS (THERE WERE A WHOLE STRING OF PRE-REQUISITES REQUIRED BEFORE YOU COULD EVEN TAKE THE CLASS - OR "INSTRUCTORS PERMISSION"). AFTER SEVERLY BURNING MY HAND THE SECOND WEEK OF CLASS (I PICKED UP A HOT, UNMARKED PUNTY ON THE WRONG END!) - I HAD MY DOUBTS.... BUT BY WEEK FOUR I WAS SURE THAT I WOULD BE WORKING WITH HOT GLASS AS MUCH AS I COULD, THE GLASS BUG BIT ME HARD!

SO, IN 1986, I GRADUATED WITH A B.A. IN GERMANIC LANGUAGES AND LITERATURES, AND A SECOND DEGREE IN THE FOLLOWING YEAR WITH A B.F.A. IN GLASS.

FOR MANY SUMMERS, I WORKED AT THE PILCHUCK GLASS SCHOOL, PRIMARILY IN THE COLD SHOP. IT WAS AT PILCHUCK THAT I BECAME EXPOSED TO HUNDREDS OF ARTISTS FROM ALL OVER THE WORLD, AND COUNTLESS WAYS TO WORK WITH THE GLASS. IT SERVED AS AN EYE-OPENING EDUCATION AND TAUGHT ME ABOVE ALL THE VALUE OF COMMUNICATION AND COLLABORATION.

DURING GRAD. SCHOOL AT OHIO STATE, I BEGAN TEACHING BEGINNING GLASSBLOWING. I ENJOYED INSTRUCTING THE STUDENTS, BUT IT WAS DIFFICULT 'CAUSE HARDLY ANYONE COULD REMEMBER ANYTHING FROM THE PREVIOUS CLASS. SO, IN 1993, I WROTE "ED'S BIG HANDBOOK OF GLASSBLOWING" TO FILL IN THE GAPS.

FOUR YEARS LATER, I COMPLETED "ADVANCED GLASS-WORKING TECHNIQUES", AND NOW THE REVISION OF THE FIRST BOOK (COMPLETE WITH AN INDEX!) - WHICH IS IN YOUR HANDS.

WHEN I'M NOT WRITING BOOKS - OR TEACHING, I LIKE TO BLOW GLASS WITH MY PARTNER - ELENA ENOS. WE OWN AND OPERATE GLASS MOUNTAIN STUDIOS HERE IN BELLINGHAM, WASHINGTON. THE WORK RANGES FROM ORNATE GOBLETS TO ENVIORN-MENTAL INSTALLATIONS, FROM FUNCTIONAL BEER BOTTLES TO UNIQUE SANDCARVED SCULPTURES.

I ENJOY ALSO: BREWING BEER & MEADS, COOKING GREAT FOOD & THE FINER POINTS OF LIVING INCLUDING MOUNTAIN BIKING, TELEMARK SKIING AND PLAYING MUSIC.

Backword

A WORD OR TWO ABOUT THIS BOOK: SOME OF YOU MAY HAVE NOTICED THAT IT IS HANDWRITTEN, AND THOUGHT TO YOURSELF "Why, he should have done this on a computer and saved himself alot of time. He could scan in his own handwriting and make it LOOK just like he wrote it by hand." WELL, THAT MAY BE TRUE, BUT... FIRST OFF - I DON'T OWN A COMPUTER ((AND HAVE LITTLE DESIRE, AT PRESENT, MUCH LESS THE MONEY - TO DO SO.).

SECOND, I'VE YET TO SEE COMPUTER-GENERATED IMAGES WHICH I LIKE, AND FEEL ARE SUPERIOR TO THOSE DONE BY HAND.

and THIRD, WHAT BETTER WAY TO ILLUSTRATE THE BENEFITS OF DRAWING TO GLASSMAKING THAN BY EXHIBITING THE WHOLE PROCESS AS A DRAWING ITSELF? MY HOPE IS THAT IT INSPIRES AND ENCOURAGES THE READER TO PICK-UP A DRAWING INSTRUMENT THEMSELVES AND PUT SOME MARKS TO PAPER.

SOMEDAY, SOMEHOW... THIS BOOK MAY BE REALIZED IN COMPUTER FORM, BUT FOR HERE AND NOW - THIS IS THE WAY IT IS.

I STILL FEEL THAT IT SHOULD CONTINUE ON AS A LIVING DOCUMENT - AND THAT IT GO THROUGH PERIODIC CHECK-UPS TO IMPROVE THE INFORMATION WITHIN.

SO.... I HAVE A REQUEST FOR YOU: IF YOU SEE OR KNOW OF ANYTHING THAT I MIGHT INCLUDE IN THE NEXT EDITION ~ PLEASE SEND ME THAT INFORMATION WRITTEN ON A POSTCARD OR LETTER TO THE ADDRESS BELOW. I'LL REVIEW IT AND MAY INCLUDE IT IN THE NEXT EDITION ((plus you'll GET A FREE COPY!). (THANKS FOR EXPLORING MY BOOK — Edward T. Schmid

INDEX